The World Upside Down

The World Upside Down

CROSS-CULTURAL CONTACT
AND CONFLICT IN
SIXTEENTH-CENTURY PERU

SUSAN ELIZABETH RAMÍREZ

STANFORD UNIVERSITY PRESS
STANFORD, CALIFORNIA

Stanford University Press
Stanford, California
© 1996 by the Board of Trustees of the
Leland Stanford Junior University
Printed in the United States of America

CIP data are at the end of the book

To John Thomas,

*who loves history
but decided to go
into business instead*

Preface

Some would describe the task of ethnohistorians as writing the history of the people without history. That definition, of course, implies a strict understanding of the word *history* as a reconstruction of past events based on written records. Many scholars now reject that definition as demeaning, ethnocentric, and not totally accurate. The history of a people can be reconstructed using many sources, including oral traditions and the material record. The absence of writing, in other words, does not necessarily deny a people a functional past.

This study uses oral traditions as written down after the first contact with Europeans, the material record as reported and interpreted by archaeologists, and early testimonies and writings of the native peoples of northern Peru to reconstruct their history. By gleaning colonial records and separating native statements from those of the Spaniards, we can construct a picture of the immediate precontact years. Often, statements cannot be taken literally, because the Andean witnesses and petitioners were using a language that was not their own, often with the help of a scribe or representative. But when such statements are considered with and compared against the behavior and reactions of these same individuals and their peers, the underlying meaning and intent becomes apparent. Statements that were incomprehensible to me at first, due to my Western cultural upbringing and training, inspired me to look deeper—as Robert Darnton did when he encountered the account he made famous in his article on the great cat massacre—to understand another perspective.

This book was a long time coming. It began some twenty years ago with my first encounters with archaeologists in the field. On many a Friday or Saturday night, we would gather to discuss our "finds." Although at the time I was working on the history of the great estates and the Indian communities of the north coast, the questions of these colleagues (such as Kent Day, Izumi Shimada, and Martha Anders) about what I was finding in the local manuscript sources regarding native shrines, cropping patterns, population, and a myriad of other topics stimulated me to start thinking about cross-cultural contact and the inevitable conflict that precipitous change usually brings. Once the first project was completed, continued probing by these colleagues and others encouraged me to narrow my subject to the sixteenth century, the era closest to the precontact past and, to my way of thinking, an era of profound and fundamental change in the way of life of the native peoples that has not received the scholarly attention it deserves.

Support, both human and material, for this endeavor has come from many and varied sources. I thank my archaeologist colleagues who were, quite literally, digging into the past at the same time I was digging into the local archives. I thank the anthropologists, art historians, ethnographers, ethnohistorians, historians, and geographers from whom I learned so much. A special word of appreciation also goes to the unsung heroes in the archives—the directors and archivists—who battle, occasionally in vain, against moths, humidity, mold, acid ink, thieves, and earthquakes to preserve the sometimes delicate papers without which much of the following story could never be told. Know, dear friends, that you too are treasured assets to your countrypersons and the world.

Support for the years it took me to gather, read, and analyze the material came from De Paul University, where one dean in particular did much to further his belief that there is a direct and positive connection between research and teaching, and from the National Endowment for the Humanities, the Ford Foundation, and the United States government through the Fulbright Commission. Without this help the following story would have remained for another to tell.

Contents

Maps and Figures

Maps

Figures

Tables

The World Upside Down

CHAPTER I

Introduction

Of a street sweeper or commoner a lady or noblewoman is
made and thus is the world upside down.
—Guamán Poma de Ayala, *El primer nueva corónica*

The old saying that "history is written by the victors" certainly applies to most of the history of European colonialism in
Spanish America. Traditionally, scholars—most of whom were from
Europe or of European descent—focused on imported institutions
and their functions and on the life of the elites. In fact, the bulk of
the scholarly output was weighted toward understanding the European presence overseas. The history of colonialism in America thus
was largely out of balance.

In the past few decades, studies of viceroys, *encomenderos* (Spaniards awarded native peoples in trust), mining, haciendas, prices,
and markets have been gradually complemented with studies of the
native Americans in an attempt to right this imbalance. Demographic analyses of censuses and tax records, though still debated
and constantly refined, have helped us estimate the size of the population. Studies of labor under the *encomienda* (a grant of natives in
trust), *mita* (a rotating system of forced labor), and migration have
also helped in determining how the Spanish incorporated the original Americans into the international economic system. Native resistance to this process has also caught the historian's eye.

Yet to date, few studies of the Spanish conquest and the very early
colonization of America have been written from the native Americans' point of view. Prominent among them are Miguel León-
Portilla's and Edmundo Guillén Guillén's retelling of the history of
the violent phase of the conquest and its well-known immediate
aftermath from the Aztec and Inca points of view, respectively. The
authors treat the topic from a native elite or centralized perspective, generalizing from the experience and events in or near the

native capitals of Tenochtitlan (Mexico City) or Cuzco to the entire empire.[1]

A closer study of everyday life and native perceptions awaited the pioneering work of James Lockhart and his colleagues. These researchers used Nahuatl manuscripts—mostly wills and other mundane documents—to reconstruct the culture and concerns of the original Nahua inhabitants of central Mexico and provide a picture of the Nahua world as conceived and categorized by the people themselves.[2]

By contrast, owing to the near total absence of sources written in indigenous languages, progress in the same direction has been slower and more meager in Peru. In this case, scholarly studies of the same era tend to be more culturally focused and narrowly defined. Such specialists as John V. Murra, Patricia Netherly, R. Tom Zuidema, and Frank Salomon have written extensively on various aspects of the pre-Spanish socioeconomic organization of the large and ethnically diverse Inca empire.[3] Others, including María Rostworowski de Diez Canseco (hereafter cited as Rostworowski), Steve Stern, Karen Spalding, Sabine MacCormack, and Nathen Wachtel deal with aspects of both the pre- and postconquest eras. Early studies tend to center on Cuzco, while more recent work concentrates on particular regions. The literature now includes specific studies from areas as varied as Cuzco and the southern highlands; Huarochirí, in the central mountains; and the central coast. Much of this literature discusses specific topics, such as natural resources, succession, or native religion. Only Wachtel and Spalding systematically cover the range of transformations occurring in native culture under early Spanish rule. The former reviews the changes to about 1570; the latter summarizes them during the entire colonial period.[4]

The work in the present volume follows in this vein. Learning from these studies and building on them, I have tried to determine some of the general principles on which the pre-Hispanic Andeans' lives were based by penetrating the veneer of Spanish institutions and structures. This book explains how the imposed Spanish colonial system altered the organization and belief systems of the native inhabitants of northern Peru during the 50 years or so after first contact with the Europeans. It shows how the Andeans' world was turned upside down (*es mundo al rreues*), to quote the Indian Felipe Guamán Poma de Ayala's letter to the king of Spain, in the aftermath of the Spanish invasion and conquest.[5]

My study is unique on several counts. First, it focuses primarily on the immediate pre- and postconquest eras, defined as the 50 years

or so before and after the fateful encounter between the Inca emperor Atahualpa and Francisco Pizarro in 1532 at Cajamarca, a period Kenneth Andrien identified as largely ignored and understudied.[6] As a result, most scholars underestimate the extent of the changes that occurred in native culture during these early years, and few emphasize the natives' perceptions of the transformation. By focusing on a limited time period, I document the changes in a detail not previously available for northern Peru. Second, by centering on an area that was incorporated into the Inca empire relatively late (in the 1460s and 1470s), my study offsets the Cuzco focus of much of the existing literature on Inca history and culture.[7] This provincial perspective is compared throughout the text with findings from the Inca capital in the southern highlands; from Huarochirí, in the central mountains; from the central coast; and from the far-north Quito area in an attempt to make meaningful generalizations. Thus, I hope to do for the northern provinces what MacCormack did in her study of native religion in the south by differentiating between Inca, imperial, Cuzco-centered ritual and beliefs and folk or provincial religion and beliefs. To this end I document and underscore the gradual process of conquest, accommodation, and resistance under the Spanish.[8]

This history is based on many types of early historical accounts, local primary documents, and archaeological and anthropological findings. I used the writings of Spanish chroniclers cautiously, keeping in mind studies such as those of Raul Porras Barrenechea, Anthony Pagden, and MacCormack, who explain their contradictions and biases by analyzing their cultural heritage and the social milieu in which they wrote.[9] Less global records—such as administrative documents, the proceedings of the judiciary, and the minutes of both Andean and Spanish *cabildos* (town councils)—were also useful, especially when analyzed document by document specifically to compare Andean and Spanish views. Administrative records often contain petitions from Indians (usually *indios ladinos*, Indians who knew Spanish), who express their concerns in their own, albeit translated, words.[10] Likewise, judicial records contain valuable testimony from native witnesses that sometimes presents a different slant on the question being argued. Cabildo records offer a marked contrast in outlook, especially on questions of land tenure. These, then, are windows—intimate glimpses that the Spanish chroniclers rarely provide—into Amerindian society, a society that had lost the power of description.

The native American statements contained in these records show that the Andeans actively sought opportunities and manipulated circumstances to defend the principles on which their community life depended. Thus, don Juan, cacique of Collique, offered buried treasure to the Spanish official who wanted him hanged for bigamy. He successfully tricked the Spanish, at least for a short while, by sending another woman in the place of his favorite mistress to the home of a good Christian woman for religious instruction. Another example is the paramount lord don Antonio, a cacique from a community near the Spanish provincial capital of Trujillo who tried to protect the burial structure of his forefathers (rich with possessions and offerings) from the greed of treasure-hunting Spaniards. When physical defense became impossible, he reluctantly settled for a share of the spoils taken from the ancestral tomb—which he promptly invested to relieve the growing tribute burden of his subjects. He thus upheld the principles of reciprocity and redistribution and continued to fulfill his guardianship role in relation to his people.[11]

In these native testimonies and in their last wills and testaments, the Andeans attempt to explain their beliefs and conception of the world. These statements also show that what the Andeans said was ignored or dismissed, discredited, and ridiculed, or at least largely misunderstood by contemporary Spaniards. To don Juan, multiple wives meant more numerous offspring to do work; more wealth, status, and power; and perhaps a longer collective memory of his achievements—that is, immortality. Most Spaniards did not understand that an index of chiefly power, prestige, and wealth was the number of followers a lord had, not the sum total of the gold or silver he had accumulated. They interpreted chiefly behavior in a strictly Christian European framework. One wife was normal, moral. Intimacy with more than one woman was sin. Because he was unrepentant and had tried to bribe and deceive the Spanish officials sent to right the situation, don Juan was condemned to death, and his sentence was carried out with uncommon haste.

The local sources I use come from an area extending on the south roughly from Trujillo, the colonial and modern provincial capital, and Chan Chan, the capital of the important pre-Inca polity of Chimor, to Motupe and the Sechura desert on the north, and eastward inland into the Andean mountains through the areas inhabited by the peoples of Guambos and Cajamarca (see Map 1). The study thus encompasses a broad area from the Pacific shoreline to the eastern side of the Andean mountains before they descend into tropical forest and jungle. Within this area, the different combinations of elevation, rainfall (or lack thereof), types of soil, exposure to the sun, and

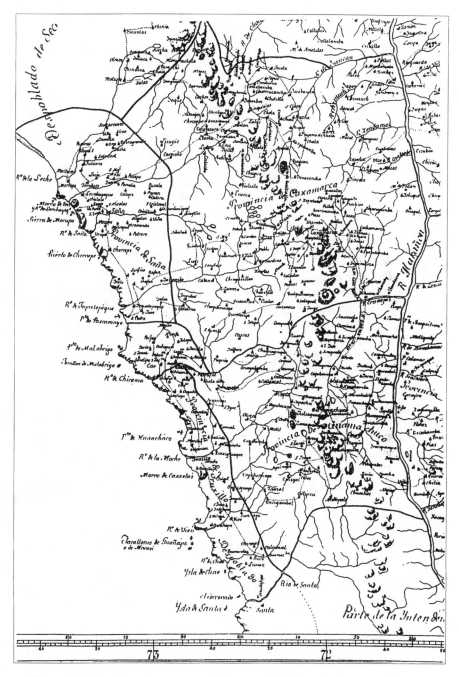

Map 1 Northern Peru

the availability of other natural resources allowed inhabitants to meet most, if not all, of their subsistence needs.

The gently sloping desert coast is punctuated at intervals by rivers that descend from the mountains. Irrigation canals distribute the water from these rivers to agricultural lands in the valleys. Beyond the sophisticated hydraulic systems, little more than cacti and *algarrobo* (carob) and *zapote* (sapota) trees grow. The agricultural potential in these valleys is also affected by a heavy mist (*garua*) that accompanies the formation of fog during the six-month winter season (from about April to September). Garua alone does not provide enough moisture for agriculture. In fact, close to the sea—an area inhabitants called the *valle nuevo*, or "new valley"—the combination of thick fog and heavy mist actually retards crop growth by diminishing sunlight and promoting the growth of harmful fungi and insects. Farther inland—an area local inhabitants called the *valle viejo*, or "old valley"—the semitropical climate and year-round sun make it possible to harvest two and even three crops a year on irrigated land. In valleys like Lambayeque, the pre-Hispanic indigenous population was concentrated in the upper or old valleys and was resettled (in the 1560s and 1570s) into the lower valleys to free up the most productive areas for expanding Spanish agriculture.[12]

Moving from the coast into the highlands,[13] the gently sloping coastal plain gives way to the foothills and mountains of the Andes. In the highland valleys, agriculture depended on both natural rainfall and irrigation systems. Here the rivers that irrigated the coast began. Colonial chroniclers describe Cajamarca as a fertile area with a healthy, springlike climate. Besides fertile soil and a temperate climate, the highlands also provided good hunting grounds for deer and fowl and mines of copper, gold, silver, and other minerals.[14]

Thus, within a few days' walk inhabitants could angle for saltwater fish; collect shellfish and seaweed; work salt pans; cut reeds in marshes for mats, baskets, and boats; hunt waterfowl and other animals; and farm. Along the rivers, people netted shrimp, fished, and dug clay for pottery and construction. At about 1,000 meters above sea level, the mines of Chilete provided silver ore. A remnant rain forest on the western side of the Andes, at a place now called Monte Seco on the trail going to Udima (about 2,000 meters in elevation), is still a source for wild honey and the feathers of brightly colored birds.

Both coast and highlands shared the experience of conquest by Cuzqueño forces in about 1470, despite a defensive coalition between the peoples of coastal Chimor and highland Cajamarca.[15] Once dominion was established, the Cuzqueños diverted tribute labor from Chan Chan to Cajamarca, balkanized the coastal kingdom of Chimor, and moved residents from one locale to another, but they otherwise had relatively little impact on the daily life of the people. Loyal local lords were usually confirmed both on the coast and in the highlands. Although sun worship and the Quechua language were mandated, on the coast non-Inca populations continued to worship their ancestors and speak local tongues—Mochica or Yunga. Resistance to Cuzco hegemony flared occasionally. Both the Penachís and Sañas revolted against southern domination before 1532.[16] This relatively recent experience of foreign hegemony probably helped forge the collective identity of the northern peoples and helps explain why many allied with the Spanish against the Cuzqueños.[17]

My own comprehension of the Andean perspective developed slowly, always keeping this history and native testimonies in mind. First, I found Andean responses to Spanish questions and behavior that did not follow European logic. Then I focused on what the natives stated and how their words compared with their behavior. Understanding these observations involved reading widely in the secondary literature in anthropology and archaeology and consulting often and at length with colleagues.[18] Only then did the contradictions between the Spanish testimony and the Andean account become comprehensible. Eventually, such study enabled me to see the impact of expanding colonialism on indigenous ideas about leadership and legitimacy, the supernatural and morality, service and allegiance, land and tenure, and wealth from an Andean perspective.

The chapters that follow deal with the impact of Spanish colonialism on indigenous institutions and beliefs. Each compares the original precontact Andean situation (to the extent that it can be reconstructed) with that existing to about 1570—in some cases before the imposition of Viceroy Francisco de Toledo's reforms. Each chapter focuses on one aspect of the indigenous mind-set and way of life, with the aim of coming closer to understanding Andean culture as it existed in the five decades before and after contact with the Spanish.

Chapter 2 focuses on the *curaca*, the paramount lord and leader of native society, and the impact of the Spanish colonial system on this native office and its bases of legitimacy. Spanish concepts of governing gradually changed the power structure and in the process subverted the original role of the curacas as leaders of and spokesmen for the local indigenous peoples. Gone was the cargo system in which lower-level lords, at the rank of *mandon* (or overseer), for example, were tested and, if successful, assumed more responsibility.

Management ability was rewarded by elevation to higher rank, such as *principal* (noble lord). Continued prosperity, hospitality, and "good government" might make a principal a consensus candidate for curaca. After 1532, these cultural brokers came under the control of the Spanish and were bent to the will of the colonials or were murdered or otherwise replaced. As a result, the product of tribute labor was not recycled back into the community as much of it was before 1532, but instead extracted to support the colonial elites and their international ambitions.

Chapter 3 unravels contradictions about land tenure. Writing it was a lesson in self-discovery as I realized what a creature of my culture I am. At first I could not imagine, much less put into words, what I saw in the data. It was only in the light of massive, irrefutable evidence that I pierced through my own cultural bias and came to acknowledge that the concept of private property need not always be present in a system based on access to naturally occurring goods like land, salt pans, and rocks. After all, land and rock do not become natural resources until someone recognizes them to be of value and uses them. What I found was that the Spanish did not initially recognize the use-value that natives gave to land or the way their tenure system reflected this value. The Andeans endeavored to control labor in order to use the land and other natural resources. But the notion of ownership in the Western sense of possessing land even when it is not used was outside the Andean cultural perspective. By contrast, the Spanish took over the land and other natural resources for their intrinsic and sometimes potential value and, later, to gain control over labor and draw it and its products into the expanding trade networks. The Spanish clearly interpreted reality according to their own legal concepts; consequently, they gradually appropriated land and other natural resources. They succeeded because the native Americans did not understand the private ownership of such resources and the process of alienation.[19]

Chapter 4 traces the evolution of the tribute system from duty and allegiance (based on reciprocity), work in exchange for management and well-being, to service and goods and, finally, to silver and gold. A commoner's obligation to work for limited periods of time for his lords was gradually transformed into a quota of physical items and measured tribute. The production of cloth was commodified as the indigenous natural economy was gradually replaced with the money economy of mercantile capitalism, which inserted the Andeans into expanding global networks of unequal exchange. This is another aspect of the appropriation by one sector of society of the surplus produced by another sector—the essence of individual and collective exploitation, of colonialism in its most elemental form—and of the process of converting various groups of Andeans into a largely undifferentiated mass of "Indians."

Chapter 5 is based on a single incident of *huaca* looting on the north coast that epitomizes the clash between the native inhabitants of the Western Hemisphere and the Spanish. This was a conflict over gold, wealth and its definition, and religion. The Spanish thought wealth could be individual and measured in bullion; the Andean peoples used population as a measure of collective strength and well-being. The Spanish took possession of an indigenous structure for the bullion it contained. The Andeans defended the structure as a "house" and resting place of their foreparents. Ancestor worship and its related edifices and rituals represented the history and continuity of communities, they claimed. But the Spanish had no respect for these beliefs, equating them with satanism.

This is the story, too, of how the Indians reacted in the face of overwhelming force. Don Antonio, the paramount lord of the native community in question, finally compromised his original defensive position to alleviate some of the oppression of his subjects. Ultimately, his part of the treasure taken from the "house" of his ancestors was used to better the chances that his community would survive in the face of a largely unresponsive legal system that favored only a small sector of Spanish society. It is, in short, the story of gold and grave looting, of the desecration and destruction of physical structures as well as the belief system on which the political economy of the indigenous people rested. In a very personal sense, this story brings us back to Chapter 2 by illustrating the contradictions faced by a paramount lord and the pressures on him to either redistribute gains for the good of his community or to divert them into Spanish hands.

In a sense, the organization of this book is inadequate, since I use European categories to analyze and describe a non-Western culture. To compensate, the concluding chapter, Chapter 6, sums up the story by bringing the analytical pieces back together again; it offers a tentative sketch of the various elements of the indigenous culture and how they functioned together. The Andeans appear uncomprehending at first (e.g., why give up polygyny in favor of monogamy?). They must have wondered, after repeatedly explaining their rationale, why their words went unheeded. Gradually, they grasped the significance of what was happening. The Spanish disregarded the natives' reasons, definitions, and procedures. Their culture and values were under attack. Some aspects of their way of life survived; others were reinvented. Because they came to serve the colonizer, native leaders were discredited. Though their peoples continued to fear them, native lords no longer commanded the respect they had before contact with the Spanish. The resources created and supplied by the gods and improved by the work of the ancestors were parceled up and cordoned off. Temples and tombs were desecrated. Homage and help were replaced by extraction, which created riches for the foreign few. With so much in flux, no wonder the population decreased, no wonder Andeans refused to work.

This story of northern Peru challenges views on continuity and change in native American culture between Inca and Spanish times in the sixteenth century. The history of the curaca of northern Peru contrasts with the continuity of that institution that Nancy Farriss found extant on the Yucatán peninsula during colonial times.[20] Like MacCormack's study of Incan and Andean religion, this study demonstrates that many aspects of indigenous life had already changed in areas of high contact with the Spanish before the Toledan era, the era usually used to begin measuring significant systematic change in the native societies in the south.[21] It thus qualifies Viceroy Toledo's reputation as the master reorganizer of the realm.

The northern experience, furthermore, argues that the Indians of the coast from Trujillo to Motupe, an area of desert punctuated by fertile river valleys, and of the Guambos and Cajamarca highlands shared views on land, resources, and the supernatural, although the names of gods and their positions in the hierarchy might be different. Thus, my findings support Murra's research and challenge, in part, Rostworowski's thinking that the socioeconomic organization of the coastal groups differed significantly from that of groups in the highlands.[22] In addition, my presentation adds perspective to the spiritual conquest often thought to be synonymous with the history of the Catholic church.[23] My work complements that of Pierre Duviols, providing earlier information on the belief systems of the Andeans in a different area of the Inca empire from a source not associated with his extirpation of idolatry records.[24] Finally, I attempt to take a step closer to understanding the cosmology and organizing principle of native society—namely the reciprocity between leaders and led, between living and dead.

This study, in sum, is an in-depth look at the interaction between Andeans and Europeans, between two distinct sets of practices, values, beliefs, and world views, that emphasizes how the natives' culture and traditions affected their reactions, or lack thereof, to the imposition of the Spanish colonial system. This is a story of Eurocentrism, of the Europeans' disregard (for the most part) of others' cultures and identities. The results offer at least the beginnings of an outline of how the Andeans of the north perceived themselves in the material world. It will remain for others to refine the images portrayed here.

CHAPTER 2

The 'Dueño de Indios'

SHIFTING BASES OF POWER OF THE 'CURACA DE LOS VIEJOS ANTIGUOS'

A lowly tribute-paying Indian is transformed into a lord.
—Guamán Poma de Ayala, *El primer nueva corónica*

Among the documents copied into the records of the *residencia* (administrative review at the end of a person's term of office) of Dr. Gregorio González de Cuenca, the judge of Lima's Real Audiencia (supreme court) and visitor to the northern provinces of Peru, is the transcript of the judicial proceedings against don Juan, cacique of the native community of Collique.[1] In these 1566 proceedings, the Indian witnesses distinguished between old-style and new-style chieftains. Don Juan was described by contemporaries as a "cacique like the ancients or old ones who used to rule the valleys whom their subjects feared." The paramount lord of Túcume,[2] a curaca who himself was identified as a chieftain "in the ancient mold [de los viejos antiguos]," declared that don Juan was worthy of the respect of his native subjects, like those chieftains of times past and very unlike those curacas who were being elevated to the position by their current Spanish overlords.[3]

In this chapter I use primary sources, some written by Andean scribes, to explore the role of the curaca during the first 50 years or so after the Spanish invasion and conquest. Using contracts, petitions, court cases, and other local documentation, together with the writings of chroniclers, administrative reviews, records of *visitas* (inspection tours or reviews), censuses, and other Spanish viceregal documentation, I will compare the old-style curaca and his function in the local political economy with the new-style curaca, who became the agent of the Spanish colonial system. In so doing, I describe the active process of transformation of one aspect of local culture. To borrow from Marshall Sahlins's analysis, the designation *curaca*, a cultural category, acquires "new functional values." In the process, cultural meanings change, the relationships between categories are altered, and the structure is transformed.[4] Thus, unlike several studies of the Mexican indigenous elite that stress continuity,[5] this discussion highlights the extent of institutional change during these years. In this chapter I also touch on the ideological bases of legitimacy of the curaca and the articulation of one curaca with another. This discussion has important implications for the understanding of indigenous settlement patterns (*"territorialidad salpicada"*) and the interdependence between polities on the coast and those in the highlands.

To Be a Chief; or, The Concept of 'Good Government,' Circa 1532

To be a chief or paramount lord *de los viejos antiguos* in the first half of the sixteenth century on the north coast of Peru (see Map 2)[6] meant that don Juan and others of his origin and generation controlled thousands of native American subjects and managed the lands and the natural resources they used to support themselves. Their subjects knew them first and foremost as leaders of men, *dueños de indios.*[7] Curacas enjoyed recognized power over the life and death of their subjects. As arbitrator of local justice, the curaca decided guilt or innocence. If a commoner were guilty of a minor infraction, the curaca determined the means of torture or other punishment. If a commoner were guilty of a grave offense, the curaca could take the offender's life.[8]

Dr. Cuenca, the Spanish career bureaucrat charged with visiting and inspecting the northern part of the Peruvian viceroyalty in 1566 through 1567,[9] tried and executed don Juan ostensibly because he had tortured and killed two of his pages for making love to a favorite mistress. In contrast to areas under stricter Inca control, where a curaca was supposed to get the Inca's permission to inflict capital punishment on his subjects, local north coast indigenous society accepted don Juan's judgment and his sentencing of the two offenders. According to an Andean witness and page to don Juan, the curaca had told the two "that because they had slept with his mistress and thus showed him so little respect, he wanted to kill them; that he was going to kill them because they were his [subjects] or had been [subjects] of his ancestors, and that he was not killing Indians of another [lord]." This statement indicates a tacit recognition of the right of a curaca to take the life of his subjects. And this was not the

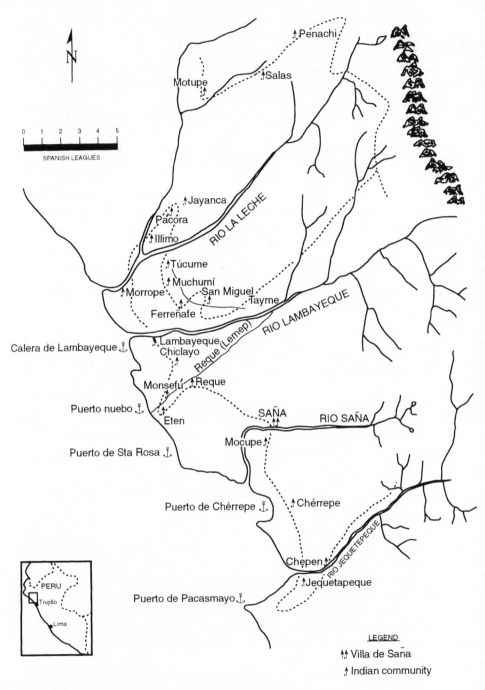

Map 2 Indian communities of the north coast. Not all the Indian communities mentioned in the text are shown.

first time. During his reign, don Juan had purportedly already executed eight to ten subjects for unspecified misconduct.[10]

In general, the curaca probably exercised this power carefully and favored leniency, because in this status-based society, his own rank, position, and prestige were equated with the number of his subjects. Many contemporary authors have commented on the fact that the rank and status of a native leader were correlated with the size of the population he controlled, not only in the north but throughout the wider Inca empire. Felípe Guamán Poma de Ayala, the early seventeenth-century Andean chronicler, for instance, says that each ranked official had to have a certain number of native tributaries to achieve and maintain his status in the Inca's decimal system of administration. An official's status and reputation directly and positively correlated with the number of his subjects, increasing as the numbers grew, and vice versa. This principle reinforces and expands the Jesuit chronicler Bernabé Cobo's classic definition of native wealth. According to Cobo, a rich man was an individual with a large family that could help him fulfill his tribute service obligations faster than a man with a small family. Although Cobo's statement refers to a commoner, the same definition undoubtedly applied to the native elite.[11]

On the north coast, as well as other areas of Peru studied by Nathan Wachtel, rank and position were directly correlated with the number of a lord's subjects. The native households under the curaca of Jayanca still numbered over 1,000 eight years after the first direct contact with Europeans. His second-in-command went by the title of *conozeque*, "lord of 1,000 Indians." Other lesser lords (*principales*, *mandones*, and *mandoncillos*) had charge over successively smaller numbers of households. In the 1560s, principales of coastal communities might hold sway over a hundred households. Mandoncillos might have as few as five.[12]

It is essential, however, to separate the curaca's *señorío* (seigniory) and *mando* (command), his position and hegemony over human resources, from a territorial base. That a distinction was made is clear from testimony concerning the lord of a group of fishermen of Jayanca. Two of four key native witnesses distinguished clearly between the señorío, *parcialidad* (part of a whole, i.e., of a group or native community) or *principalazgo* (principality), and lands. The office of curaca, then, had both demographic and geographic dimensions, though the geographic one applied more precisely to the use of resources than to land per se.

The territorial extent of an early lord's domain is still imperfectly understood and, as suggested above, often confused with the essential relationship of ruler and lord to subject. It is therefore difficult to specify the area or areas controlled by a curaca and the nature of such control. According to the oral traditions written down by early observers, the Inca or his agents and surveyors divided and marked each lord's domain when the coast was incorporated into the empire (between 1462 and 1470).[13] Guamán Poma de Ayala says the Inca divided the highlands from the coast. The seventeenth-century Mercedarian missionary Fray Martín de Murúa elaborates, saying that the Inca delegated, entrusted, and assigned land and other resources to a curaca and his followers.[14]

That this demarcation had been carried out on the north coast is evident from a petition brought before Cuenca by the cacique of Moro (a town in the modern valley of Pacasmayo) asking that the lands held by him and his counterparts of Jequetepeque, Chérrepe, and Chepén be confirmed "according to the plan [*traça*] devised by the said ancient caciques and Indians of said communities." He reiterates the need to restore the boundary markers "constructed in the time of the Inca who established them."[15]

Further evidence that the territorial domain of a curaca was indeed known and bounded comes from an official decree, dated December 6, 1567, of Licenciado Lope García de Castro regarding the founding of the Spanish town of Santiago de Miraflores in the valley of Saña. This decree locates the boundary between the valleys, and by extension the lords, of Pacasmayo and Saña "on the sandy plains that exist between the valleys of Saña and Pacasmayo . . . according to how the ancient Indians . . . had them divided."[16] These demarcations seem to have been an administrative convention designed to keep the peace and to structure relations between neighboring lords. Guamán Poma de Ayala says of the distribution of lands, "Thus were disputes avoided."[17]

These quotes do not necessarily mean that the territorial dimension of a chiefdom was one compact unit, just that each lord was delegated control of specific resources, including lands scattered along the length of a valley and in different ecological zones. Use, whether direct or indirect, however, seems a better criterion for establishing "ownership," which, as will be shown below, did not have the same connotation as today's Western concept of private property.[18] Dry lands, forests, natural pastures, and other such resources certainly fell within the lord's domain thus defined. Like the inhabitants of Canta farther to the south, whom Rostworowski studied, the peoples of the north coast told early Spaniards that irrigation water "belonged" to the curacas too. Several explained to Cuenca that if they opened a ditch and cleaned and maintained the canal, the products harvested from lands irrigated with the water, and by extension the land itself, were theirs.[19]

Theoretically, therefore, in the period immediately prior to 1532, rights to land depended ultimately on the delegated authority of the Inca. Water rights on the coast, though also ultimately dependent on the Inca, were more straightforwardly dependent on the lord who controlled the headwaters of the river or canal that ran through the coast to the sea. Augusto D. León Barandiarán, in his book *Mitos, leyendas y tradiciones Lambayecanas*, states that before the Spanish conquest, the curaca of Jayanca "bought" the ravine of Canchachalá and the water it channeled toward the coast from the lord of Penachí with "gifts" (*presentes*) or "payments" of salt, chili peppers, and cloth. Sebastián de la Gama, a visitor to Jayanca in 1540, reports much the same relationship.

> The said valley of Jayanca is large and densely populated and of many corn fields and *conico* [?]; and, during the summer, water is scarce; and because there is little [water] in the said valley, [this witness] heard from Christians and Indians that a river originates and runs through the lands of Caratache, lord of [don Lorenzo de] Ulloa [encomendero of] Guambos, with which Jayanca is irrigated, and that this cacique [Caratache] restricts the flow of water when he wants and he will not let it flow [to the coast] without [receiving] tribute.[20]

Once the water reached the coast, however, the curaca controlled it. A sentence in a court case between the lords of Jayanca and Pácora over irrigation water in the late 1530s, appealed before the Audiencia of Panama, gave the lords the right and power to name the native officials who oversaw distribution. It ordered that

> half the officials [*camayo(c)s*] that from this day forward are appointed to divide and assign [*diuidir e partir*] the said water [of the Jayanca River] should be chosen by [*puestos . . . por*] the cacique of Francisco de Lobo [encomendero of Jayanca] and the other half should be chosen by the principales of Diego Gutierrez [encomendero of Pácora]; they should divide and assign the said water as it was divided and assigned in ancient times during the reign of [the Cuzqueño] Guaina Capac.

These officials were to give the curaca of Jayanca ten days of water to irrigate his corn fields and those planted for his encomendero, lesser lords, and subjects. The lord of Pácora and his followers were allotted eight.[21]

Control of the water gave the curaca jurisdiction over irrigated agricultural land. In a now insect-eaten and incomplete notarial register of the native *cabildo* (municipal council) of Lambayeque, a

local scribe recorded the oral testimony of old men to the effect that
the lands that those born in Lambayeque still held in 1607 had been
given and assigned to them (*q[ue] les fueron repartidas y señaladas*)
by the *caciques antiguos* of the town. Again, they declared that the
lands "belonged" to the lords. They had been passed down in some
cases, according to the native witnesses, through as many as ten
generations.[22]

The curaca entrusted these lands to the lesser lords under him,
who in turn entrusted them to subordinates further down the hierarchy until individual heads of households actually received parcels.
In the land register of Lambayeque, quoted above, one entry says, regarding the lands called Colluçi, that they "belonged" to the heirs of
the principal Chum, because "in times past the said principales of
Chum rented them and paid rent to the principal of Collocçi."[23]
These statements show that in return for access to resources, the
users customarily gave the lord a gift. Thus, the lesser lord called
"Chum" gave "rent" (for lack of a better English term) to the principal Collocçi. So, too, the lord of Ferreñafe would not let a subordinate plant on lands without tribute, "as has always been done by the
Indians to this day." And the lords of Jayanca divided and subdivided
the lands among their subjects in return for an annual *terrasgo* (land
tax or rent).[24] Irrigation water, as noted above, was also "owned"
and subject to a "rental." The curaca of Jayanca, for example, "made
his [subjects] buy water and did not want to give it to them without
their paying him in good gold."[25]

The interpretation of the words *gifts, terrasgo, rent, tribute,* and
payment in the above passages must be understood first as reflec-
tions of expected reciprocity between subjects and lord and second
in terms of labor service. Rostworowski, to whom we are increasingly indebted for information on early native society, tells us that
the father of Efquen Zula (who became principal of the community
of Reque) had been a subject (*feudatario*) of the curaca of Callanca,
"and it was his obligation to bring his people to work on the traditional lands of the curaca of Callanca."[26] So, too, in Jayanca the
lesser lord apportioned lands that were to be tilled for the curaca in
recognition of his hegemony.

> In all the principalities they gave in that time [pre–Hispanic conquest] a
> plot of land to the paramount lord and that said Neptur [a principal] had
> assigned a piece of land to the cacique of Jayanca as his lord and that this
> witness has seen that in the jurisdiction [parcialidad] of said Neptur, the
> said don Francisco lord of Jayanca possesses a piece of land that he has
> planted.

The goods (corn, pepper, and cloth) mentioned in the passages quoted above as gifts or payment for irrigation water resulted from planting and cultivating these two crops and cotton and weaving the latter into cloth. Labor input was how the tribute obligations were originally assigned and measured. The payment in *buen oro* ("good gold") expected by the curaca of Jayanca in 1539 was probably a Spanish idea and imposition.[27]

Curacas also allowed subjects of other lords to use some of these resources. In addition to the many references of curacas "renting" land to subjects of other lords, we have the 1540 instructions that Pizarro gave Diego Verdejo, an encomendero and the person he entrusted with conducting a visit or inspection tour of the north coast. In these instructions, Pizarro asked Verdejo to find out, among many other things, "what [how many] foreign immigrant [*advenediros*] Indians[,] subjects of other cacique[s] and foreigners [*mitimaes*] they [the curacas] have [under their jurisdiction]."[28]

The practice of allowing outsiders, or "foreigners," to use lands and other resources probably benefited both parties. The visiting curaca and his subjects got the use of resources he might not ordinarily control, and the resident lord received part of the produce from the incoming users as rent. This practice also explains how a preconquest curaca of Jayanca could have his subjects working two days' distance away on land under the jurisdiction of the lord and community of Túcume. It also suggests that señorío, defined as the relationship between ruler and subordinates, did not necessarily correspond to the territorial jurisdiction of a lord as established for administrative purposes. In other words, the social frontiers of a *curacazgo* as defined by allegiance or loyalty were not necessarily coincident with territorial boundaries and control.[29]

The obligations of the commoners to their lord did not end with cultivating a piece of land for him. They also helped him fulfill his responsibilities to the Inca and maintain the rest of the community. Thus, they worked to open new canals and to keep the existing ones open and free of debris. They followed their lords to service and man the inns (*tambos*) and to maintain the roads. They joined their curaca, as ceremonial leader, to clean, plant, cultivate, weed, harvest, deliver, and store the commodities from the lands tilled for the state and the gods.[30]

To recruit the labor he needed for these tasks, the curaca personally visited the lesser lords and their subjects wherever they lived. Don Juan of Collique, on trial for his life for killing his two pages in 1566, insisted to Cuenca that he needed to go "to see the towns by

the sea." Sometimes such journeys entailed traveling long distances
and making frequent stops. The existing early censuses and the to-
ponyms of the settlements under the various lords show clearly that
a curaca's subjects were spread out in hamlets. In 1540, the subjects
of the curaca of Jayanca lived in about 250 settlements scattered
over a two-league radius from his administrative center. In other
valleys, villages and hamlets whose inhabitants recognized the same
lord might be one, two, or sometimes several leagues away. One curaca declared that he had subjects "in a district of over 30 leagues
from the sea to [the highlands of] Cajamarca."[31] Other curacas with
known groups of subjects living at great distances from them included Copez (Copis), who lived on the coastal plain and had some
principales that lived next to the Guambos (in the Cajamarca highlands); the curaca of Controilico, "who lives on the coastal plains
with another [subject] principal [Penachí] in the highlands"; and the
curaca of Saña, who had subjects living in nine towns in Cajamarca.[32]

A curaca who went to visit distant subjects would be accompanied by suitable pomp and circumstance. Rostworowski, basing her
remarks on a sixteenth-century manuscript dealing with succession
of paramount lords in the community of Reque, notes that when the
coastal curacas left on these trips, they were accompanied by "a
great ostentatious show [*gran aparato*] of people." Two to three hundred bearers sometimes carried the chief's hammock or litter and
supplies. In addition, trumpeters came along to play and announce
his approach, and there were jesters or buffoons to amuse and enter-
tain the retinue. Pedro de Cieza de León also describes the court and
retinue of the paramount lords of Jayanca, a few kilometers north of
Reque, and the surrounding valleys:

> And there were [in the valley of Jayanca] large apartments [*aposentos*] and
> warehouses [*depositos*] belonging to the principal lords in which were
> stationed their highest-ranking mayordomos. . . . The natural lords of
> these valleys were esteemed and venerated by their subjects: those who
> have survived still are: and they are accompanied and well-served by
> women and servants and they employ porters and guards.[33]

Another characteristic of these visits was *chicha* (maize beer)
drinking and banquets. Wherever the curaca stopped, "all had to
drink of his chicha," according to the notable native defender Bartolomé de Las Casas. Fray Buenaventura Salinas y Córdova wrote
that when the female curaca of Tumbes received Francisco Pizarro
and his men, she offered them a banquet under a lean-to. Northern
curacas lectured Cuenca on the need to provide chicha and food to
their subjects as part of ritualistic exchange for services. Guamán

Poma de Ayala speaks of an indigenous "law" of compassion, mercifulness or loving-kindness (*"ley de misericordia"*) that predated the Incas whereby "all ate in the public plaza." And, he adds, "in every community and town they observed this law."[34]

It was precisely for the festivities, banquets, and beer; the occasional gifts of clothing, beads, and fine alpaca slippers; and, more important, the access to land, water, and other natural resources that the commoners and their lesser lords participated in communal labor under the curaca's direction, even if it meant leaving their homes and traveling some distance. In one account, the principales and commoners living three leagues away agreed to the curaca's request "to obey him and do what he asks." Another commoner had to travel two leagues to see the curaca "to obey him and do what he orders . . . in the public works projects."[35]

Without those incentives subjects would not obey. Cristóbal Payco, principal of the community of Jequetepeque and town of Lloco, asked for permission to provide chicha to the workers on community projects, explaining that

> the Indians obey their caciques and principales because of that custom [*mediante aquella costumbre*] that they have of giving them drink . . . if it were not because they gave drink to the Indians who will work [*benefiçiar*] [this land] and the others who will plant the field of the community to pay the tribute, they would not cooperate [*juntar*] to do it.

The cacique principal of Moro and others reiterated and confirmed this statement for their communities as well.[36]

Thus, for the use of the resources, the beer, banquets, and other ceremonies and festivities, and the exchanges of gifts, the commoners produced a surplus that the curaca could use to fulfill his obligations, reinforce relationships, and build his reputation. The curaca was the prime mover of the entire regional redistributive exchange system, as shown schematically in Fig. 1. On his organizational, motivational, and administrative skills rested his largess and hospitality and ultimately his reputation as a great man and leader. His generosity was a measure of his success and the strength, productivity, and prosperity of his people.[37]

The obligations between ruler and ruled were mutually reinforcing and interdependent. The better the curaca's organization, coordination, and direction, the greater the productivity, the larger the surplus, the more abundant the feasts, the more frequent and richer the gifts, the higher the standard of living of the populace, and the larger the community. The curaca delegated authority to the lesser lords to aid him in organizing the communal labor force and in

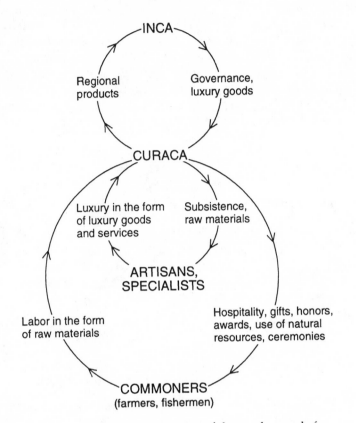

Fig. 1 Indigenous socioeconomic organization of the north coast before 1532

redistributing goods. The more the curaca gave away, the greater was his subjects' obligation to reciprocate with labor service and the easier it was to "request" aid and manipulate, coax, and cajole them into obeying his commands. The more they produced, the higher the standard of living of the community as a whole, and the more likely the curaca could attract others to his ranks. For serving the Inca well, a curaca often received gifts of women, who would expand his immediate household by having more offspring and thus increase his productivity. A relatively prosperous community would encourage subjects of other lords to marry into the local curaca's service and embolden others to ask the curaca for protection or help in return for their labor.[38] Theoretically, it follows that a curaca's power and reputation could expand, subject to the approval of the Inca and the limits of the natural resources under his control, as shown in Fig. 2.

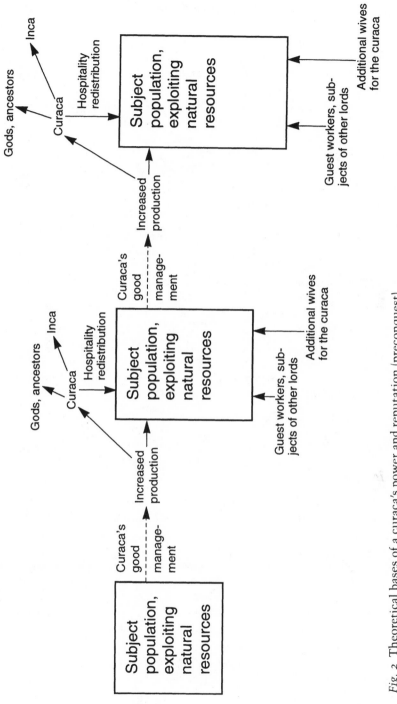

Fig. 2 Theoretical bases of a curaca's power and reputation (preconquest)

Indeed, the curaca's ability to facilitate the functioning of the economic system was perhaps the most important reinforcement of his rank and position. Early testimonies clearly establish the ability to maintain or improve the well-being of the community as a criterion for legitimacy and succession to high office. In the sixteenth-century court battles over the political leadership of north coastal communities, witnesses agreed that birthright alone was not sufficient to ensure succession to the office of curaca. In the early sixteenth century, a curaca was chosen from among several contenders by the incumbent curaca or a council of principal persons. Candidates for the office of curaca in Reque were "able and sufficient, capable and kind." In Catacaos, too, a chieftain's sons did not necessarily inherit office. If capable sons existed, the curaca might choose "the one who had the best judgment." If no sons survived to adulthood or seemed worthy, the curaca might choose another able Indian "of his kin or of others of more ability and qualifications [*suficiencia*] without giving them the right of succession because they were named and supported according to their capability and talent to fulfill the said position." Up and down the coast, natives agreed that one needed "a lot of understanding to govern the *cacicazgo*."[39]

Licenciado Hernando de Santillán, in summarizing the succession principle on a kingdomwide level, also defines ability, understanding, and sufficiency.

> All those who were lords showed great zeal that they be succeeded by a person who was sufficient enough to govern [*bastante para mandar*] and who would conserve his dominion [*señorío*] and thus during their lifetime they would choose from among the principales of their jurisdiction [*provincia*] the one who was most capable [*más hábil*] and of the best customs.

The key phrase of Santillán that explains the object of a lord's "capability" is "conserve his dominion." "His dominion" referred to his subjects, without whom the natural resources he controlled were of little use.[40]

Murúa sums up the role of the curaca from an indigenous perspective, observing that "curacas and lords of Indians they call caciques, that really means lord who is responsible for the people." The curacas of the coast saw themselves in exactly these terms: "We are caciques and we have Indians to command and visit." Their subjects, the people and their sheer numbers, were an index of the curacas' wealth, power, and reputation, as noted above.[41]

Guamán Poma de Ayala further states that population growth was rewarded in late pre-Hispanic times and provided opportunities for upward mobility. He tells us that an individual could become a principal simply by having children, for his status increased positively with the size of his family. If he had five children, he received jurisdiction over them and was named a lesser lord, a "little overseer" (mandoncillo). If he had ten children, he was granted the status of mandón (overseer). If he had 30 to 50 children, he could found a community and be given jurisdiction over an area in his own right. To amass large numbers of progeny, a man would have to have several wives, which we also know to have been possible and customary for the elite in northern Peru and elsewhere.[42]

Rostworowski found that on the north coast, as numbers grew, communities divided and each segment chose a leader, subject to the approval of the Inca. In their 1558 manuscript, Fray Cristóbal de Castro and Diego de Ortega Morejón discuss the periodic censuses that the Inca ordered taken and state that "as the people multiplied they made [new] lords." Although great mobility in one lifetime was probably a rare accomplishment, the reward structure existed. In these cases, wealth and mobility rested on achievement, defined as population growth and, by extension, good management and "institutionalized generosity," to use a phrase favored by Murra.[43]

If the curaca failed to live up to his subjects' expectations, he was removed by rebellion and murder. Rostworowski recounts the oral traditions of the north coast that tell how curacas were eliminated if they did not provide for the well-being of the community. In one instance, tradition recalls, Fempellec, a lord of Lambayeque, decided to move an idol from its temple. This angered the gods, who sent thirty days of rain followed by a year of sterility and hunger. Fempellec was blamed for the disaster and drowned by the priests. Likewise, curacas could be deposed from office if they did not provide food for public banquets in the plazas or if they failed to be just—that is, if they violated the principles of "good government." Without this "institutionalized generosity," the entire community was "in danger of losing everything."[44]

The curaca redistributed goods, then, as much for his own self-interest as for the material benefit of his people. Perishable foodstuffs could not be stored indefinitely, given the technology of the day. There was a limit on the cloth he could personally or ritualistically use. There was no value in hoarding, so he invested his surplus in goodwill, by giving it away. Although the early curacas were renowned as rich men, their last wills and testaments show they died materially poor, judged by Spanish standards. Most of these documents mention houses, cattle, beads, cloth, and occasionally one or more silver or wooden drinking mugs (*cocos*). Few curacas, however, had all these goods at the time of death.[45]

The curaca was truly the *dueño de indios*, with life-and-death power over them. But he had no reason to kill or to restrict the use of resources. It was to his advantage to share. By so doing, he enhanced his reputation as a good, generous, and able provider; reinforced his legitimacy in the eyes of his people; and thus secured as his reward a place in the collective and selective memory. He would be celebrated in song, become a revered ancestor, and thus achieve immortality.[46]

Socioeconomic Disarticulation and Collapse to 1572–73; or, Why the Indians Stopped Singing Songs in Praise of Their Curacas

The Spanish invasion and conquest, which the curacas were powerless to stop, quickly changed the circumstances within which a curaca acted and in so doing changed the nature and function of the office and destroyed the basic premise on which the curaca's power rested. Thereafter, he was no longer identified as the guarantor of the well-being of his people. In less than 40 years, those who were invested with high office became foremost, though sometimes ambivalently, accomplices and functionaries of the Spanish colonial state.

Several factors—all acting to destroy the functional balance between curaca and subjects—operated simultaneously. The first and perhaps best documented was the demographic collapse. The populations of both coast and highlands had already been decimated by disease that spread from Mesoamerica into South America years before Francisco Pizarro's first voyage down the coast in 1529. The chroniclers tell us that Guayna Capac died of a strange illness (assumed by many to have been either smallpox or measles) in Quito in 1524–25. Some scholars estimate that the population had fallen by 50 percent before the arrival of the Spanish. Table 1 shows that the population continued to drop dramatically through the sixteenth century.

Depopulation is also certainly evident in the town-to-town census of Jayanca in 1540. On Tuesday, July 27, 1540, Sebastián de la Gama arrived at a town where twelve of the twenty dwellings had collapsed. Farther along his route, he noted another town where only eight, less than half the original number, remained standing. During the next two days he visited several more settlements with

TABLE I

Population of the North Coast Region (Sixteenth Century)

Encomienda	Year	Tribute payers	Total population
Chuspo-Callanca	1572	716	2,972
(Monsefú)	1578–80	624	2,443
	1592	375	—
	1593	358[a]	2,101
	1593	250[b]	2,131
	1597	356[c]	—
Chérrepe	1564	200	650
	1572	290	934
	1573	197	—
	1576–83	131	—
	1580	216	—
	1581	199–201[d]	—
	1582	212	—
	1583	278[e]	918[e]
	1584	293	—
	1588	136	—
	1591	144[f]	—
	1593	102	718
	1597	115	—
Collique	1570	582	—
	1572–82	518–82	2,325
	1581	577	—
	1582	518[f]	—
	1596	381	—
	1597	386	1,869[g]
Eten (see also Collique and Sinto)	1593	96	937
Ferreñafe	1532	—	c. 2,000
	1572	398	—
	1572	535	1,985[h]
	1561–76	241	—
	1575	350	—
	1591	398[f]	—
	1593	214	2,261
	1599	260	—
Illimo	1541	300	—
	1572	834	3,335
	1593	357	2,762
	1597	390	—
Jayanca	1540	680[i]	4,000[i]
	1558	c. 1,362	—
	1566	1,700	—
	1572	1,248[k]	6,068
	1567–89	530	—
Jequetepeque	1530	3,584	17,920
	1572	896	3,787[l]
	1580	74?	—
	1581	72?	—
	1582	714	—

TABLE I (*continued*)

Encomienda	Year	Tribute payers	Total population
	1582	757[m]	3,785[m]
	1591	687[f, n]	3,435[o]
	1598–99	623	—
Lambayeque	1572	—	8,000–9,000
	1575	1,584	5,854
	1591	1,453[f]	—
	1593	1,009[p]	10,416
	1597	1,070	4,070
Mocupe	1572	317	—
	1593	190[a]	1,327[a]
	1593	176[b]	—
	1597	230	—
Reque	1566	c. 700	—
	1572	650	2,572
	1582–88	530[q]	—
	1591	536	3,506
	1593	326[b]	2,744[b]
	1593	358[a]	—
	1597	360	—
	1599	318–24	1,928–34
Saña (town of)	1532	3000	—
	1549	1,300–1,500	—
	1563	400–600[r]	—
	1563	500–900[s]	—
	1566	c. 300	—
	1572	320[t]	1,223
	1591	219[u]	—
Sinto	1572	644	—
	1572–75	731	2,373
	1579	613	2,247
	1583	—	4,698[v]
	1590	—	2,431
	1593	770[w]	5,502[x]
Túcume-Mochumí	1540	1,190[y]	—
	1566	1,935[z]	—
	1572	1,554	5,779
	1576–1604	744	—
	1581	528	1,400–40
	1582	1,080	—
	1591–92	820[f]	—
	1593	381[aa]	1,246[aa]
	1593	330[bb]	—
	1597	400	—

SOURCES: Ramírez, "Land Tenure," appendix 1, pp. 535–44; Mogrovejo, pp. 232–34; AGI/P 97, r. 4, 1569, 16v; AL 320; AL 464, 1583; J 418, 1573, 3, 115v, 203v, 256v, 301, 309, 312v–15, 323, 339; J 420, 1574, 2, 152v, 154v–55; J 455, 1317v; J 457, 701v, 851, 867v, 870; J 460, 486v, 154v–55; ART/CoO, 13-VII-1570, 96–99v; CaO, 1.3, exp.65, 15-X-1573; LC, 1558; Mata, 9-XII-1562, 28-VII-1565, 24-X-1565; ANP/SG, 1.2, c.12, 1587; R, 1.2, c.5, 1582, 132, 135; R, 1.3, c.7, 1582, 95v, 164, 507; BNP/A310, 1584, 35v; Rostworowski, "Visitas," p. 90; Busto, p. 325; Centro de Estudios, vol. 1, p. 122; Lecuanda, p. 240; Burga, p. 195; Pérez and Carmona, p. 602; Gama, pp. 224, 227. The data contained in this table overlap with those presented by Cook. Much of my data predates his and in general comes from local-level sources rather than viceregal reports.

*a*According to the corregidor. Note that when more than one figure has been found for one year, all are shown.

*b*According to the priest.

*c*Includes 66 tributarios (tribute payers) in the town of Ranuca.

*d*Only 179 tributarios were actually present. The missing included 8 dead and 13 who had fled.

*e*Includes both Chérrepe and Mocupe.

*f*These figures were taken from a revision of Viceroy Francisco Toledo's tribute lists of the mid-1570s.

*g*For both Collique and Sinto.

*h*The date may be 1583.

*i*Without 118 mitimaes absent or sick within two leagues of Jayanca.

*j*Maximum.

*k*300 Indians were moved from Jayanca to Pácora.

*l*Includes 150 tributarios and 542 other people from Chepén, and 189 tributarios and 728 other people from Moro.

*m*According to Burga, p. 63.

*n*Including San Pedro de Lloc.

*o*According to Burga, p. 63, including San Pedro de Lloc.

*p*966 paid tribute; 23 were absent; 20 were excused from paying tribute.

*q*Burga gives this figure for 1578–79.

*r*Without mitimaes.

*s*Counting mitimaes.

*t*Excludes 219 mitimaes of Saña.

*u*Excludes 44 mitimaes of Saña.

*v*Including Eten.

*w*Includes the tributarios of Eten and Farcap; the tributarios of Eten numbered 96; those of Farcap numbered 67.

*x*The population of Sinto was 4,160; Eten, 937; Farcap, 405.

y"Married Indians."

*z*These are probably tribute payers.

*aa*Mochumí only.

*bb*Túcume only.

"demolished" and "fallen" dwellings and passed many "ruined towns."[47] Not all the evidence of population collapse can be attributed to disease. In 1543 the native officials of Conchucos (in the hinterland of Trujillo) assured the visitor Cristóbal Ponce de León that some of their number had been killed fighting or forced to go to places far away (such as Los Bracamoros, Quito, Chachapoyas, and Cuzco). Pedro de Cieza de León, on the road between San Miguel de Piura and Trujillo in 1548, also noted that the wars had reduced the population.[48]

The second major factor that affected the power of the curaca was the granting of encomiendas, which gave a Spaniard the right to appropriate the labor of native inhabitants of specific communities in return for his protection and religious instruction. As I have shown in more detail elsewhere, the Spanish did not respect indigenous administrative units when they distributed the population in encomiendas. Pizarro, perhaps pressured by the number of his followers who sought grants, frequently divided the subjects of one curaca between two or more Spaniards. In 1536, for example, he divided the peoples of Túcume between Juan Roldán and Juan de Osorno. Pacasmayo was divided into four encomiendas: Chérrepe, Moro, Chepén, and Jequetepeque. Fray Domingo de Santo Tomás also remarked on this phenomenon in 1550, noting that the Spanish often divided a province into as many as three or four encomiendas.[49]

This division often led to rank inflation. Lesser lords, convinced that the Spanish did not understand the preconquest power structure, seized the opportunity to make themselves "curacas" of newly created encomiendas. They adopted the titles, insignias (*duo* [throne or seat] and *vara* [staff of office]), and privileges (being carried in a litter) originally reserved for the paramount chief alone. In so doing, they quickly outnumbered the "old-style" curacas and immensely complicated the task of delimiting the original curacazgos in 1532.[50] Moreover, the dismembering of the curaca's demographic unit reduced his economic base and the productive capacity of the community.

The most serious crisis for the old-style curacas came during the 1560s, when the Spanish began systematically to settle the northern coastal valleys. The first of a series of events designed to permanently attract Spaniards to the area was the founding of a Spanish town in the valley of Saña in 1563. The king's agent chose the site of the inn at the customary ford in the river for the settlement. He then segregated the native residents of the valley to one side of the river, with the Spanish occupying the other; each of the 40 or so Spanish *vecinos* (citizens) of the new town was given 40 *fanegadas* (approximately 115 hectares) of land on which to begin farming. The establishment of Saña coincided with a marked expansion in agriculture and cattle raising in the surrounding valleys.[51]

Next, a series of *reducciones* (reductions) concentrated scattered hamlets into nucleated towns, greatly altering the indigenous settlement pattern and thus facilitating the expansion of the Spanish agricultural sector. Scholars are increasingly aware that Viceroy Francisco de Toledo was not the first to carry out reducciones in Peru. In the north the first systematic reducciones of which we have record were ordered by Cuenca, whose public pronouncements justified the procedure as beneficial to the native peoples. Concentration would facilitate their conversion and do them no harm, he stated emphatically. They need not fear moving far from their ancestral homes and lands, he continued, because he would reassign them lands close to their new settlements. Cuenca therefore ordered the scattered subjects of one lord after another to move to several centralized locations.[52]

In fact, however, concentration often benefited the Spaniards more than the native peoples. A nucleated population facilitated conversion and also tax collection and control. Native communities were reassigned lands close to their new settlements, as promised, but these sites were often in the lower parts of the coastal valleys, near the sea. The lands given them in the "new valleys" were usually inferior to the ones they had lost, having a high water table, salination problems, and fog and cloud cover that effectively reduced the growing season. Furthermore, the lands tended to be contiguous, being one or a few parcels. This often meant the loss of access to a range of scattered ecological niches and the variety of products these had provided the curaca and his people.

Thus, a hidden agenda of the reducciones was to open up land coveted by the Spanish. Cuenca had ordered that no new *estancias* (cattle stations) be established near Andean settlements because of the potential damage cattle could do to the peasants' unfenced crops. Concentration, therefore, was essential if additional ranches were to be established. Moving clusters consisting of one or two families into larger settlements opened up a great deal of the best land in the northern coastal valleys to cattle raising and later to cultivation of such cash crops as wheat and sugar cane.[53]

Both encomenderos and the natives themselves realized that the reducciones were not in their best interest. One encomendero complained that the reducciones ordered by Cuenca removed Indians to "sickly" (swampy?) terrain where 200 succumbed. One group of fishermen, despite a campaign of organized opposition symbolized by a notarized petition against the move and authority to approach the viceroy with their request, were resettled two leagues inland. They abandoned their new homes, scattered, and wandered about until allowed to reestablish themselves on the sea coast where they had lived previously. In 1572, six years after the process was begun by Cuenca, it was completed under Viceroy Toledo. The known results of the reducciones on the north coast are summarized in Table 2.[54]

Only a hint of the widespread changes occurring during this time can be provided by the references summarized above. There were about 55 named towns in fifteen encomiendas created by the Spanish by the mid-1570s. Even when compared, for example, to the original visit of Jayanca in 1540, which lists some 250 hamlets and towns in that one community, this is an inadequate reminder of the changes that must have taken place within the first few decades of the Spanish conquest, many of them even before the systematic Spanish settlement of the northern coastal valleys. Regardless of the effect of individual moves on the native peoples, the overall result was the same: fewer and fewer Indian towns.[55]

But the undermining of a curaca's traditional power did not end with the disarticulation of communities into multiple encomiendas or the concentration of scattered homesteads into reducciones. In the 1560s the colonial state systematically applied pressures designed to further restrict the power of indigenous lords. In the north,

TABLE 2

Reducciones of Lambayeque

Settlement before reduction	Settlement after reduction	Source
14–15 pueblos in Chicama	4 pueblos in Chicama	AGI/J 460, 365v
Tecapa	San Pedro de Lloc	AGI/J 458, 1419
Chérrepe, Choloc, elderly Indians from the royal way station	Chérrepe (new location of)	AGI/J 459, 3062v
Quincala	Culop(o)	Ibid.
3–4 pueblos in Licapa	2 pueblos in Licapa	AGI/J 460, 365; J 457, 790
Noquique	Chérrepe	BNP/A310, 1584
100 Indians from the royal road to Saña	Moro	AGI/J 460, 461
Mitimaes of Saña	pueblos*a*	AGI/J 459, 3064–65v
Mayna	Reque	AGI/J 457, 792v
Callanca	Monsefú	ART/ICompa, 11-XII-1787
Pueblo of fishermen, Callanca	Callanca	ART/Mata, 1587, 2v
Moclla	Pololo	AGI/J 455, 1689v
Chacchacalla	Llomonte	AGI/J 457, 727v
3 pueblos in Collique	1 pueblo in Collique	AGI/J 457, 732v
Sinto	Chiclayo	AGI/J 457, 818v
300 tributarios of Pololo	Chiclayo	AGI/J 457, 832–34
Collique	Chiclayo	ART/CoCompa, 15-I-1781, 13–14, 44v
San Miguel de Picsi	Chiclayo	OCI/Monsefú, 110 5345, 73
Sinto	Picsi	ANP/DI, l. 19, c.483, 1793, 31v
Corñan	Lambayeque	ART/CoCompa, 15-I-1781
Repartimiento de San Salvador (de Jayanca)	3 pueblos*a*	AGI/P 189, r.11, 1566–67

NOTE: The table is ordered by valley, south to north.
*a*The sources give no further information on these sites.

curacas suffered a further reduction of authority when Cuenca implemented several decrees that, among other things, restricted the
travel of the lords by prohibiting them from riding horses and forbade
them to provide maize beer to their subjects. The lords protested
these measures and petitioned to be exempted in return for a fee.
The curacas argued first that they were loyal subjects, implying that
they would not use their horses to mount a rebellion as the Andean
peoples in the southern highlands had done. Second, they argued
that without horses they could not visit their subjects. If they could
not travel they would lose contact with their people, especially
those who still lived far from their administrative center. And, more

important, if they lacked the ability to provide subjects with maize beer, the people would not work. Because the curacas, individually and as a group, were quickly becoming the intermediaries between the Spanish and the native commoners, having been approved or chosen precisely for their ability to get the natives to produce tribute goods, the curacas' petitions for exemption from these decrees were usually successful. But the damage was already done.[56]

Furthermore, the curacas complained that Cuenca increased the tribute the commoners had to pay while listing the young, the old, the dead, and those who had fled as tribute payers to increase the number of individuals liable to contribute to the support of the Spanish. In the community of Lambayeque, for example, Cuenca increased the tribute due to the encomendero from 1,500 to 2,500 pieces of cloth per year and raised the quotas of silver to 1,000 pesos (2,117 patacones 5 reales), of corn to 3,000 fanegas (each approximately 1.5 bushels), and of chickens to 4,000. This was "much more than they used to give."[57]

At the same time, Cuenca cut the personal services, and hence the support, the curacas could expect from their subjects. The curacas complained that their income had dropped to the point that they were reduced to living at the level of commoners. Further, they maintained, they could not fulfill their obligations, and consequently their authority was being undermined. The lords were in danger of being "lowly esteemed and not obeyed by the rest of their subject Indians." Don Juan claimed that Cuenca's allocation to him and his peers was so low that "the cacique[s] pr[incip]ales are like commoners, who no longer wanted to obey them like they used to." The lord of Túcume similarly complained that his subjects did not obey him as they did in the time of the Incas.[58]

The old-style curacas who tried to explain the traditional system to Cuenca and the Spanish became a threat to the evolving administrative structure and its ends. Outspokenness and defiance provoked the Spanish and hastened a curaca's removal. It may have been don Juan's defense of his traditional rights and those of his community, located in one of the most fertile of the north coastal valleys and the heart of new settlement, that provoked Cuenca's wrath and hastened the curaca's execution.[59]

Increasingly, the Spanish appointed curacas and lords who would carry out their instructions and best serve them. Francisco Pizarro began the practice, and later encomenderos continued to impose anyone they wished as curaca—"not the person that should have succeeded according to the Indians' rights and privileges [*fueros*] and customs." Guamán Poma de Ayala confirms this, saying, "They made a poor, tax-paying commoner paramount lord."[60]

In general, if the cacique did not deliver the required goods to the Spanish, he was replaced, regardless of circumstances, by one who would. Thus, in Pácora, don Cristóbal's lands were "rented" out to commoners from Jayanca by the encomendero, who received cloth and other goods from them in return. Don Cristóbal complained that he, therefore, could not pay tribute or fulfill his obligations to his people. In response, his encomendero, who also happened to be an authority of a nearby Spanish town, replaced him with a boy who presumably would cooperate.[61]

As this practice spread, commoners were asked to work for lords chosen not according to their ancient custom but by fiat of the encomendero or local Spanish authority. They were asked to obey not to guarantee the security and well-being of their community, but to support a growing number of Spaniards. Over time, the encomendero increased his exactions, appropriating more and more of a community's surplus. The exchange was skewed to the benefit of the Spaniards. The cost to the encomendero of religious instruction was a small fraction of the total tribute the natives gave him. And often, especially in these early years, the encomendero failed to provide any catechism at all.

Before 1532, most goods produced by tribute labor recirculated through redistribution. Few were "lost" to ritual burning or ceremonials. Even time spent producing goods for the Inca was compensated with gifts of women and luxury items and commodities that were often unavailable locally. By contrast, after the Spanish conquest more and more labor was directed to producing large quantities that were siphoned out of the indigenous economy to supply a growing market demand in the Spanish sector. As this process continued, the aura of the good and able native leader diminished and with it the reason to respect, obey, remember, and praise him.[62]

The colonial cacique was increasingly squeezed, to an extent unparalleled under the Inca. Caught between his responsibility for the well-being of his subjects and the demands of the Spanish, he sacrificed, in some instances reluctantly, the former. As exactions increased, the curaca, to remain a curaca, began to mistreat his subjects, and the level of recalcitrance, discontent, and resistance on their part rose accordingly. Frustrations grew because commoners had no effective recourse against the spiraling demands of the colonial system, which were transmitted and interpreted through the curaca.[63]

One response was to rebel and, as in the past, remove the leader. Records from the end of the sixteenth century tell how Xancol Chumbi surrendered to the Spanish in 1532 and became their agent, as cacique of Reque. Rostworowski recounts that Chumbi's excessive subservience to the foreigners forced him to demand from the people under his charge more labor than they were accustomed to giving under the Inca. The inhabitants of Reque came to hate their curaca, who had not been chosen according to their customs but instead imposed by the encomendero. Lacking legitimacy in the minds of his subjects, Xancol Chumbi was murdered by two members of his community.[64] Edeco, who had been a lesser lord (principal of the cooks) under Xancol Chumbi, was elected curaca soon thereafter. Edeco himself, however, did not last more than a few months because "he showed himself to be incapable of exercising his responsibility and was deposed."[65]

Over time, rebellion became less possible, for the curacas installed by the Spanish were also protected by them. Vastly outnumbered by the natives, the Spanish countered the slightest disobedience with severe punishment, as much in warning as in retribution. Furthermore, even if one curaca was removed from office, the Spanish would quickly replace him. Hope of change through this traditional means seemed in vain.[66]

Increased labor exaction; increased pressure from their lords, whom they no longer saw as legitimate, to meet production quotas; and the associated mistreatment and abuse (i.e., "bad government") also caused commoners to flee in great numbers. Because flight was an individual or family response to a deteriorating situation and apparently could be accomplished with relative ease, it became the favored alternative.[67]

The local manuscript record is full of complaints from curacas of subjects who left their service and fled. In about 1566, the natives of Pácora fled to Túcume and other places to avoid weaving 600 pieces of cloth per year, which they considered too much, given their rapidly dwindling numbers. Chuyen, a native woman married to Lloren, who was from Saña, had "fled and [they] are now with don Gonzalo, principal of Collique." Pedro Mollipe, a principal of Túcume, claimed twelve to fifteen subjects who had fled to the valley of Motupe. There were people from the province of Cajamarca and parcialidad of Chontal in Chuspo and Collique.[68] One Spaniard described the situation in 1558, saying, "The Indians wander from one town to another without settling in any one, especially not in the town where they were born."[69]

By 1558, the frequency of these movements led to a major meeting of the curacas of the north coast to resolve their claims. In attendance were the curacas of the communities of Sinto, Túcume, Ferreñafe, Lambayeque, Collique, Chuspo, and Saña. At this meeting, the curacas agreed to return refugees to the jurisdiction of their original curaca. Thus, the curaca of Reque got subjects who were living under the protection of the lords of Collique, Chuspo, and Lambayeque. The lord of Chuspo received subjects who had fled to Lambayeque, Túcume, Sinto, and Reque. The lord of Ferreñafe recovered natives who had earlier fled to Raco, Reque, and Chuspo. The lord of Sinto recovered commoners from the lords of Lambayeque, Collique, Ferreñafe, and Chuspo. The presiding Spanish judge (alcalde ordinario) then ordered the people of Sinto to remain there and deliver their tribute to the encomendero of Sinto and prohibited curacas from the nearby communities of Ferreñafe, Túcume, Chuspo, Lambayeque, Collique, and Raco from luring them away or encouraging them to leave.[70]

But, despite the above order and another stipulating "that no cacique have another's Indians [indios agenos]," Andean peoples continued to leave their original communities. Petitions to Cuenca indicate that in 1566 there were many disputes among curacas and principales for the control of subjects, with encomenderos often taking part to claim that particular Indians "belonged to their principales." When these absent subjects were located, they lived on land and presumably under the protection of another lord. Thus, the curaca of Callanca found his principal, Lanpe, residing in Lambayeque. When questioned by the authorities, however, Lanpe declared that he was from Lambayeque. The matter was settled when the curaca of Lambayeque admitted that Lanpe was from Callanca.[71]

Records of this dispute and others, though often incomplete, seem puzzling on two counts. On the one hand, the vehemence with which two lords both claimed the subjects is surprising if one assumes that one lord was lying. On the other, neither lords nor subjects, as in the case of Lanpe, seemed to know for certain to whom they rightly owed service. This confusion may be due to the fact that in preconquest times, one subject owed allegiance to more than one lord. A commoner might serve by cultivating plots for both a lesser lord and the curaca. After the conquest and the dismemberment of the original units, former subordinate lords became curacas in their own right. Since a commoner had previously served both, both claimed him; both had rights.[72]

The example of Lanpe also illustrates another facet of the migration phenomenon—that is, that some of the peoples who fled were encouraged to do so, as competition between curacas for subjects increased. As early as 1539, Jayanque, the curaca of Jayanca, "was served by the Indians of others," and he continued to "usurp" them for a decade or more thereafter. The lord of Túcume was known to have taken an entire town from the lord of Ferreñafe. Two years later, the same lord complained that a principal took sixteen of his subjects. In 1566, the cacique of Ferreñafe tried to get Indians from don Diego Mochumí in Túcume, and don Martín, curaca principal of Lambayeque, accused don Antonio, curaca of Sinto, of enticing several principales and their subjects to leave Lambayeque. An informant alleged that "caciques go around taking Indians from other communities."[73]

Enticements, or pull factors, included access to land, such as Lanpe was given in Lambayeque, since it was established custom that curacas could assign land and provide irrigation water to subjects of lords other than their own. In addition to land, immigrants were offered other rewards for moving. Cuenca stated: "They are used to gathering and bringing Indians from other parts that they call yanaconas. They give them lands and other advantages and they excuse them from paying tribute." Others insisted that the usurping lord "worked and gave food to poor Indians." Some natives preferred another lord and stayed "because the Indian or cacique where they stay gives them chicha or clothes in order to avail himself of their work."[74]

Those who left were promised a better situation. As a consequence, then, we find subjects who had fled mistreatment and exploitation by their curacas living in the settlements of other lords and being censused there, not where they were born. Because of the different rates of tribute assessed by the Spanish and the differential rates of sickness and disease, it was possible to move and find a better situation.[75] Curacas likewise took advantage of natural disasters that destroyed irrigation systems and of the disorientation and dispersion following the death of a lord to recruit the subjects of another.

Curacas attracted these subjects when "they did not have a cacique and they wandered about lost like those who do not have anyone to look out for them [*como no tienen quien buelva por ellos*]."[76]

Once settled, however, they did not stay.

Many of the same Indians who once had settled down with one principal and cacique in one community or town afterwards went to another town and community and with another cacique and principal and overseer, and they were again settled and censused there and they go around moving from one place to another because of their fickle nature [*por ser de su condiçion mudables*].

To establish order, Cuenca decreed that the Andean peoples should return to their birthplaces.[77]

The north coast was not the only area where Andean peoples were fleeing their places of origin. Guamán Poma de Ayala tells us that the phenomenon was occurring elsewhere in Peru. They flee, he notes, as if they had no regrets about living in a different town. Stern and Karen Powers report similar situations in Ayacucho and Ecuador, respectively.[78] Among the reasons given for the wave of "runaway Indians [*indios cimarrones de sus pueblos*]" was excessive tribute exaction, which Guamán Poma de Ayala blamed, with some exaggeration, on the abuses of multiple lords: "Because they have in one little town 20 paramount lords. Each one of them makes him work and tries to punish him." And he reminds his readers that when natives have enough land to subsist and enough to eat, they remain in their towns. These statements suggest that the north coast situation was typical of the central and southern highlands as well.[79]

The problem of migration was in sharp contrast to the usual situation before 1532 under Inca overlordship, when, at least theoretically, the Andean peoples had to remain in their place of origin. Santillán maintains that they could not move from one province and town to another without permission. Murúa notes that the bridges and fords of rivers were watched so that "neither a runaway nor an absent Indian could pass from one town to another and they were safe in their towns and kin groups [*parcialidades*]." Both Santillán and Murúa list the punishments—from torture to death—meted out to those who left without authorization.[80]

Competition and disputes between curacas over subjects increased as the population declined and productivity fell. In the 1560s the commoners were already falling behind on tribute payments, precisely because they were so few. Also, Cuenca redistributed land according to the number of a curaca's subjects.[81] Numbers of subjects and what they could produce were so important to these lords, caught between the increasing demands of the encomenderos and the declining population and resource base of their communities, that they reached the extreme of denying their own subjects access to resources in order to attract others who would give them a better return. As one contemporary wrote,

> The caciques and principales have usurped and appropriated all the lands and water of the communities, and to allow the Indians to plant them and

to give them irrigation water they exact a very high tribute, and they brought Indians from other parts to whom they gave land and water of the community so they could work them for them, taking them [the resources] from their Indians and renting them to foreigners if they would give more for them.[82]

It should be pointed out, ironically, that this floating population—what Guamán Poma de Ayala calls "absent and runaway Indians, become yanaconas"—in the middle and late sixteenth century did not enjoy the same status or play the same role that their predecessors had under the Inca. Santillán observes that the Inca chose yanaconas from each valley or province from the best, most able people, most of them children of curacas. He made them autonomous of the curacas so they could do his bidding. Sometimes he made them curacas in his domains. The Spanish, Santillán goes on to say, broke that order: "Everyone has become yanaconas without regulation or limit."[83] They were ultimately reduced to the status of landless servants or retainers, the mobile native work force that, over time, would come increasingly under the control of the Spanish. Those who remained in the rural areas, living on haciendas and estancias, continued to be called yanaconas. Those who moved to Spanish cities or native towns became known as *forasteros*.[84]

Colonial Contradictions

In some peripheral areas of colonial Latin America, scholars have emphasized the survival of native culture and institutions. Farriss, in her recent study of Yucatán, states that the Spanish and Mayan worlds remained largely separate: because much of the contact was fleeting and indirect, acculturation and change were slow. Native leaders cooperated if they wished to remain in power, but few, except for the first generations in the sixteenth century, assimilated into Spanish society. Tradition triumphed, she implies, simply by surviving. William Taylor also emphasizes the continuity rather than change of a cacique's prestige and authority, at least to 1650, although Taylor's work, unlike Farriss's, traces a colonial cacique who quickly became highly acculturated and was therefore better able to defend his office, rank, and wealth within the Spanish institutional structure. Both of these well-known authors treat the subject structurally and from an etic or outsider's point of view. Their long-term analysis finds that the office and the personnel filling the office continued.[85]

On the north coast of Peru in particular and, as the chroniclers' statements suggest, throughout Peru in general, change was rapid.[86] The institutional transformations outlined above took place for the most part within four decades, and certainly within five, of the conquest. This fact suggests that the reorganization credited to Viceroy Toledo was already late and that many of the traditions on which he based his plans were already fundamentally different from what they had been a half century before.

By the 1570s, the concept, role, and basis of legitimacy of the curaca had been altered. The old-style, preconquest curaca, although obliged to support the Inca state with some of the labor of his people,[87] filled a primarily redistributive function on the local level. His legitimacy was based on his ability to effect "good government." Achievement meant looking after the well-being of his demographic trust. Under his management, society remained relatively stable or grew, because the people, on the whole, supported him.

The new-style, postconquest curaca's role, in contrast, during this early period of transition, was riddled with inconsistencies and contradictions. Increasingly, his purpose became one of siphoning off surplus for the Spaniards. Achievement was still a criterion for office holding, but the definition of the word had changed. Achievement, as defined by the Spanish, implied mobilizing the community to produce, but less and less for the community's benefit. A colonial curaca's jurisdiction became concentrated in a core area by the combined effects of population decline, disarticulation caused by the establishment of the encomienda, reducciones and their attendant land reassignments, and limitations on travel and hospitality, which may explain why some lords lost control over subjects living at a distance. The curaca became, in the eyes of his people, only a dim shadow of his former institutional self. Although sometimes lip service was paid to genealogy and noble blood, a curaca's legitimacy became tantamount to the support of the encomendero and, later, of the corregidor and other Spanish colonial officials. Mistreatment of his subjects, resulting almost inevitably from the curaca's new role, bred mistrust, eroded the curaca's traditional basis of authority, and made the society unstable and unhappy.

Spalding describes the colonial curaca's alliance with the Spanish as a new basis of prestige that also opened avenues for opportunistic lords to amass considerable personal fortunes. Her research shows that the curacas did this by appropriating community lands and renting or selling them as their own. Colonial curacas on the north coast did this too. Also, as early as 1556 they entered into contracts with Spaniards to establish mixed farms. Some began to emulate their Spanish masters, spending significant proportions of their dwindling resources on imported cloth to enable them to dress in peninsular fashion. They developed a taste for wine, eschewing chicha, and became dissatisfied with their wooden drinking beakers or mugs, preferring costlier goblets made of silver and even gold. They also acquired horses and plows to work the land more easily.[88]

Some curacas did increase their wealth, power, and prestige under the Spanish, especially in the long run. But it should be emphasized that only some accomplished this and that it took them more than four or five decades. Furthermore, the prestige they gained was in the eyes of the Spanish, not in the eyes of their former followers, as the expressions of awe and respect for the *curacas de los viejos antiguos* showed. Reciprocity had been the proverbial glue holding the community together. Once the bond was broken, Andeans either rebelled (a possibility of dwindling importance as the colonial regime became more firmly established) or eventually fled. Thus, though the office continued—and the personnel changed or survived depending on the degree of collaboration with the Spanish—the traditional basis of a lord's legitimacy, reputation, and support diminished. In the short run and from an emic or insider's perspective, the essence of the position had radically changed.

Finally, because the coastal curacazgos were dependent on the lords of the highlands for water and perhaps other resources as well, the economy and society of the coast cannot be clearly and completely understood without also studying the situation in the mountains and the interactions between the people of the two regions.

CHAPTER 3

Indian and Spanish
Views of Land and Tenure

By taking away said lands [from the Indians] and giving
them to Spaniards and the very same Indians are forced to
work the same lands that they lost so that they [the
Spaniards or Spanish authorities] say that they confiscate
the lands because they [the Indians] cannot cultivate them
and then they force the same individuals to till them,
then what can an Indian feel when they take away his
land and they deprive him of his freedom to have it
worked for him and they force him to work it for the person who confiscated it?

—AGI/AL 316, 1584, 178

The study of the system of land and tenure is crucial to an
understanding of the political economy and social structure of any
agrarian society. Not surprisingly, then, many scholars trying to reconstruct the workings of the indigenous societies of early colonial
Peru have focused on the differential rights individuals and groups
had to this resource. Some scholars describe the situation in general; others analyze it by categorizing and cataloguing. Recently,
some have also focused on systems of land measurement.[1]

Progress in such understanding has been difficult because of the
language barrier. Postconquest sources, on which we rely, were written in Spanish, with an occasional Indian word or two included.[2]
The Andeans' inherent symbolic and representational understanding
of their reality suffered in translation into Spanish from Quechua,
Aymara, and the five separate native languages reported to have
been spoken on the north coast.[3] Translation was doubly difficult in
the north, where court records reveal that sometimes two inter-
preters were needed: one translating from Spanish to Quechua and
another from Quechua to Yunga.[4] Juan Diez de Betanzos, although
undoubtedly referring to the southern highlands, early complained
about the difficulties and frustrations of accurately describing Andean life and customs in translation.

I had decided not to compose or translate another book of similar material on the events [*hechos*] and customs of these indigenous peoples of Peru in an Indian language because of the great amount of work that informing myself of these things entailed and of the discrepancies between the conquerors' descriptions of these things and those of the Indians and this I believe to be so. Because back then they [the Spanish] spent relatively little time in finding things out as compared to subjugating the land and acquiring it and also because as newcomers in dealing with the Indians they did not know how to inquire and question since they could not speak the [native] language and the Indians, distrustful, would not dare give a full and simple account. . . . To be a true and faithful translator I must take care of the manner and order of the natives' speech.[5]

Spanish words carry inherent European thought patterns and underlying assumptions that did not accurately convey indigenous reality. Other chroniclers admitted that because the Spanish did not know the Andeans' history, they could not understand their customs.[6]

As a consequence, contemporary observers disagree with one another on indigenous access rights to land. This has been confusing, as pointed out above. Chroniclers, most of whom were more familiar with the highland area (and especially the Cuzco region) than they were with the north, contradict each other when they discuss whether or not the Inca "owned" the land and, by implication, the resources thereon. At the risk of overgeneralizing, I have divided chroniclers into two groups of opinions on the land rights question.

One group states that the Inca "owned" the land. Santillán, for example, is representative of the group (which also includes Betanzos and Blas de Valera) when he says that the Inca's claim was based on the right of conquest. From an empirewide viewpoint, this claim makes sense because the Inca could control the land and resources by threat or use of force.[7] Contemporary observers who argue this first position base their belief on the fact that they were told that the Inca allocated these resources, ultimate control and disposition being the hallmarks of ownership in the mind of the Spanish.

Moreover, most chroniclers state that the Inca divided the land into three parts to support the Inca and his government, religion and church personnel, and the community or people.[8] Clearly marked boundaries, so this first version of the official story goes, codified the land distribution. The Inca assigned guards to the boundary markers so that they could not be moved or violated. Anyone who dared change or move a frontier marker, according to one source, was tortured for the first offense and executed for the second at the

spot where the mischief was committed.[9] The Inca proved so concerned with the inviolability of these boundaries that he committed
a lieutenant governor to each town (if we can believe the source)
charged with ensuring their integrity.[10] Furthermore, if unresolvable
disputes developed, the Inca ideally would designate a special judge
to settle the problem and reestablish order.[11] Santillán says that another official managed the land and assigned it in parcels to the curacas and Indians in each valley and made sure the Indians worked
this land. In addition, imperial bureaucrats (*tucuyricos*) managed
the lands of the church and government in each province.[12]

A second group of chroniclers and scholars question whether
the Inca considered land his private property in the Western sense.
Although manuscript sources attest that Topa Ynga Yupanqui and
Guayna Capac actually spent time "in the field" reorganizing their
spatial domain and that lands dedicated to the sun and the Inca existed in many locations, other accounts assert that historically Inca
lands were tilled by individual communities and that, once conquered, local lords and their subjects worked for the Inca as a sign of
obedience.[13]

Damián de la Bandera, writing in 1557, epitomizes the argument
of the second group of chroniclers, noting that the lands sowed for
the Inca were called *del Inga*, a phrase implying ownership to the
Spanish mind, though the lands really belonged to the local people.
He continues by explaining that the natives worked certain lands
to grow corn, coca, chili peppers, and other vegetables for the Inca as
a sign of vassalage. Acosta agrees, stating that the lands belonged to
the peasants, who only *worked* them for the Inca.[14]

Castro and Ortega Morejón, writing in 1558, describe the same relationship in coastal Chincha, but they phrase it in a more suggestive way, saying that each *guaranga* (census unit of 1,000 households) tilled a *chacara* (planted plot of land) for the Inca.[15] Polo
agrees, saying that some of the lands worked for the Inca and the sun
belonged "to the Indians themselves and to their ancestors and to
their same communities, from which one will understand something that has been misunderstood until now." This second group of
chroniclers also contradicts some of the assertions of the first. For
example, the fact that the Inca and/or his agents did not redistribute
lands each year, as Santillán claims, is discussed in Castro and Ortega Morejón's account of Chincha. They declare that Topa Ynga
Yupanqui had once assigned land on the south central coast, but
"since then the agricultural plots [*chacaras*] have not been distrib-

uted again" either by the Inca or his agents.[16] Likewise, Licenciado Francisco Falcón states:

> It is necessary to note that those, and even the caciques, who say that the Inga granted and confiscated lands from whomever he pleased are misleading, it does not happen thus, except during the beginning [*entrada*] and conquest . . . and it does not take into consideration that in some places until today [1567] lands are distributed by the Indians, because this is customary in those provinces even before the time of the Inga and the Inga allowed them [the customs] to continue.[17]

My purpose in this chapter is to resolve the seeming contradictions by establishing how the natives themselves conceived of land and its use. Access to land cannot be rightfully separated from indigenous ideas about their past, their kinship system, and their functioning political economy. In fact, indigenous land tenure patterns were manifestations of these values and beliefs.

To demonstrate these associations I will first discuss the meaning of land and land rights before 1532, relying heavily on early local manuscript sources, as opposed to the chronicles that often reflect the southern highland experience. In contrast to the chroniclers' general observations, I will pay particular attention to Andean testimony in court cases, petitions, and wills. A close reading of these and other early local sources suggests that natives defined preconquest and early postconquest rights to land by occupation, use, and possession. Once their precontact understanding is established, I will show (in an admittedly long postscript) that diachronically later and more acculturated natives, usually lords rather than commoners, and most Spaniards considered occupation, use, and possession to be "ownership," with all the Western connotations implicit in this term. The indigenous system, characterized principally by traditional and customary usufruct rights, coexisted and then was gradually displaced by the concept of private property in the fee-simple European sense. Finally, I will show, to the extent that the documentation permits, how rights to land that before the conquest were flexible, reciprocal, and often temporary became, under the tutelage of the Spanish, inflexible, codified, and permanent.

The geographical focus of this chapter is the same broad area described in Chapter 1. The majority of my primary sources deal with the north coast. The significant minority come from the Cajamarca and Guambos highland hinterland of this area (see Map 3). For perspective, I make use of secondary material from all over Peru as well as the Cuzco-centered information found in most of the chronicles.

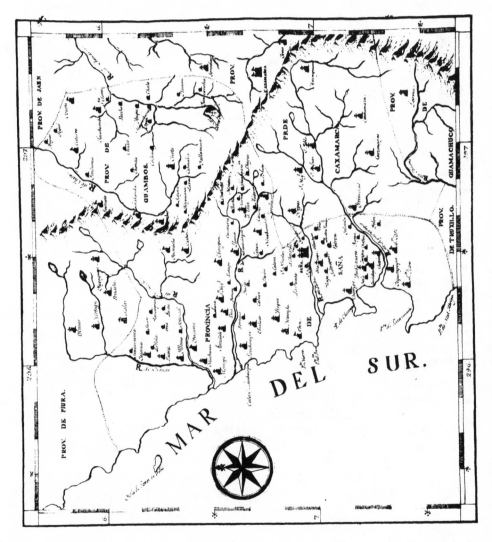

Map 3 Provinces of Saña, Cajamarca, and Guambos (as drawn in 1784)

The available information is strongest at the provincial or individual community levels. As will be shown below, many of the generalizations accepted as true for the Inca empire are not accurate at the regional level. Unfortunately, data on the preconquest land rights of yanacona and mitimaes are sparse. There were, of course, yanacona and mitimaes in the north, but local-level information on the exact function of these groups is often lacking. Although more data on these specific categories of individuals would be welcome, their absence does not greatly affect the objective of the chapter.[18]

Rights to Land in Precontact Peru

In early local primary sources, the expected references to private property are missing. In sixteenth-century petitions to local authorities, natives, when they spoke for themselves, use such words as occupation and possession (*asentada, aprovechamos de, ocupamos*) to describe the rights they enjoy to lands. In 1562, for example, don Pedro Rocxa (or Ocxa) Guaman, who identifies himself as a cacique of the Chimu, submitted a brief to authorities in a court case against Diego Gago over land. He asked for

> support [*amparo*] in the possession that I and my community have of the arable lands in which Diego Gago and Hernando de Angulo have entered. . . . We are damned . . . because it is time to prepare the said lands to plant them and the said [men] have usurped them. . . . We ask that you confirm our possession of the lands we have.[19]

A few months later, several brothers, in a petition to authorities dated August 31, 1563, stated that they had possessed disputed lands (*las quales las abemos poceydo yo y mis hermanos*) at least for two generations.[20] In 1564, don Hernando Efquiq, a lord of Túcume, in a petition denouncing don Francisco, the paramount lord of the valley, used words such as *occupation, possession*, and *dominion* (*señorio*) to describe his tenure and that of his subjects.[21] Finally, in 1566, the cacique of Ferreñafe claimed lands "on which he was settled."[22] Such language in no way implied that they had exclusive, long-term rights to particular parcels of land.[23]

In addition, that the lords did not understand rights to land as property—communal or private—is evident from the bequests they made to heirs in early colonial times. Native lords did not leave specific plots of land to their survivors in their wills until over 30 years after the conquest, when the large-scale, systematic settlement of the area by the Spanish began. (Saña was founded in 1563.) In the

1560 inventory and sale of the belongings of the lord (*principal*) don
Diego Quispe of the coastal community of Tecapa, for example,
no land was listed. He left gold, silver, clothes, furniture, and cattle
(5 to 6 mares, 1 colt, 2 oxen, 50 goats, and 60 pigs) but no land. He
mentioned a field of corn (*chacara* [planted field] *de mayz*) measuring 5 *fanegas de senbradura*[24] that was dry, ready to harvest, and expected to yield more than 100 fanegas (258 bushels). The context
(here and elsewhere) makes it clear that the word *chacara* (or *chacra*)
referred solely to the corn plants growing on the land, with an emphasis on the former, not the latter. The fact that the expected harvest, not the land per se, was inheritable makes land seem of little
and only passing interest.[25]

Another will, dated June 22, 1565, of the curaca (*yndio cacique y
señor principal de las provincias*) don Melchor Carorayco of highland Cajamarca is the first to make a clear distinction between
planted fields and lands and to mention the latter in the sense of a
delineated plot of soil. His testament is significant because it shows
that his major asset and preoccupation were his retainers. He explicitly enumerated 86 individual subjects and the residents of three
entire towns (not counting two in dispute) who served him. He
mentioned lands almost as an afterthought and always in connection to planted crops. He listed

- · 2 pieces of lands and chacaras in the town of Contuamasa;
- · 5 pieces of chacaras and lands in the town of Chaden;
- · 1 chacara and lands; and another chacara;
- · 6 pieces of chacaras and lands in the town of Chanquys.

In each case, the word *chac(a)ra(s)*, following contemporary usage,
refers to plants or crops and *tierras*, to the land. An unplanted (unprocessed) plot of land is not a chacara. One chacara that is mentioned without lands may have been sown on lands within the jurisdiction (domain or homeland)[26] of another lord. No mention is made
of fallow or otherwise unused land.[27]

Likewise, a principal of Túcume left a will in 1574 that again included the yield of a field of corn (*chacara de maiz*) as part of his estate, but lands are not left to anyone. Unlike his houses (other real,
tangible "property" in the Spanish or Western sense), the lands in
and of themselves are not mentioned. In the auction of his possessions, no land was sold.[28]

As late as 1582, some curacas were making no mention of lands in
their wills and final dispositions. The lord of Moro, don Garcia Pilco

Guaman, for example, left a field of corn (*sementera de maíz*) measuring three *acequias* (an indigenous measure of land based on the amount of water running through irrigation ditches over a specified period of time) *de maíz sembrado* and two cattle stations (*estancias*), one at the site (*asiento*) de Chule and one at Hiço.[29] Neither cornfield nor corral implied any perpetual or exclusive rights to land. In the subsequent auction of his worldly goods, his cattle were sold without reference to any corrals, pastures, or lands. His executor describes the field of corn in terms of yield:

> Item. There remain three measured units [*acequias*] of planted corn belonging to said don garcia so that said Juan Rodrigues [the executor of don Garcia's estate and guardian of his infant son] can have it worked [*benefiçiar*] at the cost of the said corn and once harvested he should pay 20 fanegas that the said don garcia ordered paid to the principal of Pucala and his Indians for damage resulting from his oxen as appears in a clause of his last will and testament and the net, after the said debt is paid, should be given for what the Indians requested, mindful that what might be left might be little.[30]

Lands on which the corn was planted are not mentioned; they were neither sold nor left to anyone. Inherent in this testimony and the others cited above is the idea of land used to plant a field—that is, as a place and a medium, not an "item" or "possession" belonging to anyone in particular, not even a lord.

Likewise, evidence from Jayanca as early as 1540 indicates that traditionally the curaca had no perpetual residual rights to the lands that his subjects tilled to support him.[31] Authors who claim that *señores* (lords) had personal title to lands (*a título personal*) misrepresent the preconquest situation.[32] Instead, the curaca's office was associated with the labor to work the lands.[33] Rostworowski's short classic, *Curacas y sucesiones*, reminds us of the consensual nature of the political system in which a council of principales played an important role, if not always in naming and choosing, then certainly in confirming and legitimizing (or, conversely, delegitimizing and overthrowing) one of their number as curaca.[34] Once accepted, he became the first among equals and as such the representative and trustee of the larger group, being always subject to the advice and consent of his counsel of peers. As a sign of vassalage and obedience, principales, as representatives of their subjects, agreed to support the curaca, their chosen spokesman. Thus, an early local account that is part of the testimony in a court case between two Spaniards over groups of native farmers and fisherfolk on the coast attests to

the active and discretionary role of principales in supporting the curaca. Principales (Neptur, in particular) designated subjects to work
land for the curaca. Thus, the curaca used and controlled as much
land in the principalazgo (the area, or principality, occupied by subjects of a lord) of Neptur and in the area occupied by his own kin
group as he had subjects (labor) to till it. Willingness to serve was
the indigenous criterion for hegemony.[35]

But neither the service nor, less still, the lands the subjects worked
"belonged" to the person who occupied the office. They were "office
lands," perquisites of the position meant to free the curaca from
subsistence activities and allow him to dedicate himself to the more
important tasks of administration and promotion of the public welfare. The service (and the lands) supported the chief, whomever he
might be. Because of the need to rotate crops and to allow even irrigated land to lie fallow, "service" was what counted, not specific
lands. Tribute labor could be applied to any of a number of sites to
support the lord.[36] On the transfer of power to the next curaca, the
kin group of the past curaca lost all rights to the service unless the
new chief came from the same lineage. When the curaca don Francisco died, his widow (doña María Pircos [or Adpen]) had no claim to
the service or the land her husband's subjects had worked for him.[37]
Thus, when queried by the Spanish, curacas, according to one interpretation, said that they transmitted land *en forma de fideicomiso*
(as a trustee or fiduciary, one who holds anything in trust for another) to their successors in the office if they were from the same
kin group.[38]

Thus, the curaca claimed an administrative jurisdiction over his
subjects and the area they improved and occupied (much as a modern governor might have jurisdiction over the area of an existing
North American state). He did not "own" land himself. He had use
of lands reserved to support the office holder in each of the domains
of his subordinate principales and had access to lands of his own
principalazgo as would any common member of the community.

In precontact Peru, the curacas and principales only managed the
labor that worked the land. A lord's subjects had traditional and customary rights to use lands that had been occupied and worked by
the group and its predecessors. The lords respected these rights,
confirming the usufruct or actually ceremonially entrusting parcels
of the collective domain to individual households in the name of
the lineage or community. Ideally, a family of commoners enjoyed
rights to various plots, which could change from time to time (e.g.,
year to year).[39] In reality, other local sources, like a register of the re-

distribution and possession of lands within the domain of the community of Lambayeque, suggest that individual families worked the same land for longer periods.[40] This was probably the case with irrigated land. Elsewhere (for example, in the highlands, where crops had to be rotated and land had to lie fallow to recoup fertility) a family might work different plots each year or so.

A head of household was entitled to work as much land as he could with the help of his family, his wider kin group, and anyone else he could persuade to work for him. Each family received an allotment of land proportional to the family's size. As the family matured, sons, once married, cultivated some of this allotted land for themselves and their own dependents. Alternatively, a son might take over his father's rights once the latter was too old to work, was otherwise incapacitated, or had passed away. If the family died out or for some reason no longer used the land, it reverted to the community domain and was eventually reassigned to another head of household:

> And thus as is the custom [Xuñtoc] had had distributed [to him] some acequias of lands for planting as an Indian of the parcialidad, because of his end and death [and] because he left no male son who could cultivate and plant and enjoy them, they should be consolidated [be reunited with] the rest that belong to the principalazgo [not] just to me as principal but to all the rest of the Indians of the parcialidad.[41]

This custom was followed both on the coast and in the highlands.

Don Juan of Collique and other lords also allowed subjects of other leaders to use land near that worked by their own followers.[42] As Chapter 2 shows, lords permitted and sometimes actively encouraged and recruited subjects of other lords to work such resources in return for part of the produce of their labor; this practice created a system of "resource sharing." The same principle applied to other resources, such as mineral deposits and irrigation water. In 1540, coastal Indians mined the ore at the silver deposits of Chilete even though the deposit itself was managed by the highland lord of Cajamarca. Such permissions were analogous to the "licenses" some chroniclers say the Inca gave to use certain resources.[43]

Likewise, highland curacas "shared" water with coastal curacas, who acknowledged that the irrigation water was responsible for the growth of their crops on the coast. Therefore, it was the obligation of those who enjoyed the water and harvested the plants to reciprocate with some of the yield. In one instance, coastal Indians gave their highland counterparts presents of chili peppers, cotton, and

corn in exchange for water. Representatives of the parcialidades of
Túcume said that they worked for (paid "tribute" to, according to the
Spanish) the owner of the irrigation ditch in exchange for water.[44]

This system of resource sharing among lords was mutually beneficial. It made use of resources that might not otherwise have been
exploited by a lord's own subjects (especially in a situation such as
the demographic collapse during the fifteenth and sixteenth centuries) or would have been lost (e.g., the river or canal water "lost"
in the sea if not diverted for irrigation). By increasing use and sharing the yield, both recipient group and grantor lord benefited by having additional goods (called "tribute" by the Spanish) to bolster the
well-being of the group. Thus, the system—in keeping with the
ideals of reciprocity, generosity, and hospitality—was the essence of
good government.[45]

The common thread here is labor, which conditioned the way precontact peasants regarded the land. In Chapter 2 the definition of a
curaca's authority was shown to be the size and quality of his subject population. The basis of his continuing legitimacy and power
was his ability to manage his subjects' labor to sustain and improve
their standard of living and general well-being. As population defined
a curaca's authority and gave it a territorial manifestation, so too did
the labor of that population give value to resources. Put simply, resources and land, divorced from a population to work them, had no
value for precontact native peasants because there was no market
for them.

This principle fits two key native concepts related to resources.
By studying a *quipu* (a knotted series of strings used as a memory
aid under the Inca), Murra realized that Andeans divided resources
into two categories: *crudo* (crude, unworked, raw, uncooked) and
cocido (cooked, processed, worked).[46] Resources like unimproved
land, natural pastures (as opposed to planted pasturage like alfalfa),
forests, and salt deposits were crudo. Unimproved land, like other
unprocessed things, was available "free" in nature and had no immediate worth. Only by being cleared, irrigated, plowed, or planted
did the land become valuable; it was then cocido. Work turned a
good of no immediate value into a productive natural resource and
established for its developers a claim to it.[47]

Precontact Andeans venerated their ancestors, even those too far
back to be remembered by name, because they had settled the land
and overseen the gradual building of the infrastructure of irrigation
canals and other improvements that brought more and more of the
otherwise often barren (crudo) landscape into production and made

it fruitful (cocido).[48] Indeed, the geography of the north coast is one of fertile but narrow river valleys running through desert from the Andes Mountains to the Pacific Ocean. Vegetation, except for a few lichens, cacti, and other drought-resistant flora, ends just beyond the reach of fresh water. Archaeological remains and manuscript sources indicate that a curaca with vision, engineering skill, and labor at his disposal could increase the area available for farming by directing the building of additional irrigation canals and the digging of wells. The ancestors had done this and bequeathed the improved land to the living. For this and other legacies, the ancestors were worthy of song and praise, offerings and sacrifices.[49]

Although the domain occupied by a community or ethnic group was loosely defined,[50] shrinking or expanding with the capacity of a given subject population to use and maintain it, that domain became the group's physical manifestation—its homeland—as continued long-term use became intimately bound to the group's sense of identity. From the resources of the area the group occupied and used, life was maintained. Productivity provided an appreciable index of the community's well-being, status, and reputation vis-à-vis other groups. The domain and, by implication, the resources within it were available to every member of the community and at the same time to no one in particular. The community retained residual claim to an area even after it had lain fallow for some time. Only when abandoned, when it reverted to the crudo or unprocessed category, could it be again improved and subsequently claimed by others.[51]

The curaca was the heir to this legacy and its chief executive. The control of the labor of his subjects made him the trustee, manager, and caretaker of the land they worked. Thus, the natives' conception of rights to the land was not equivalent to the Western conception of land ownership (denoting exlusive individual or institutional control of a delineated piece of earth, whether occupied or worked or not). To the natives, land itself was unimportant; they conceived of it only as a medium.

Indigenous systems of measurement corroborate this way of thinking. Indians used seed and time as a reflection of their labor to measure the lands they used.[52] A fanegada de sembradura (*de maiz de indios* [Indian corn]), for example, was the land that could be planted with a fanega (or fraction thereof; e.g., an *almud*, or one-twelfth of a fanega) of seed. This was not an absolute and constant measure, because the amount of land that could be sown with a fanega of seed was a function of the type of seed (e.g., corn, cotton, chili pepper, or yucca), each of which could be planted closer or farther apart, depending on soil fertility, climate, water availability, and other factors.[53]

For this reason, early colonial efforts failed to establish exact and uniform correspondences with Spanish measures. The Spanish defined a fanegada as 288 by 144 *varas* (a unit of measure equal to 33 inches)—that is, 41,472 square varas—as early as 1579. Rostworowski reports that near Lima three indigenously defined fanegadas (*de sembradura de maiz de indios*) equaled one Spanish-defined fanegada. In Lambayeque, a field planted with three almudes (a fourth of a fanega) of (seed) corn (*chacara de sembradura de tres almudes de maiz*) was measured at two Spanish fanegadas in the eighteenth century. Thus, the native fanegada, despite repeated exact Spanish measurement, continued to be based on a relative concept that varied among regions. The precise Spanish system was very unlike the Andean way of reckoning.[54]

Likewise, the measurement of a native *topo* differed in various localities. Garcilaso de la Vega reports that a topo equaled one and a half Spanish fanegadas, while according to Bernabé de Cobo, a topo (*tupu*) measured 50 by 25 *brazas* (300 by 150 feet). As early as 1713, one topo measured 96 by 48 varas near Cuzco. At this rate 9 square topos equaled 1 Spanish fanegada. Yet another source equates a topo in Arequipa with two-thirds of an acre, not even a fourth of a fanegada. Rostworowski also reports that a topo for potato planting in the high tablelands (*punas*) of the Andes was distributed in unequal plots depending on the climate: cold, colder, or frigid. What seemed like discrepancies to the Spanish mind fit the native definition of a topo: the amount of land needed to provide subsistence to a household, which would vary according to the quality of the land, the subsistence crops planted, and the labor available in the household.[55]

Likewise, other measures common to the north varied. Some *carretadas de tierras* (literally, cartloads, or great quantities, of land), for instance, measured 164 by 94 varas; others measured 90 by 125. Similarly, an acequia of land was an imprecise measure that varied with the diameter and depth of the irrigation channel, the soil type, and the crop planted. In the eighteenth century, the natives claimed that seven acequias equaled seven fanegadas. According to the local Spanish corregidor, a man by the name of Pedro de Seijas, three asequias equaled one fanegada. Eventually, the dispute was settled by the viceroy, who agreed with the peasants. Finally, some pieces of land were reckoned by the number of plants, or *montones* (mounds), that could be grown on it. Again this measure varied by crop and locality, thus supporting the native notion that land was measured according to what was needed to sustain a given socially or culturally defined group.[56]

All these systems of measure reflect the amount of land necessary to maintain, through their work, a given unit of society. That land was measured at all indicates the need to allocate an equitable share of resources to people to provide for their subsistence and prosperity along the lines called for by institutionalized generosity, the ideology of cooperative work for the common good—that is, the expectations of good government.

The significance of this interpretation of the Andean conception of land as a medium that could be claimed and was of value only when improved and used is threefold. First, it is imprecise to speak of indigenous "ownership" of land in the Western fee-simple sense. Much of the confusion on this point can be traced to the accounts of chroniclers. The claims associated with the first position—that the Inca owned and distributed clearly delimited parcels of land for the exclusive use of different groups—have a basis in fact, but seem to be exaggerated, a part of the royal propaganda that emphasized the idea that Inca domination promised the greatest good for the greatest number—a pax Incaica and uniform good government. These claims reflect the political myth current in colonial Cuzco in the early sixteenth century that became enshrined in the popular mind as chroniclers recorded oral tradition (a process that also involved "inventing" tradition according to the chroniclers' own cultural norms). Informants probably viewed Inca expansion and reform from the top down, and as heirs themselves of the indigenous imperial elite, they were sure to enhance and emphasize their (or their ancestors') pivotal role to any Spanish or mestizo listeners. For these claims to be accurate, Inca administration would have to have been much more centralized and effectively established than now seems likely, although these claims were probably truer for the Cuzco area than for the provinces, especially distant ones conquered late, like those on the previously Chimu-dominated north coast and in the adjacent highlands.[57]

Furthermore, if the Spanish-perpetuated, top-down biases of the remnants of the Inca bureaucratic elite are acknowledged, it is feasible to interpret the Inca's initial efforts at division and allocation, not as a preoccupation with creating exact limits of "ownership," but as an attempt to administratively order the growing empire to promote peace and to establish a system to channel surplus into the state redistributive system. In "reordering" an area on conquest, the Cuzqueños established, or perhaps more often only reconfirmed, boundaries primarily for jurisdictional purposes to prevent wars over access to potential resources. According to Pedro de Cieza de León, Falcón, Murúa, and others, boundary markers were placed to avoid such altercations. Guamán Poma de Ayala explains that such spatial preoccupation was tantamount to "so much order [*tanta pulicía*], with this they avoid quarrels."[58]

If no one owned land, how must we interpret reports of *mercedes* (grants) of private property to individuals for extraordinary services to the Inca? First, we must note that "lands" are not often mentioned in lists of such grants. Women, cloth, gold, and silver are much more commonly listed.[59] The few land grants that the Inca made to individuals might be interpreted not as private property, but rather as jurisdiction over a relatively large domain or sphere of influence, which was a great honor precisely because it implied the chance to become a lord in the grantee's own right. With access to enough resources, the honoree could become the founding father of a lineage (especially if the grant was further enhanced with gifts of women). If he managed his lineage and used the labor to work the resources to advantage, his family might grow and prosper. Both Licenciado Juan Polo de Ondegardo and Cobo discuss land grants in these terms. Guamán Poma de Ayala relates how a commoner with increasing numbers of children could become a mandoncillo and principal and eventually be allowed to found a town on vacant land (*tierra valdía*), with the Inca's express blessing and permission, of course. Castro and Ortega Morejón also state that "as the population increased, lords were made [*como yva (multiplicando) la jente yvan haziendo señores*]." In recognition of his feats or merit, the Inca's attention, and his accorded privilege, the lord would be enshrined in the living memory of his descendants and of the other retainers and adherents he could attract. If this interpretation is correct, these "mercedes" could give an ambitious, capable, and generous individual a chance to become immortal.[60]

Besides establishing jurisdictions and peace, a second reason for concern over geographic limits is suggested by Guamán Poma de Ayala when he states that the highlands were separated from the coast "so that order would be established between the Indians of the highlands and the coast [, so] that each could fulfill their duty." This division is confirmed by an independent source that states that each town of each province supposedly knew its boundaries and responsibilities (e.g., to repair roads). As the empire expanded, the Inca ordered roads, bridges, and other facilities built; and as part of their tribute obligations, the people of a district built and maintained the infrastructure within their domain.[61]

In sum, the Inca's goal, according to the second interpretation, was not necessarily to appropriate private property for imperial functions, but to separate and allocate specific areas (called *marcas* and *llactas*), representing administrative jurisdictions, to end conflict and wars, thus legitimizing his rule by establishing peace. Once this goal was accomplished, he could dictate the duties and responsibilities of each ethnic lord and his subjects to begin the process of channeling a group's surplus labor and its attendant production into the state redistributive flow, thus, theoretically, guaranteeing prosperity for all his loyal followers.

On the ownership issue, the differences between the two groups of chroniclers is reduced to one: one set holds that the Inca "took" land; the other, that the Inca was assigned or "given" labor to work certain tracts that had traditionally been worked by the community. In both cases, the arrangement was probably negotiated between the Inca conqueror and the surrendering lord and took into consideration traditional rights. What is more important is that the advocates of both positions describe the Andean land tenure situation in European terms, which split ownership between ultimate control and disposition (*dominio directo*) and usufruct (*dominio útil*). The proponents of the first position argue that the Inca took dominio directo, leaving the communities to enjoy dominio útil. This represents a top-down, Cuzco-conqueror, Inca-omnipotent point of view. Those who advocate the second position hold that the communities enjoyed dominio directo and that the Inca had the use of some lands for as long as he dominated (dominio útil). The second position more accurately reflects a local perspective as well as the actual reality. This view also fits the ideal, consensual nature of indigenous rule and the concept of good government—namely, that a lord must "ask" for "help" (labor to work resources). In reality, the distinction made little practical difference. In both cases, the Europeans described the Andean indigenous situation in their own terms, failing to clearly address the inherent meaning of lands and rights in Andean cultural terms and thereby overlooking the labor dimension of land.

The second reason the native conception of land as medium is important is that this interpretation contradicts a well-known statement in the *Relaciones geográficas de Indias* that asserts that in certain hot valleys of the north the curacas "owned" the land. Wachtel mentions this declaration in *Vision of the Vanquished*, and Rostworowski uses it in claiming that the basic pre-Spanish tenancy systems were fundamentally different on the coast and in the highlands.[62]

This statement is suspect first because of its relatively late date. Marcos Jiménez de la Espada, the editor and author of an extensive introduction to the four *Relaciones geográficas de Indias* volumes, reconstructed the temporal and geographical context of the report and concludes that it was written by Governor Juan de Salinas about 1571.[63] As I showed in Chapter 2 in this book, by that date the re-distributive function of the curaca had begun to change fundamentally, collapsing at a rate proportional to the loss of population and of the valuable resources the people could work. Subsequent generations of curacas, their traditional source of legitimacy seriously weakened, who risked removal by not accommodating to the Spanish, became perforce more domineering locally in an effort to maintain a semblance of order and mobilize their subjects to produce tribute for the Spanish. As cultural brokers between the Spanish and their subjects, the curacas assumed a greater role in the administration of the local economy and sometimes began to claim "possession" or "ownership" of the land, especially as a market in land developed in this and other high-contact areas; this claim to exclusive possession or ownership, in time, revolutionized the meaning of land to the commoners.[64]

Moreover, the purported author of the "Relación de Piura" (volume 2 of *Relaciones geográficas*) reported that the curacas "owned" the land because they received rent (terrasgo) in return for its use. This, I believe, is another case of a Spanish term that misrepresents the indigenous practice. The natives probably allowed the Spanish into their domain, acting according to their cultural norms and the custom of "resource sharing," expecting and accepting in return part of the produce from the activity on the land. Thus, the terrasgo referred to in this context probably alluded to deliveries of goods (the results of working the resource), which seemed like a rental payment to the Spaniard writing the account. But to the Andeans, terrasgo was not rent (*alquiler*) in the Spanish sense, at least not at first.[65] *Presentes* probably expresses the true indigenous sense of the relationship better. This example of a group interpreting the present in terms of its past cultural norms is what Sahlins calls a "structure of the conjunction."[66]

A final reason that this use or labor value of land, associated as it is to the concepts of crudo and cocido, is important is that it explains the scattered, interspersed, noncontiguous, and sometimes overlapping settlement pattern of ethnic populations. Resource sharing gave the subjects of the curaca of Jayanca the opportunity to work lands in the area occupied principally by the Guambos people several days' distance from Jayanca's administrative center. It may also explain the presence of mitimaes of Saña and Moro in Cajamarca and others in areas far from their own administrative centers.[67]

Land Is to Rule

What is of paramount interest is not land, but subjects and their labor; in sum, land is to rule.[68] In fact, "loyal subjects" were really what was of interest to the Inca, his administrators and imperial officials, curacas, principales, mandones (lords with fewer subjects than principales), and on down the hierarchy. Chroniclers report that the Inca took possession of people, not land, in newly conquered provinces: "He seized possession of the said lords and peoples and provinces who were subject to him."[69] Loyal subjects and peaceful, ordered relationships between them, not land per se, were the real basis of authority, power, and prosperity. The empire, like the curacazgos (discussed in Chapter 2), had social frontiers as well as physical ones. Curacas competed for subjects. The Inca's overtures to ethnic group leaders in the path of expansion can be interpreted as competing for the loyalties of subordinates of another ruler too.[70]

Betanzos, writing in 1551, recalls that Pizarro asked the Inca in Cuzco to inform him on the extent of the empire. The Inca instructed his agents to provide a list of lords and their subjects; they did not draw maps or give Pizarro an account of boundary markers or describe their jurisdiction in terms of land. Land and territory alone were worth little to the Inca, except perhaps as an abstract index of the peoples he governed and thus a reflection of his prestige. Curacas did not claim territories. Persons, not land, were important and the source of wealth. According to Cobo's well-known definition, wealth was people. If one controlled the people, one controlled the land, the resources they used, and the surplus they produced. This principle is hinted at by some of the chroniclers holding the second position.[71]

What the Inca and in turn the curaca claimed were the allegiance of people and the right to put them to work exploiting resources, which did not necessarily have to be all in one location or, in the case of land, remain the same size year after year. The curaca's responsibility mirrored the legitimizing claim of the Inca, which, as Chapter 2 establishes, was to provide for the common good of the individuals in his community or empire, respectively. Therefore, the curaca, like the Inca, confirmed individuals', families', or groups' access to lands and other resources. In return, they were obliged to use the resources productively and come to his aid when asked. Each curaca routinely visited the homesteads of his people to request this help. He asked them to till the land that accrued to him when he assumed the office of curaca. Or he might assign them to clean an irrigation ditch or make adobes for construction. While they worked on such projects, he provided them with food and maize beer. When they came to serve, they brought him gifts, as custom dictated. Some tended crops for him; others delivered the harvest to his administrative center. Might not this be the "rent" (terrasgo) that was reported by those Spaniards who claimed that curacas "owned" land in certain hot valleys of the north?[72]

Thus, the Europeans missed the main point. From an emic point of view, the distinction between dominio útil and domino directo did not matter, because exclusive right to private lands was not a concept the natives understood. Unexploited lands—like veins of copper, salt deposits, water, and natural pastures—simply existed; they did not become resources until used. There was, in short (to paraphrase Alberto Ulloa Sotomayor), no individual or collective ownership, only collective and delegated individual use of resources.[73]

What could more properly be said to have been "owned" in the European sense was the fruit of one's labor. A native peasant owned what he planted (or had planted) with his own seed. Recall that when commoners worked for the Inca, the state supplied the seed. In wills, fruit trees were owned, inventoried, and listed individually. Peasants "owned" the plants that grew with irrigation water that their labor channeled to the land; ownership was subject only to reciprocal claims if the water originated in the domain of another. As will be discussed in more detail, in the eighteenth century natives still claimed that they owned what grew as a result of their cultivation and irrigation.[74] Individuals "owned" house sites, and lords "owned" *huacas* (indigenous sacred places or objects, such as a temple or tomb; see Chapter 5) because they were built with their own labor or labor they controlled. But before 1532 one did not own the land. This legacy persisted to the middle of the seventeenth century, when use was still the basis of possession among the inhabitants of Chiclayo. From an emic point of view, it is imprecise to say that the product of the land belonged to the landowner. More precisely, one could claim that one owned the product of one's labor on the land used.[75]

In short, the work or labor principle was the tribute system (as we will see in more detail below) and defined access to land. The prestige and status of a lord was based on the amount of work and good-will he could muster. The natives valued people; only the Spanish conquered the land.

Postscript: The Introduction and Imposition of the Idea of Private Property

THE CONQUEST ERA

The first two decades of Spanish presence in the north saw three changes that began to shift the native understanding of land and tenure from one of use-value to one of ownership of a specific piece of property, whether used or not. During these first decades, not many Spaniards lived on the northern frontier. To administer the area, Pizarro awarded native chiefs and their subjects to his loyal followers in trust (encomienda).[76] The encomienda, as the trusteeship of a group of people under specific native lords, was remarkably coincident with the natives' own concept of jurisdiction or domain.

Over time, however, the area where an encomendero's wards lived and worked was ascribed by the Spanish to be the property of a chief. In contrast to the wording of the grants of 1535, for example, the wording of some encomienda grants as early as 1549 gave this impression. La Gasca's confirmation of an encomendero's wards states that he was granted control of the Indians and the chacaras and estancias "that belonged to them [*a ellos pertenecientes*]."[77] What went unstated is that the chacaras and estancias moved from one year to the next and that use did not imply or convey ownership of the cultivated area indefinitely.[78] Such midcentury wording gave the encomienda a territorial equivalent (in the eyes of the Spanish) that obscured reality until only 30 or 40 years ago.[79] When the peasants and their leaders spoke for themselves, however, they continued to speak in terms of possession and occupation.

Encomiendas were granted with the condition that the conquerors settle down and live in the area. Most of the encomenderos with charges in the north therefore took up residence at Trujillo, the Spanish town (*villa*) founded near the old Chimu capital of Chan Chan in 1534.[80] The foundation and settlement of the town was the first opportunity the natives had to understand the concept of private property as it applied to land. Available sources do not describe the natives' reaction to the cordoning off of the area of Spanish urban settlement. Judging from records of later foundations (e.g., that of the town of Santiago de Miraflores de Saña in 1563), it seems probable that the Spanish received permission from the curaca to use the land. Pizarro then granted citizens house sites around the central plaza and garden plots on the periphery of the town.

The encomenderos' preference for urban living meant that they did not spend much time in the countryside with their native wards. The contact most of these Spanish encomenderos maintained with their subjects therefore remained formal and distant, usually mediated by the curaca or, eventually, by a Spaniard or mestizo mayordomo and, years later, by royal authorities. The encomenderos expected the curaca to provide them with the labor to maintain their households. Perhaps unwittingly at first, they asked—or (more accurately) ordered, following accepted Andean tradition—their encomienda workers to provide labor to build their townhouses.[81] In addition, the Spaniards asked indigenous lords to apportion subjects to build the church, municipal hall, and other public facilities of the town. Native inhabitants also cultivated the suburban garden plots around Trujillo for their Spanish masters.

This first generation or two of Spanish encomenderos and settlers showed little interest in land ownership outside the immediate environs of the city of Trujillo. Many did not believe that native lands had much value.[82] They seemed content with their urban residences and their garden plots, which provided the peninsular foodstuffs they preferred to the native corn. Actually, there was no need to produce basic foodstuffs directly and therefore no need to use, hold, or own extensive tracts of cultivatable land, since the encomienda population produced the required amounts of goods on lands they and their ancestors had tilled off and on for years. The Spanish became collectors of goods, content to receive shipments of such items as cotton, wool, corn, beans, and fish at home in their urban strongholds.[83]

The main economic activity in the countryside was cattle raising. During the first few years after the conquest, European livestock (horses, beef cattle, sheep, goats, and pigs) was scarce and therefore expensive (see Table 3). Supplies of these animals had to be shipped from older points of Spanish colonization, sometimes long distances by sea from Panama and Nicaragua,[84] so encomenderos began raising them in a conscious effort to avoid imports. Cattle raising was already organized in the Saña Valley in 1537 and in Pácora in 1539. Herding quickly spread to other valleys up and down the coast and into the highlands.[85]

Spaniards established estancias, a word most commonly translated in the literature as "ranch." These first estancias, however,

TABLE 3

Prices of European Livestock (Early Postconquest)

Date	Description	Price	Source
Horses			
1530s	Horse	3,000 pesos	Lockhart, *Men of Cajamarca,* p. 283
c. 1542	Horse	825 pesos oro	Angulo, p. 199
1543	Mare	350 pesos oro of 450 maravedís each	ART/Alvarez, 5-IV-1543, 12v
1543	Horse	180 pesos oro de minas de ley	ART/Alvarez, 10-V-1543, 41–41v
1559	54 mares	918 pesos plata corriente	ART/LC, 21-IV-1559
1560	Mare	25 pesos	ART/CoO, 6-XII-1560
	Colt	25 pesos	Ibid.
	Mare	20 pesos	Ibid.
1560	Working horse with a halter	100 pesos plata corriente	ART/LC, 4-XI-1560
1561	Mare	38 pesos	ART/CoO, 20-X-1561
1564	Horse	50 pesos	AGI/J 459, 2438
1565	Horse	150 pesos oro plata corriente de 5 pesos/marc	ART/Mata, 14-VIII-1565
1566	Mare	60 pesos (fiada for 2 months)	AGI/J 458, 2326
c. 1566	Horse	90 pesos	AGI/J 460, 481
1576	Mare	12 pesos	ART/CoR, 30-VI-1576
	Pregnant mare (among Indians)	30 pesos (at auction)	Ibid.
1582	Mare, filly	23 pesos	ART/CoO, 11-VII-1582
1582	Horse	36 pesos 4.5 reales	ART/CoO, 11-VII-1582
1582	Horse	20 pesos	ART/CoAG, 24-XII-1582
c. 1586	Horse	39 pesos	ART/CoO, 18-XI-1596
	Mare	30 pesos	ART/CoO, 18-XI-1596
1611	60 mares	360 pesos de 8	ART/Palacios, 16-I-1611
1611	3 stallions of mares	270 pesos de 8	ART/Palacios, 16-I-1611
Pigs			
1562	230 pigs	460 pesos de 9	ART/CoAG, 24-XII-1582
1574	Pigs	3–6 tomines plata corriente	BNP/A157, 101, 130–130v
1575	1,175 pigs	441 pesos 3 tomines plata corriente	Ibid.
1582	Pigs sebados	14 pesos each in Trujillo	ART/CoAG, 24-XII-1582
1582	692 pigs	12.5 pesos corrientes in Pacora	Ibid.
1605–1606	405 pigs	24 reales each	ANP/RA, 1.24, c.82, 1609

TABLE 3 *(continued)*

Date	Description	Price	Source
1606	Pigs, large and for slaughter	22–24 reales each	Ibid.
1608	Large selected pigs	12–14 reales each	Ibid.
	Castrated pigs for fattening	22–24 reales each	Ibid.

NOTE: For sheep and goats, see Ramírez, *Provincial Patriarchs*, pp. 78–79.

were not ranches in the modern sense, with defined boundaries and a precise area.[86] They began as wooden, brush and scrub, and adobe corrals where a herd could be enclosed for the night. Huts were sometimes built nearby for the comfort and protection of the herders and the Spanish administrator or overseer. Gradually, the administrator's residence and adjacent corrals became the de facto center of the herding operation, or *hato*.[87] Over the years, additional corrals were built one, two, or more days' distance from this center.[88] The "estancia" of Picsi, for example, included corrals at Terrán, Pomap, Cusian, Chullamcap, and Sonconsech.[89] In time, the hato and the surrounding corrals became associated with the name of the place where the hato was located or of the local lord and people in whose midst it was established.[90] Thus, the estancia called Raco was named after an early principal of Túcume who claimed jurisdiction over the inhabitants of the principalazgo of Raco, and it was established at the principal's original administrative center.[91] A better translation for estancia, at least at this early stage of its development, would be "cattle station" (an *estancia y guarda de ganados*,[92] a way station or resting area, from *estar*, "to be" or "to be at/in"). In short, until the second half of the eighteenth century, *estancia* technically referred to the named hato and the corrals at varying distances from this center.

These hatos were not established on land "owned" by the Spanish. Land so far from their urban center had practically no value to the Spanish.[93] Instead, encomenderos began their cattle-raising ventures using their native wards as shepherds.[94] In the valley of Licapa, 60 Indians from that community herded mares for their encomendero, Francisco de Fuentes.[95] Pedro Gonzalez de Ayala raised cattle in Jequetepeque as early as 1554, where he employed a significant number of peasant families from his encomienda.[96] Pedro de Barbarán, Lorenzo de Samudio, Juan Roldán, Salvador Vasquez,

Captain Francisco Perez de Lezcano, and Luis de Atiencia all charged the natives under their control with grazing their animals.[97] Inevitably, these shepherds kept the animals on pastures near their residences.[98]

This practice was coincident with both Spanish and indigenous traditions. David E. Vassberg reports on the fifteenth- and sixteenth-century communal grazing practices of Extremadura, Spain, the birthplace of many of the first immigrants to Peru.[99] As early as 1541, the concept of the communal use of pastures, broadly defined as fields of stubble left after the harvest or vegetation growing on fallow or unused ground, was transferred to Peru and regulated there by innumerable royal decrees following Spanish models.[100] One statement sums this up: "[The] pastures and water are open to all animals and building corrals and huts is unregulated and free as much by right as by royal provisions of the emperor and other decrees of the Royal Audiencia and Viceroys."[101] Use of the natural pastures in the area occupied by the subjects of a lord by individuals other than his own subjects was also coincident with the established indigenous view of natural pastures as an unprocessed (crudo), wild, or free good and the established practice of "resource sharing." Implied in the encomendero's request to the lord to furnish him shepherds was the use of "their" pastures, because the Spanish ascribed to the curaca's population-based authority a territorial dimension. As we have seen, Europeans equated native land use and possession with ownership, however unclear the terms and limits of this control were at this early stage of encounter.[102]

Judging from other early negotiations for use of land (e.g., the founding of the villa of Saña), the native peoples expected reciprocity, some sort of return for their labor. The Spanish institutionalized reciprocation, calling it a rental, or terrasgo.[103] The natives called it "gifts" or "tribute."[104] Each saw the exchange in their own terms. Since the peasants were doing all the physical labor, it was not always clear whether the gifts or terrasgo the encomendero brought to the curaca was for their labor or the use of the land or both. But these arrangements should not be understood as rental in the modern sense—as contractual for a specific amount of goods or specie. More likely, the Spanish reciprocated in kind and in unspecified amounts of goods (i.e., "presentes"). Arrangements must have been mutually satisfying, because there is little indication that the native communities opposed grazing before the end of the 1550s. Not until the problem of cattle foraging in unguarded and unfenced peasant fields became acute in the 1560s were protests voiced.[105]

Many encomenderos who used the services of the commoners and, indirectly, their resources may have reciprocated inadequately; to relieve a guilty conscience, they often left their charges bequests for services rendered. Among the items Diego de Vega left the natives of Sinto, for example, were 900 patacones "for being without catechism and [for] service in [my] house and [for] working on my estates."[106] Francisco Luis de Alcántara, one of the 80 original founders of Trujillo and a town councilman, left houses and stores to the people of Chuspo "by way of restitution."[107] Pedro Gonzalez de Ayala, who died on February 15, 1559, left the yearly rent of 550 pesos from three houses and four stores and 4,000 gold pesos to divide among the subjects of his encomienda "to relieve his conscience."[108] Captain Pedro de Lezcano eased his guilt regarding his encomienda subjects—"for having taken, in whatever form, their belongings or services, work and skills and too much tribute"—by leaving money to support a hospital and ordering masses said for their souls.[109]

Later, nonencomenderos followed the encomenderos' lead in raising cattle. Pedro de Morales used native shepherds of Chérrepe to watch over his animals, which they kept about half a league from the asiento of Nuestra Señora de Guadalupe, next to their fields.[110] The corrals of the estancia of Picsi were built on lands near Collique, Eten, Chiclayo, and Reque.[111] The young men of Chicama shepherded animals for the Trujillo-based Ortiz brothers.[112]

Thus, in this early era two systems of tenure operated. On the one hand, the indigenous system guaranteed usufruct of the area that a family or individual needed for subsistence. Community members also worked land to produce for their encomendero. License to use cleared or otherwise improved (e.g., irrigated) land was given liberally to community members not directly under a lord's control and to the Spanish, with an expected, but probably negotiated and largely unspecified, return. The Spanish, on the other hand, established an urban enclave for European colonial society, where the land granted for house sites and garden plots was considered private property and was duly surveyed, with marked physical boundaries. At a time when the indigenous population was declining precipitously, lords were competing for subjects, and the Spanish had not increased their immigrant population significantly, few seemed concerned about defining precise rights to and limitations on the ownership of the land outside the immediate suburban radius of Trujillo. Natural pastures were free for all to use by both Indian and Spanish systems of reckoning. Thus, what had value were native labor, slaves, cattle, and the use of natural pastures and subsoil minerals.[113]

FIRST LESSONS IN THE CONCEPT OF PRIVATE PROPERTY

Neither the establishment of an urban enclave at Trujillo, the granting of encomiendas, nor the start of cattle raising during the first two decades after the conquest was sufficient to convey the full meaning of private property to local peasants. Starting in the 1550s and continuing through the middle of the 1570s, however, the founding of more cities, the Indians' forced resettlement (*reducción*) in new towns, and the advent of large-scale commercial agriculture by the Spanish reinforced this idea. The resources of the area continued to be shared, but gradually the Spanish began appropriating land and other resources for their exclusive use while assigning the natives lands and other resources as communal property and corporate domain. The most acculturated lords began to claim "ownership" (based on occupation since the conquest) and to sell plots.

Although the effective settlement of the frontier or hinterland of Trujillo, especially north along the coast and into the interior toward Cajamarca, was a gradual process, already by 1541 and certainly by 1550 late-arriving immigrants were becoming a problem for royal authorities as vagabondage and banditry rose.[114] There were not enough encomiendas, pensions, and other suitable rewards to satisfy late arrivals who claimed to have honorably served their king.

The families of the first conquistadors and encomenderos effectively dominated the urban societies of Trujillo and Lima. The encomenderos ordered their charges to build enough housing to accommodate this growing population and to produce enough foodstuffs and other articles to supply them. Because of the hold encomenderos had on labor, latecomers had few prospects for making an independent living, much less a fortune. A few settled in the cities and earned their keep in the employ of the encomenderos or as skilled artisans. For most, however, such jobs were not fulfilling.

European demand for specialized foodstuffs and the uncompensated frustrations of those who believed they had "served their king" initiated an intensive reorganization of the countryside. The Real Audiencia and the Marqués de Cañete began the systematic distribution of agricultural land. Both encomenderos and settlers welcomed the allocation as a way to increase agricultural production, reward latecomers, and settle the land. In the mid-1550s the Real Audiencia granted 50 fanegadas of agricultural land to the brothers Pedro and Alonso Ortiz.[115] The marqués gave Francisco Luis de Alcántara, an encomendero, "certain lands" that the local inhabitants said "had no owner."[116] Few native communities protested this gift. High mortality continued to plague the Indians, and by this time, large tracts of the once-blooming countryside had been abandoned and allowed to revert to the wild, or crudo, state.

Between 1550 and 1563 encroachments by the Spanish on this previously worked but increasingly empty land rose sharply. The town council of Trujillo continued to make land grants in the immediate environs of the city in addition to those made by the viceroy and the audiencia. Nonencomendero grantees, or *labradores*, began cultivating land to produce the specialty foodstuffs that the increasing Spanish population demanded. Farms began to pockmark the countryside, and estancias proliferated. By the middle of the 1560s, cattle regularly grazed on the countryside, sometimes damaging unfenced and unguarded peasant fields.

In the mid-1560s the pace quickened when the crown's policy of urbanization actively encouraged settlement of the northern frontiers. In 1563 Viceroy Conde de Nieva issued a royal decree ordering the founding of the villa of Santiago de Miraflores in the Saña Valley. Saña, as the villa came to be called, was laid out on the north side of the river on lands occupied by the people of the community of Mocupe, who were relegated to lands on the southern bank.[117] Saña became a thriving Spanish agricultural enclave based on the concept of private property in the middle of native communities that still only recognized a use-right to land. Duplicating the practice of Trujillo, a royal deputy assigned to the first settlers of Saña not only house sites and garden plots, but also 40 fanegadas (*de sembradura de maiz de indios*).[118]

Encomenderos, although explicitly enjoined from moving north to Saña, did so anyway to be closer to their charges. Many were already using arable land and pastures near the administrative center of the native lords they controlled either indirectly, by using the labor of their subjects to produce or by establishing partnerships with the lords, or directly, as renters.[119] As they invested to increase agricultural production, they became concerned about establishing legal claim to the land they occupied. Therefore some, like Francisco Perez de Lezcano, purchased a plot of land to erect buildings and pens at the center of his herding activities.[120] Renting seems to have been the more common mode, especially from the 1570s onward, because by then encomienda grants and other official documents clearly stated that the encomendero could not own land among the agricultural plots used by those of his encomienda.[121] Nevertheless, encomenderos subsequently cited the "rental" as payments toward the purchase of the land.[122]

Settlers of Saña could not match the encomenderos in capital investment. Their 40 fanegadas were often underutilized at first, but some of them, over the next 30 years, accumulated enough to intensify and diversify agricultural production. Many financed farming with cattle raised on communal, free-to-all pastures on land that was now abandoned but had once been used by a lord's subjects.[123] Thus, Gaspar de Coría bragged in 1580 that he had two estancias: one within the jurisdiction of (*en terminos de*) don Pedro Cuynamo, principal of the town of Nuestra Señora de Guadalupe, and another within the jurisdiction of the principal don Miguel Faclo.[124] Over time, these activities became large-scale. Coría eventually grazed 4,000 head of cattle. His neighbor Francisco Gomez Montalvo raised 12,000 sheep in the Pacasmayo Valley and 1,200 cows and 600 mares in Cajamarca.[125] Another settler, Andrés Martín Pizarro, had up to 16,000 head of cattle, according to the tithe collector, grazing on pastures "rented" from Collique and Chiclayo.[126]

It is difficult to judge the indigenous reactions to these activities. Since the conquest, curacas and other lords had assumed the power and prerogatives of the once seemingly omnipotent Inca.[127] The Spanish assumed that these local survivors and heirs of the once-powerful Inca empire "owned" the lands, and it was with their acquiescence, if not outright permission, that the Spanish used them. Such license would have been customary practice as long as pre-Columbian usages survived. When the Spanish began to move into the northern valleys, the first rentals and "sales" were negotiated with the curacas.[128]

Neither lords nor commoners fully understood the rights such arrangements gave the Spanish. Natives sometimes reacted with surprise that rentals and sales—as well as grants from the cabildo, the audiencia, and the viceroy—deprived them of the use of a resource that had previously been open for all to use. Some complained to Dr. Gregorio Gonzalez de Cuenca, the Real Audiencia judge who was inspecting the area in 1566, that certain Spaniards would not allow them to use such land.[129] But such lessons merely hastened the acceptance of the concept of private property. Beginning in the mid-1560s, a few of the more acculturated curacas began claiming private possession, if not outright ownership, of plots of their own, basing their claims on occupation since the conquest.[130] Subtle changes in the wording of petitions document this thinking, as possession and use (*asentada, aprovechamos de, ocupamos*) turned into ownership.[131]

Yet the natives rarely protested Spanish land usage. A review of the extant court cases from the mid-1560s shows that most of the cases involving natives were over water, not land.[132] As discussed above, the Andeans believed that the plants (and, by implication, the land) irrigated through their efforts (opening, clearing, and cleaning irrigation canals) belonged to them.[133] In five different instances, involving the communities of Chepén, Chérrepe, Reque, Ferreñafe, Sinto, Jayanca, and Túcume, suits were fought over rights to water, not land.[134] In two instances—one involving Illimo and Túcume; the other, Lambayeque and Chuspo—lands and water were at issue.[135] In only one instance did natives dispute the use of land, and their grievance may have had something to do with the 1566 reallocation by a Spanish official.[136]

It is noteworthy that these cases are between native communities; the Spanish are not implicated. When natives objected to the Spanish presence, they complained of damage done by cattle to their fields of corn and cotton or to their irrigation ditches. A principal of Lambayeque, for example, protested to Cuenca that Andrés Martín Pizarro's sheep, although centered (*asentada*) within the jurisdiction of Collique, grazed on pastures growing on Lambayeque's lands, where they damaged fields and destroyed irrigation canals.[137] Likewise, inhabitants of Chérrepe claimed that Pedro de Morales's animals damaged their canals and crops.[138]

To quell increasingly desperate pleas and petitions from local people regarding damage caused by livestock belonging to Gaspar de Coría, among others, Cuenca issued ordinances regulating the use of lands by Spaniards in 1566.[139] He established, for example, minimum distances between estancias and community holdings to eliminate the damage of the transhumanant, migrating herds of uprooting pigs, overgrazing sheep and goats, and foraging and trampling horses and cows. Gaspar de Coría was ordered to establish his corrals "on lands that did not belong to Indians," and Andrés Martín Pizarro was ordered to move his hato half a league from the nearest peasant fields.[140]

Cuenca also ordered some encomenderos to stop cultivating in certain locations, because such activities were prejudicial to the communities. He ordered others who said they had bought native lands to "make new payments and compensate them [*hacer nuevos pagas y recompensas*]," implying that the communities did not understand the consequences of allowing Spaniards to work lands traditionally used by their members.[141] These efforts were the first attempts to codify and regularize tenure in the area.

Cuenca's impact on the area did not end with these regulations.

During this second, more intense, era of colonial presence and reorganization (see Chapter 2), he also began to resettle the natives in nucleated villages (reducciones).[142] The implications of this effort were twofold. First, the affected native communities were moved to a different site, sometimes far from their original homes. In such instances, they gave up, often reluctantly and under protest, the use of lands that they had worked previously in return for plots closer to their new Spanish-designated homes. Cuenca redistributed the land in rough proportion to the population of each community.[143] This invariably meant a restriction on the variety of resources under one lord's control.[144] It also meant that native communities were assigned the usufruct of specific lands that the Spanish residents of the area should recognize. Second, the resettlement meant that land (often the best land) was cleared of Indian settlement and thus opened up for further Spanish development.[145]

Six years later, the prospects for expanded Spanish agricultural production brightened when Viceroy Francisco de Toledo mandated a second, more comprehensive, reshuffling of the indigenous population by ordering another series of reducciones. In the north, these reductions were carried out between 1572 and 1573 by the *corregidor* (district governor) Juan de Hoçes. Like the Cuenca reducciones, Hoçes's efforts often placed the new native settlements far away from their original homes, meaning that again the affected Andean peoples had to abandon their ancestral domains (when more than one league from their new homes).[146] To compensate, the crown promised them equivalent lands near their new towns.[147]

In some documented cases, the reducciones systematically shifted the native administrative centers from the upper to the lower valleys and changed the layout of administrative centers by requiring a grid pattern. The effect was to assign native farmers to lands in low-lying areas close to the ocean where the water table is high and the land is salty and therefore less productive. The lower valleys also suffered from higher humidity and denser and more prolonged seasonal cloud cover than the original lands. Humidity increased the probability that fungus and disease would wipe out the crops. Cloud cover meant that only one or two crops could be raised per year instead of the two or three that were possible in slightly higher elevations inland and to the east. Moving closer to the sea also meant that some communities lost control of the intake to their irrigation systems. Since the Spanish could get to the water first, native communities at the end of the irrigation system would be left without enough water for even personal and drinking purposes during droughts.[148] Finally, by ordering the farming population to give up their scattered homestead settlement pattern and live in concentrated agricultural villages, the reducción policy opened up additional land—the best, most fertile land with the longest growing season, closest to the headwaters of the river and irrigation intakes—to Spanish settlers.

The reducciones also impinged on the range of resources available to the community. By concentrating native land in one or several areas, the Spanish policy cut native chiefs and their subjects off from reeds, essential for making mats, or from the salt pans they once exploited. But the second series of official reducciones, like the first, gave the local peoples claim to specific lands (i.e., administrative jurisdictions), and the right to exploit resources where they lived was replaced with usufructory rights to specific lands.

Thus, by the end of the 1570s, there were still two systems of land tenure operating concurrently: the Spanish system based squarely on the rights to private property as it applied to arable land, and the native system of repartimiento land, to which they enjoyed the usufruct. The king, as the communities' ultimate guardian, theoretically retained direct dominion. Internally, however, the Indians administered repartimiento land in their customary fashion, redistributing individual plots according to changing household needs, although, as discussed above, some of the more acculturated curacas had begun to claim certain lands as their own.[149] Both Spaniards and natives still regarded pastures as open for use by everyone.

AGRICULTURAL 'DEVELOPMENT' AND CONFLICT OVER LANDS AND PASTURES

Local and international circumstances coalesced in the 1580s and 1590s to initiate a phase during which the expansion of the hacienda meant a concomitant encroachment on native lands and reserves. Beginning in the last quarter of the sixteenth century, arable lands and water in the north were increasingly appropriated by one Spanish hacienda owner after another. The natives gradually accepted the idea of exclusive rights to land, even to land they legally held in common and only in usufruct. Curacas remained in the vanguard, establishing or expanding their own private estates in imitation of the Spanish or purchasing additional land from the crown for communal use.

The land tenure situation was closely associated with demographic trends. Locally, the native population continued to fall, although at a less precipitous rate than immediately after the conquest.[150] Only about the middle of the seventeenth century did the population begin a slow recovery. Thus, until that time the native population used fewer resources than they had used or would use thereafter. In contrast, the numbers of Europeans, mixed bloods, and blacks continued to rise, increasing demand for foodstuffs, textiles, and other consumer products. In response, farming and cattle raising expanded, escalating conflicts over the right to use arable land, irrigation water, pastures, and other resources.

The process by which encomenderos and settlers became *hacendados* (estate owners) and *estancieros* (ranchers) began in a technical sense with the first herding activities in the 1530s. In the mid-sixteenth century, encomenderos and settlers received land grants from viceroys, the *audiencia* (supreme court), and town councils or, perhaps more commonly, took up what amounted to squatters' rights on lands not used by the natives. In the latter case, some Spaniards gave the natives "gifts" of part of the produce, transforming the interaction between Spanish and Indians into what the Spanish called rentals. As the Spanish invested in permanent facilities, especially wheat and sugar cane mills and facilities to make soap and to tan hides, legal "ownership" of the land became a concern. The Spanish then claimed that "rental" payments had indeed been installment payments for purchase. In other cases, individuals took advantage of legal loopholes to dispense with rental transactions and to purchase lands from the curacas, who acted as representatives of their communities.[151] In other cases, Spaniards claimed that the natives donated lands to them. Complicating this picture, the pastures remained common.[152]

Spanish acquisition of arable lands by legal or quasi-legal means was far less significant, if measured by area, than the illegal means used to appropriate arable lands. In the sixteenth century, the most common method was to occupy untilled, sometimes fallow land that had until only recently been cleared and used by indigenous peasants.[153] The Spanish then went to elaborate lengths to defend their possession—using force or arguing in court that they really owned it. Cases of collusion between hacendados and royal officials—who were often related by marriage or blood or allied by common interests—delayed legal proceedings, sometimes long enough to frustrate the willpower and exhaust the financial resources of the native community.[154] Allegations of bribery and intimidation of witnesses abound in the transcriptions of these cases.

Cattle raisers sometimes used the animals to harass and eventually chase indigenous people from their fields. Untended cattle continued to damage peasant fields. After many unheeded complaints and unpleasant incidents, the native farmers usually moved their fields outside the range of the roaming beasts.[155] In other instances, intruding cattle broke down canal walls, allowing soil and brush to dam the flow of irrigation water. Once an irrigation ditch ceased to function, the native peasants could no longer sow the land, and brambles, weeds, brush, and trees eventually covered it.[156] Once the peasants abandoned the land, the Spanish moved in permanently and grazed it or cleared it, cleaning and repairing the canals if necessary to resume cultivation under their control.[157]

Outright appropriation of irrigation water was another tactic that can be traced back to at least the second half of the sixteenth century, when the city council of Trujillo allotted itself water from the Moro canal, thereby depriving some native communities of irrigation water farther downstream.[158] Later, the Spanish rented land to use the water that irrigated it.[159] Since the coast was a desert, unirrigated land was not cultivatable. More than one community on the coast abandoned land to the Spanish under such conditions, maintaining that it was useless for planting.[160] Others who claimed that they had no arable lands (*de pan sembrar*) simply had no water.[161]

With time, the struggle over land became a struggle over water.[162] The Spanish established their farms above the communities on the lands left open by the reducciones. These were the most fertile lands, with the longest continuous growing season and closest proximity to the canal intakes. The Spanish began introducing crops, such as alfalfa and sugar cane, that required more irrigation water than did the indigenous crops of corn and cotton, sometimes leaving the native farmers stranded at the end of the irrigation infrastructure without enough water for their fields and sometimes without enough even to drink.[163]

Finally, in frustration, a few peasant families sold their fields. Such sales were supposedly illegal,[164] but some took advantage of a loophole in the law that sanctioned such transfers when the natives (1) had sufficient other lands to work, (2) needed the money to pay tribute, and (3) had the express permission of the corregidor and other officials.[165] Such sales consequently contain a conspicuous statement declaring that the lands under consideration were, in fact, not needed to sustain the household and that the money was needed for one purpose or another.[166]

The appropriation of water and lands and such sales were sanctioned by local officials, who themselves sometimes had interests in the land, and then legalized by a series of land visitations and title reviews, or *visitas de la tierra*, the first of which took place in 1594–95.[167] Before this time, New World revenues, especially from increased mining, financed the Spanish crown's European adventures. A few years short of the hundredth anniversary of Columbus's fateful discovery, Spanish adventurism came to an end in the naval debacle of 1588, the defeat of the Spanish armada. This embarrassment, which some historians consider the turning point in Spanish history, initiated a steady decline in world power status and hastened a call to increase revenue collection in overseas kingdoms. Among the measures the crown subsequently took was a review of land titles.[168]

This visita and the four others that followed had two purposes. Ostensibly, the visita was to rectify the "great disorder that there has been in the distribution and alienation of the vacant lands in Peru."[169] Another goal was to raise money, which according to the official justification was to defend the Indies from foreign enemies.[170] The decrees ordering the visita began 200 years of defining and consolidating rights of lands and other resources throughout the viceregal territory.

The five crown-mandated land title reviews (1594 to 1595, 1641 to 1642, 1655, 1711 to 1712, and 1787) were designed to check legal holdings against an on-the-spot survey and measurement of the area claimed by an individual or community. If any discrepancies in areal extent or in boundaries were found, title holders were given the chance to *componer* (fix, remedy, or legalize) the problem by paying a "moderate" fee to the crown treasury. This fee was not set, but negotiated by the title holder and the visitor, depending on the extent of the problem, the quality of the land, and its use and productivity. This freewheeling entrepreneurial process, designed to allow the visitor ample flexibility, also gave the unscrupulous opportunities for bribery and wholesale fraud because it favored the highest bidder and those with the best connections. In three of the five visitas, the visitors blatantly favored the Spanish and creoles in important transactions against the peasants. The natives' outcries resulted, sometimes years later, in a remeasure to their advantage. By the second and third reviews, the native peoples understood the concept of private property and the need to defend it.[171] But it was not until the last visita that pasture lands were "sold." Establishing the right to own uncultivated and unprocessed resources further destroyed the indigenous distinction between crudo and cocido and gave the estancias, which until that time had not enjoyed ownership of any more than a few units of land, a true territorial dimension and hastened the day when they would be ranches in the modern sense.

The first systematic visita de la tierra got off to a bad start. The viceroy initiated the visita reluctantly and apparently without much forethought years after it was originally ordered in the 1580s by King Philip II.[172] In the north, he appointed as visitor the corregidor of the district, don Bartolomé de Villavicencio, who also happened to own land there.[173] This proved a mistake, because Villavicencio systematically legalized the holdings of the Spanish without due regard for the community's holdings and needs. So blatant were the excesses that the viceroy replaced the corregidor with a more disinterested royal bureaucrat from outside the district who had few ties to the existing landholding interests. He completed the review with some semblance of impartiality and legitimacy.[174]

The records of this two-part review and other titles show that before the mid-1590s few parcels of land were titled and those that were had been described imprecisely.[175] In fact, one suspects that news of the impending visita prompted a few who did not have a title dating from an original grant from a viceroy, audiencia, or town council to ask native lords for a bill of sale.[176] This was particularly true of many cattle raisers, for example, who bought the right to build corrals and adjacent structures on a few fanegadas of lands (one to twelve in the known cases)—which was technically illegal, because sale of native lands was proscribed. That such sales took place illustrates how unevenly colonial legislation was enforced at the time. Of the 49 estates with well-documented histories in the northern valleys, only 22 (about 45 percent) date from this period. Of these 22, 9 originated in a recorded purchase or grant, and of these only 2 (or 9 percent of the 22) were subsequently legalized and confirmed, which reveals problems with insufficient title and other irregularities. Another 9 (41 percent) are first referred to in their confirmations, which indicate earlier occupation without recognized title. The remaining 4 (18 percent) were occupied in the 1590s or earlier—perhaps sporadically (as rentals?) and without title. These were later reviewed and legalized. Owners of the known estancias, among them Picsi, were little concerned with title because pastures were considered common and corrals represented minimal investment.[177] Thus, the visita gave the owners of 68 percent of these estates legal title.

In the north and elsewhere, visitors interpreted the instruction of the Spanish king in a way that hurt native communities. The instructions said to take lands from those who had more than they needed and, Robin Hood fashion, give or sell them to those with too little. The proceeds were earmarked for the royal treasury. These instructions, under the circumstances, meant that the lands long occupied by the original inhabitants but then left vacant by the Andean peoples' high mortality rates were declared "surplus." Some of these were auctioned to the highest bidder (invariably Spanish); the rest were claimed as the patrimony of the crown. These sales allowed the wealthy and powerful to obtain the "best" lands, relegating the original inhabitants to less desirable ones.[178]

During the first review, the visitor sometimes gave communities a choice of keeping certain lands in exchange for allowing him to declare others surplus. To the people reduced to the town of Mocupe, the visitor gave lands sufficient for their needs. But because so many of them had died, areas called "Sarapo" and "Isco" were declared vacant and surplus and sold to a Spaniard named Sancho Casco.[179]

The first visita established a precedent that allowed owners to obtain or legalize titles to native lands they usually had already occupied. The records give the impression that except for the reallocations, the Indians did not take or were not allowed to take an active role in the proceedings, nor were they often consulted. Apparently, they still did not fully understand the implications of private ownership.[180] They also did not understand the implications of the visita. Furthermore, few natives spoke fluent Spanish, and many more were ignorant of Spanish law and practice. They were therefore dependent on colonial administrators.[181] In the beginning they were apparently left with sufficient lands. But such transactions meant that they lost access to traditionally used resources. The periodic reviews were thus established as an institution that often ignored legal safeguards for native communities and disregarded their interests.

The second land review (1642–43) was entrusted to don Pedro de Meneses, a name that proved anathema to the natives and synonymous with corruption.[182] The law was designed to remedy abuses and, particularly, illegal annexation. It was clear to authorities that Spaniards, mestizos, and mulattos harmed the natives "because if one foot entered [native lands] they exceed and enlarge their holdings and take their [irrigation] water causing them harm with their cattle[;] and [royal officials] rarely make due restitution."[183] But Meneses zealously implemented the law, which again meant that the declining numbers of native peoples received a smaller land allocation. Meneses interpreted his instructions literally, giving the natives arable land according to the number of their population.[184] Generally, a curaca received 12 fanegadas (or 36 fanegas de sembradura); the second person (*segunda persona*) got half that amount. Each tribute payer received 2 fanegadas; orphans, widows, and others who were exempt from paying tribute received one. Meneses did not give lands to those who had not been born in the community (*forasteros*). Speaking about Mochumí, he said, "And although in this town of Mochumí there are more Indians, they are outsiders [forasteros][;] and so they are not given any lands because they are allocated lands in their towns even though they are absent."[185] Most communities also received lands to work communally to pay their tribute.[186] But they alleged that Meneses left them with too little land, of the worst quality ("tierras infructiferas y sin utilidad," "arenales y pedregales"), and too far from their homes.[187] The rest he declared "excess." Table 4 shows the extent of this reallocation. In each case, the communities lost over half their lands, which left them without reserves for crop rotation.[188] Meneses sold as much of the "surplus" as possible.[189]

But irregularities marked the Meneses visita. For example, he sold lands of Collique without first consulting or even notifying the residents.[190] He accepted Spanish bids without measuring land.[191] Some alleged that the same piece of land was sold to several people.[192]

TABLE 4

Meneses's Reallocation of Arable Indian Lands (1642–43)

Community	Confirmed	Surplus	Percentage lost
Callanca-Monsefú	408	653[a]	61.5
Ferreñafe	290–400	600–1,000	67.4–71.4
Illimo	500	600	54.5
San Pedro de Lloc	250	350[b, c]	58.3
Lambayeque	7,022[d]	8,360	54.3
Pácora	200	800	80.0
Reque	600	2,500[e]	80.6
	192	1,847	90.6
Sinto	700[f]	1,560[g]–2,000[h]	69.0–74.1
Túcume	400	500	55.6

SOURCES: AGI/AL 100, 1646, 30–33; E 511A, 1648, 10–11; BAH/ 9-26-1, 9-4763, 1707, 24v–25; ANCR/1808, 162.

[a]Lands only. Years later, the pastures on these lands were sold to the hacendado don Bonifacio de Gastelú y Pereda.

[b]Usable (*utiles*).

[c]Another medidor with Huerta found 1,780 fanegadas and 2,400 fanegadas of unusable land (Torres, 12-V-1959, 1 and 3).

[d]In four separate locations, fanegadas of cultivable land.

[e]Includes Callanca and Monsefú.

[f]Spanish fanegadas.

[g]In at least six parcels.

[h]2,000 were claimed in the visita of 1711–12 (discussed in the text).

He allowed others to buy fanegadas in excess of those indicated in earlier documentation, thus sanctioning previous usurpation.[193] He also allowed Spaniards to confirm titles of questionable origin.[194]

Likewise, he discriminated against natives who wanted to "buy" (componer) some of the surplus for themselves or their community. Blas Núñez Lobo bought 36 fanegadas near Chiclayo for 320 pesos. Don Gerónimo de Villalobos purchased another 2 fanegadas for 20 pesos. Other lands between the irrigation ditches of Pácora and Jayanca were sold to General don Joseph de la Parra for 400 pesos, although Jayanca opposed this sale as late as 1762.[195] Juan de Arriola purchased 20 fanegadas of former community lands for 160 pesos. For 510 pesos, Meneses allowed don Gerónimo Puiconsoli, the curaca and governador (governor) of Ferreñafe, to buy back 52 fanegadas of his community's own "surplus" land, which he redistributed back to the residents.[196] He also sold 20 fanegadas of Chiclayo's land to the native governor of the community of Lambayeque for 500 pesos, which was at least two and a half times more per unit of land than any of the known sales to Spaniards.[197] On the (weighted) average, then, natives spent 14 pesos per fanegada and Spaniards only a bit more than 8 pesos to obtain "surplus" land.

The records of this visita show that by the middle of the seventeenth century, native leaders had grasped the idea of exclusive long-term rights to property. Among themselves, community members still calculated their land holdings using indigenous measures, but Meneses codified their allotment in Spanish-defined fanegadas, which on paper reduced their holdings by one-third and replaced the need-and-subsistence criterion with the precise measurement implicit in private ownership.

The native outcry over Meneses's notorious abuses was loud and prolonged enough to cause the viceroy to order an investigation and remedial visita in 1655. The visitador (royal inspector), a priest by the name of Padre Maestro Fray Francisco Huerta Gutierrez, confirmed Meneses's distribution of lands to tribute-paying male commoners at the rate of two fanegadas each, but he also gave communities extra land for the elderly, widows and widowers, and unmarried females.[198] Despite claims that Jequetepeque had enough land to accommodate its tributaries, Huerta restored the lands of Coscupe to the members of the parcialidad of don Martín Tamayo that Meneses had denied them.[199] He also nullified the sale of the lands of Canchape and restored them to Chérrepe and San Pedro de Lloc.[200] Such corrective measures quieted peasant protests and reestablished the authority of local bureaucrats. By the end of this visita even the tribute-paying commoners understood and accepted the concept of private property.

Don Antonio Sarmiento de Sotomayor was the next visitor to review land titles in the area. In 1711–12 he adjusted the land according to the native population. But at this juncture, officials realized that many forasteros' families had lived in the area for several generations and that they would not return to the birthplaces of their forefathers, as had been previously assumed. Therefore, unlike the previous visita in which only *originarios* (original inhabitants) had been given lands, this visita marked the first time landless forasteros were given "vacant" lands in an effort to justify charging them tribute at the same high rate as the original inhabitants.[201] Surplus lands—like those of the communities of San Francisco de Mocupe, the 2,000 fanegadas of Sinto, and the 4,713 fanegadas of Lambayeque—were auctioned off, sometimes to native lords.[202] Sarmiento was careful to avoid the worst excesses of his predecessor Meneses, although in the review process he alienated some individuals, who did not hesitate to voice their allegations in Lima.[203] Yet he followed his instructions and generally allowed native communities to retain some extra land to accommodate future growth of their population, which had already reached its nadir and was beginning to recover slowly.

Sarmiento de Sotomayor visited the north during (but admittedly toward the end of) the heyday of agricultural production. Arable land had an obvious economic value. Other lands were valuable, even though they remained uncleared, because they had an allotment of water that could be diverted to irrigate elsewhere. But by the beginning of the eighteenth century, new efforts were made to acquire native lands, even marginal lands of no obvious economic use, because if the peasants lost their lands and access to others, however marginal, they could more easily be convinced to work on the Spanish estates. Their availability was an advantage to the Spanish, since native labor was less expensive than importing and maintaining African slaves.[204]

Natural pastures, whether on owned land or vacant scrub land, were still common in theory, but hato and estancia owners increasingly wanted to establish exclusive spheres of influence, especially during the late 1720s when labor scarcity, depressed sugar prices, and flood damage to sugar mills led to an increase in cattle raising.[205] Conflict continually arose when one individual grazed cattle on land owned by another.[206] In the mid-seventeenth century, the lords of Collique and Reque protested the Jesuits' possession of the estancia of Picsi "by saying [that] said lands of the said estancia of Picsi belong to the Indians of the said communities of Collique, Eten, Chiclayo, and Reque."[207] The owner of the estate of Tumán grazed cattle on pastures growing on lands of Lambayeque.[208] In other words, as late as 1787, estancias were hardly more than theoretical constructs based on rights to graze common pastures, often on other people's lands. As community members acquired their own cattle, they protested Spanish use of the pastures on their repartimiento land, usually on the grounds that the pastures grew as a result of their labor and irrigation water.[209]

The scarcity of pastures, combined with population growth and the resulting pressure on land and other resources, prompted another change in the land tenure picture in 1787. The backdrop of these changes was the era of enlightened rationalization of the Bourbon rule in Spain. The Bourbon kings had begun to reform their realms after the War of the Spanish Succession in the early eighteenth century. The reforms were gradually introduced with the main aim of increasing the revenues flowing into Spanish coffers. Among the measures designed to do this were tax hikes and other fiscal maneuvers, the introduction of new technology to spur production, and a far-reaching administrative reorganization.[210]

Among the fiscal reforms adopted by the crown was the redefinition of a taxpayer.[211] The crown decided to include more individuals on the formal tax roles as a way to collect more revenues. To this end, new population censuses were ordered. Population censuses of the sixteenth and seventeenth centuries had counted only Indians.[212] Under the Bourbons, civil authorities began to count other sectors of the population in the census, and for the first time, census records listed numbers of mixed bloods (*castas*), slaves, and Spaniards (including creoles). Table 5 shows the relatively small numbers of individuals of mixed blood living in native communities at midcentury. Around 1760, Eten recorded 13 mixed bloods among 1,069 Indians.[213] In Illimo at the same time only 1 mulatto lived among 80 Indians.[214]

However, as can be seen in Table 6, the population of mixed-blooded individuals was increasing. Callanca, which had no casta residents around 1760, had 16 by 1789. Chiclayo's population of mixed bloods rose from 680 around 1760 to 1,518 in 1789, or 123 percent. In 1792 a total of 2,452 mestizos and castas lived there, according to an independent source.[215] In Ferreñafe, the native population increased 13 percent between 1760 and 1789, while the rest

TABLE 5

Population of Indian Communities (Mid-Eighteenth Century)

Date	Community	Indians	Mixed	Spanish	Slaves	Other non-Indian	Total
c. 1760	Chiclayo	1,817	680	169	156		2,822
c. 1760	Eten	1,069	13				1,082
c. 1760	Ferreñafe	2,800				666	3,466
c. 1760	Illimo	80	1				81
c. 1760	Jayanca	204				89	293
c. 1760	Lambayeque	3,002[a]				4,104	7,106
c. 1760	Reque	302	8				310
c. 1760	Túcume[b]	130	8				138
1756	San Pedro de Lloc	754	40	23			817
c. 1760	Mocupe	21					21
c. 1756	Callanca[c]	931					931
c. 1756	Pacora	148				39	187
	TOTAL	11,258	750	192	156	4,898	17,254
		(65.25%)	(4.35%)	(1.11%)	(0.90%)	(28.39%)	(100%)

SOURCES: BP/2817, 5–7; BM/Add. 17588, 44v–58v.   [b]Includes Mochumí.
[a]I counted only 2,992.   [c]Includes Monsefú.

of the population grew from 666 to 1,278, a 92 percent increase. In Illimo the number of Indians declined during those same years from 80 to 54, while the number of mixed bloods rose from 1 mulatto to 10. The numbers show that except for Lambayeque and Chiclayo, which were major administrative and commercial towns, the non-Indian population was increasing at a higher rate than the native population.

TABLE 6

Relative Increase in Indian and Non-Indian Populations

Indian Community	1760		1789		Percentage increase	
	Indians	Others	Indians	Others	Indians	Others
Callanca	931	0	1,516	17[a]	63	—
Chiclayo	1,817	1,005[b]	4,244	1,937[b]	134	93[b]
		680[c]		1,518[c]		123[c]
Ferreñafe	2,800	666	3,160	1,278	13	92
Illimo	80	1	54	11[a]	−33	1,000
Jayanca	204	89	313	403	53	353
Lambayeque	3,002	4,104	5,902	6,872	97	67
Reque	302	8	481	14	59	75

SOURCES: BP/343, 1789, 5; 2,817, 5–7; Table 2.   [b]All others.
[a]Includes one Spanish (creole) priest.   [c]Mixed and mulattos.

Armed with this data, the visitor don Isidro Patron de Arnao did two important things in the north. First, he effected land reform that gave land to the tiller.[216] Lambayecanos and Motupeños had been complaining of scarce agricultural lands for years.[217] By 1784, most of the 3,000 Lambayecanos did not have access to arable land. Although Lambayeque still claimed 7,022 fanegadas of "usable" land in 1712, in 1783 over half of these lands were in private, nonnative hands. Patron's review revealed that neither the Lambayecanos nor the hacendados had legal title to these lands; the community had written title to only 115 fanegadas.[218] Titles held by the hacendados covered 2,181 fanegadas, although they actually occupied over 4,100 fanegadas. Therefore, without hurting third parties, the visitor "composed" the excess for the possessor for two *patacones* (worth eight reals each) per fanegada.[219] The visitor confirmed native possession of 3,781 fanegadas and reserved 660 fanegadas for population increase. In another instance, the community of the port of Chérrepe complained to the visitor that they had no agricultural lands (*tierras de labor*) or pastures for their beasts of burden and cattle. So the visitor ordered the corregidor to give the community possession of the lands and pastures of "Chinto" and "Lagunas" that had originally been used by the natives but had subsequently been usurped by doña Juana de Estrada, the owner of the estate called Rafán.[220] Following Sarmiento de Sotomayor's example, the visitor expropriated excess land from some and reapportioned it to landless forasteros, thus giving them the equivalent of originario status and making them liable for paying full tribute instead of the lesser amount assessed on the landless.[221]

Also, he allowed individuals to buy (*componer*) the pastures that grew on the land and that had until then been regarded, at least in theory, as common.[222] This was the last resource that could be alienated to quickly increase revenues. Furthermore, this course was deemed desirable because it would lessen conflict between those who grazed pastures and those who owned the land.[223] The visitor therefore allowed both natives and Spaniards to "buy" exclusive rights to pastures on land. In 1712, 653 fanegadas of the lands of the community of Monsefú were declared surplus. As such, the dominio directo reverted to the crown. Pastures on those 653 fanegadas were open to any and all herds. In 1787, Monsefú bought the lands, while the owner of the estate of Collús purchased the pastures on those same lands.[224] This measure allowed Spanish estancias to become, for the first time legally, ranches in the modern sense because it implied a given right to the vegetation on a given unit of land. The results of this last colonial land title review deprived the communities of yet another resource that they had been accustomed to using and had always regarded as crudo and therefore open to all. Yet, as this example and others attest, there was not always a one-to-one correspondence in the ownership of resources. In this instance, one owner owned the land and one the pastures; the trend, however, was toward consolidation of both rights in a single owner.[225]

Thus, by the late eighteenth century, the natives were increasingly forced by royal mandate into the Spanish sphere as far as land and tenure were concerned. The process of assigning exclusive, delineated rights for land and the pastures growing on them was complete. The last facet of the precontact indigenous idea about access to resources had been repudiated. In the wake of the 1787 visita, the two tenure systems were still functioning concurrently, but even in their communal sphere the native peoples had to adopt more and more of the Spanish notions of private property. Increasingly, peasants sold, donated, or left one another parcels of communal lands they had been working. Some even alienated their communal plots to Spaniards, mulattos, and mestizos, with the consent and even at the suggestion of royal officials and their erstwhile protector.

By this time, too, native communities were more apt to take an active role in their own defense in the courts, where so many times in the past their efforts had been unproductive. They also took action in the streets, as an incident involving the natives of Illimo in 1820 demonstrated. They protested the rental of their pastures to Spanish and creole cattle raisers, eventually chasing renters' animals off the pastures. In Lambayeque, their insubordination to crown officials was punished with jail.[226]

Land and Tenure

Before 1532 the native inhabitants of the north divided resources into two categories: crudo and cocido. Crudo referred to wild or unimproved resources, theoretically open for anyone to use; cocido referred to improved or worked resources, implying recognized rights. Improved land was seen to be a medium, becoming valuable only when in use and occupied. Use gave an individual or a corporate group claim to the resource. Abandonment eventually meant that an improved resource would revert to the crudo or wild category and be open to others for exploitation. Neither individuals nor groups owned a particular delineated area, whether used or not.

In the context of early sixteenth-century Peru, when Old World diseases were already decimating the population a decade or so before Pizarro's fateful encounter with the Inca, land scarcity seemed not to be a problem. The population decline, in fact, resulted in competition among curacas for subjects. They were eager to attract as many followers as possible to increase the labor at their disposal. Curacas, therefore, not only distributed and confirmed the right to use land to their traditional followers, but also gave permission— that is, safe conduct or license—to subjects of other lords to use lands that had once been used by their traditional subjects or to use previously unexploited resources within their administrative jurisdiction. (This is much like the way the Peruvian government today licenses and taxes foreign oil companies to explore and drill within the national territorial limits.) Such resource sharing was in keeping with a lord's mandate to be generous and hospitable, and it also had two other consequences: first, reciprocity required the licensees to produce gifts for the granting lord; and second, such gifts increased the supply of goods the lord could distribute to his traditional followers. There was also the possibility that residence in the area would make the other lords' subjects want to stay in their new homes and in time join the group of the granting lord's traditional followers, thereby increasing the labor supply at his disposal. This situation implies that the settlement pattern was much more fluid than many scholars have previously assumed.

The Spanish described what they saw, and they saw that the curaca controlled the labor of his subject population on the land they used. Misinterpreting this situation, the Spanish were soon stating that the curaca owned the land where his subjects lived. The Spanish mistook administrative and jurisdictional boundaries as the limits of land ownership. Likewise, they saw subjects of the curaca and other lords delivering produce to the curaca. They did not realize that such deliveries were unregulated, voluntary gifts, part of an indigenous reciprocal gift-giving tradition. Especially when the subjects of other lords had been working resources near the subjects of a lord not their own, the Spanish called such gifts rent (terrasgo or alquiler).

Within 50 years after the conquest, curacas had begun to claim ownership of certain lands in order to sell them. Thus began the process of change. Over the next few hundred years, natives lost land through (1) rental or sale to others, (2) usurpation of land and water, (3) reducciones or reassignment, and (4) land title reviews that legalized these changes.

All of these mechanisms culminated in the native communities' losing the resources they traditionally occupied and used—the co-cido. Ultimately, too, they lost the crudo, which had been theoreti-cally open to all, as the Spanish finally sold the rights to natural pas-turelands. By the mid-eighteenth century, the haciendas of Pomalca (and its annexes) and Luya occupied the lands of the community of Chiclayo, and the owner of the hacienda of La Otra Banda had ac-quired a piece of land called "Leviche" that had belonged to the community of Mocupe.[227] In this process, the Indians' concepts and categorizations were challenged, changed, and replaced. Their way of thinking and their way of life were thus permanently altered.

CHAPTER 4

The Evolving Tribute System in Northern Peru

In olden times 1,000 served 100 Spaniards and now
100 Indians are to serve 1,000 Spaniards.
—AGI/AL 316, 1584, 176

Most of the adventurers and others who traveled to Spanish America in the sixteenth century expected to better themselves in a material way. The promise of great economic rewards spurred men to risk life and limb in the European invasion, exploration, and settlement of the New World. Lockhart detailed for students the fulfillment of peninsular dreams when he provided an accounting of the gold and silver ransom Francisco Pizarro apportioned to those who accompanied him to Cajamarca. After the gold and silver of Atahualpa's ransom was melted down, assayed, and distributed, the Spanish almost immediately began to purchase land, buildings, and other investments in the homeland. Thereafter, those who remained in America faced the problem of transforming the wealth of Peru into salable products that promised them at least subsistence and possibly great profits and riches. Building on the labor obligations of commoners to their lords of the precontact indigenous tradition, the encomienda became the institutional vehicle after 1532 for mobilizing an indigenous labor force and translating it into commodities for an expanding European market.[1]

For favored individuals, the right to control labor and exact tribute through the encomienda made them the masters of Peru. But the phase of encomendero omnipotence did not last long. As early as 1536, the state began to rethink the relationship between Spanish encomenderos and indigenous peoples. In Peru, the encomenderos proved so powerful that they challenged and temporarily thwarted the state's efforts in the 1540s to regulate this intercourse. The resulting civil wars probably accelerated the colonial bureaucrats' efforts to realign the priorities of the state. Manifestations of the resulting policy changes were restrictions on the interaction of the encomendero and his native charges and limitations on the amount and type of tribute exacted from the indigenous population. In fact, this regulation and the history of tribute in the sixteenth century parallels and even epitomizes the shifts in crown policy and the organization, elaboration, and centralization of the colonial state. The story of tax collection also shows the indigenous peoples to be reluctant and sometimes recalcitrant contributors to the royal treasuries.

The early story of the encomienda and tribute has been told often, in parts, by diligent researchers over the years. Ronald Escobedo Mansilla has published in the last decade a meticulously researched legal history of the tribute regime. About the same time, Robert G. Keith published a comparative study of the encomienda. Such work has been complemented by the publication of actual tribute lists, some dating from the late 1540s. Teodoro Hampe Martínez, Jorge Zevallos Quiñones, Mercedes del Rio, and others have done empirical studies of tribute in various locales.[2]

My purpose here is to build on these efforts by documenting the changing tribute demands on the native peoples and their response during the sixteenth century in the context of increasing state centralization and control. The dimensions of the tribute system evolved according to a dialectical process of give-and-take between the degrees of willingness and possibilities of the indigenous communities and the claims and aspirations of the Spanish. In the process—punctuated by demands, threats, and force, on the one hand, and negotiations and compromises, on the other—tribute became more burdensome over time and gradually forced the native population into the market economy.[3]

Pre-Hispanic Tribute

The Spanish chroniclers claim that tribute under the Incas was calculated in labor or time, in contrast to the Aztec system in which indigenous tax obligations were assessed in quantities of goods. In Peru, the commoners (called *indios parques y mitayos* in the north), under direction of their lords, supported the state and religious hierarchies with a rotative labor tribute or service called the mita, or turn. Murra, in summarizing the types of categories the Inca system included, notes that it involved working lands, herding camelids, weaving cloth, and gathering "raw" products of forests and lakes.[4] In the north, more specifically, commoners took turns clearing land, planting fields, and weeding and harvesting crops; delivering produce and finished goods to storehouses; spinning cotton and wool thread and weaving it into cloth;[5] constructing walls, buildings, and canals; and guarding llamas and alpacas for their leaders. Craftsmen, some resident at the curaca's court, worked to provide the curaca and, indirectly through him, the Inca with their own specialties: weavers presented fine textiles, silversmiths offered bracelets, fishermen delivered fish, feather workers sent feathered objects, and so forth. Other forms of tribute known in Cajamarca, for example, included service in the army. "Personal service," celebrated in sometimes elaborate ritual, reinforced an individual's feeling that he or she worked for a member of a larger kin group, lineage, and community and, indirectly perhaps, for the imperial state through the persons of the curaca and the Inca.[6]

That the state expected service from local peoples is evident in Gama's visita to Jayanca in 1540. Confusion reigned when the visitador asked the cacique of Jayanca about tribute in Inca times. The cacique denied knowing "Guaynacaba" (the Inca),[7] and when asked "if his father the cacique of Xayanca gave tribute to Guaynacaba and what items he gave," he said that he did not know. Perhaps the form of the question, asking about goods rather than labor, confused the cacique. The probably imperfect translation of don Hernando—the "tongue," or interpreter—may not have helped either. The lord did, however, understand the question about what items he gave to his encomendero. When another "cacique principal"[8] was asked similar questions, he also claimed not to known anything about pre-Hispanic tribute, although he could enumerate the goods and quantities given to his encomendero.

The Andeans would have been better able to understand had the question been asked about labor, not goods per se, as tribute. Indeed, in the 1541 visita of Cajamarca, Pru calla, the lord of the highland mitimaes, gave a detailed accounting of labor tribute:

> The caciques guaman and chico who are from the area of the chachapoyas served the ynga in the said tanbos [tambos] of caxamarca; the caciques of Caxas mayo [Pacasmayo] and saña and col[l]ique and chuspo and çinto [Sinto] and tuvone [Túcume] all of the said caciques, said the said Lords of caxamarca, had sent [tenian puestos] mitimaes to the said lands [or jurisdiction—tierras] of caxamarca so that each of the said caciques [of coastal peoples] could serve the ynga with less work and deliver the tribute

because they contributed to the ynga in the tanbos of caxamarca . . . ; and that [people] from the guanbos also served the ynga in the said tanbos of caxamarca; the cacique of Cacazmayo [Pacasmayo] and sana [Saña] and collique and chuspo and çinto and tucume all the said caciques, said the said lords of caxamarca, had sent and placed [_tenian puestos_] their miti-maes in the said lands of caxamarca so that each of the said caciques could serve with less work [_mas sin trauajo_] the ynga and deliver the trib-utes with which they contributed to the ynga in the tambos of cajamarca and that they have been there a long time and that the coastal mitimaes always assisted and served the ynga under their own caciques and not un-der the lords of caxamarca.[9]

Other early sources, such as tribute lists from Cajamarca (see the next section below), were enumerated in labor, confirming the above point.[10] According to the standard writings of the chroniclers on the period, when the commoners worked on the lands set aside to sup-port the Inca or their religion, they were supported by those institu-tions. The state, for example, provided them with seed and other material and rewarded them with food and drink in exchange for their labor. In the Chimu Valley, for example, the curaca probably supplied these items, perhaps using goods that belonged to or had been previously produced for the Inca. Commoners did not have to give the Inca or other leaders goods harvested on the land cultivated for personal use. They also did not have to give anything that did not grow or could not be produced in their own area. Therefore, at least in theory, the majority of native peoples (with the exception of some yanaconas and mitimaes) worked near their birthplaces.[11]

Local sources, however, show some contradictions to this last gen-eralization. Coastal communities were often responsible for goods from temperate areas, and highland peoples often produced goods known to come from warm lowland areas. This seeming contradic-tion can be explained in two ways. First, as Santillán states, the only exemption to the no-exotic-produce rule was the license given to certain skilled workers to go to a neighboring jurisdiction to obtain raw materials. Second, many communities included members liv-ing in various ecological niches. For example, Saña and Moro, two coastal communities, included members living and working in high-land Cajamarca. Thus a given community might have access to both cool- or cold-weather and hot-weather products. In other words, An-deans had much greater geographical mobility than the general ac-counts have led readers to suspect.[12]

Tribute service also implied transporting the product of one's la-bor to storehouses, usually nearby. Reference has already been made to the Inca's request to have coastal communities deliver goods produced through tribute labor to Cajamarca instead of the old Chimu capital of Chan Chan. Goods taken outside a region were usually war materiel or supplies or items intended to be presented directly to the Inca or his representative. In general, goods carried a long distance "were few in number and very valuable things and they did not weigh much, and they considered whatever the Inca might give them an honor and a privilege." This statement proved true for Cajamarca as well as other areas of the Andes.[13]

Under the Inca system, completion of the assigned task fulfilled the individual's obligation to the state or religion. Whether the crops a person planted thrived or failed, for example, a person owed nothing more than the labor already provided. The state and religious hierarchies assumed the risk of production.[14] The responsibility for providing labor fell on the entire community, and the curaca and principales directed the efforts. Lords might instruct a few people to go to a mine or a riverine site and with their work or industry (*grangeria*) bring back ore; others might procure the hemp (*cabuya*) needed to make sandals. Some received wool to spin thread, while others wove cloth. The community planted and harvested fields of corn or other agricultural goods. Thus, the entire community worked together to fulfill its obligations.[15]

Surviving records indicate that the labor exactions under the Inca system were relatively mild compared with those the Spanish imposed after contact. One manuscript source that specifically describes the precontact tribute regime states that the natives were "less burdened . . . in paying their tribute" because they had to serve only one ruler (señor).[16] Although this statement is technically incorrect—natives in fact had to serve leaders on several rungs of the indigenous hierarchy (Inca, curaca, principal, etc.)—it is true that every able-bodied adult male commoner served (with the help of his wife) except for the Inca, the top officials (*justicias mayores*) of provinces, and the highest local lords. Thus, since the general populace supported only a tiny tax-exempt hierarchy, the service was not burdensome.[17] The light tax obligation is also reflected in the relatively small portion of the community involved in "personal service." One source says that only 1 (in the case of mining) or 2 of each 100 served at a time.[18]

In theory, Andeans worked for the state and their gods in part because the work was not all consuming and in part because some of what was produced for the state eventually returned to the local community in the form of gifts, rewards, and succor in times of need. The natives also knew that the surplus was available to provide for the poor, aged, and infirm. Furthermore, community efforts produced goods and services to support individuals performing specific jobs for the state, such as soldiering. Falcón sums this up, albeit in an exaggerated manner, saying: "All that the Indians produced eventually benefited them." Santillán echoes this finding with the same sweeping optimism: "All the said tribute and services that the Inca mandated and took, . . . were under the pretext and for the use of the government and benefit of all." Labor, then, was the common basis of the reciprocal and redistributive system that guaranteed not only the survival of the population and its individual communities, but also the continuity, expansion, and grandeur of the state. The communal welfare implied by this system served as the basis of legitimacy and empire.[19]

Encomiendas and Tribute to 1549

The Spanish misunderstanding of the indigenous tribute system, perhaps colored by expectations based on the Aztec experience in Mexico, where tribute was specific quantities of goods rather than labor, meant that they introduced a new relationship to superiors and a new way of thinking, though probably not a totally new method of production and procurement, to the Indians in the first years after the Spanish invasion of 1532.[20] Grants of encomiendas in the north date from March 1535, only months after Pizarro received authorization to grant them in May 1534 in Jauja. These grants made the Spanish grantees or encomenderos the masters of entire native communities. Since encomienda grants did not specifically establish the tribute the subjects had to give the encomenderos, the Spanish could and did request both labor service and goods from their charges. These unregulated exactions—unlike those of the Inca, who had usually respected local customs (at least to a degree)—rarely acknowledged ancient practice and usage.[21]

In the highlands of Cajamarca, the lords directed their subjects to work for their encomendero Melchor Verdugo. They provided labor in 1539 to shepherd large herds of llamas and alpacas (*auquenidos*) and guard wheat fields. They also

> gave to their master [*amo*] Melchior Verdugo Indians to make wool clothes and very fine pieces of tapestry [*paños de corte*] and . . . gave him corn and chili peppers and coca, and potatoes and camelids or sheep [*ovejas*] and sandals and male and female yanaconas, enough for his household and . . . did not give him gold or silver that they did not have.

The last statement is of particular interest because we know that the lords of Cajamarca sent 100 subjects (*personas de servicio*) to the silver mines in Chilete as early as 1540. This testimony thus clearly shows how the natives interpreted requests for tribute in terms of labor. They did not give gold and silver per se, but they did provide a number of workers to mine the ore, a clear distinction to the indigenous mind but one that was often lost on the Spanish.[22]

The Spanish, and Verdugo in particular, measured their production in market terms. Verdugo estimated his yearly income in 1536 as 5,000 to 6,000 castellanos (12,811 patacones 6 reales to 15,374 patacones 1 real);[23] by 1549 his encomienda charges produced 80,000 ducados de buen oro (at 375 maravedís, or 11 reales, per ducado, the equivalent of 110,000 patacones). This interpretation of tribute as measurable quantities of goods is the Spanish bias and the one most often reflected in the manuscripts.[24]

On the coast, where contact with the Spanish began earlier and was more constant and direct than in the highlands, the encomenderos of Jayanca, Francisco de Lobo and Diego Gutierrez, received a greater mix of items, as shown in Table 7. In addition, Lobo received fourteen small thin disks or plates (*tejuelos*) of gold (weighing 37 pesos) and small bars (*barretillas*) of silver (weighing 107 pesos) every two months (*cada dos lunas*). Gutierrez likewise received every three months nine small bars of silver and four or five small thin disks or plates of gold. Here the Spanish view of tribute as "things" prevails, although native labor produced them. It should be noted, however, that because there were no known mines of either gold or silver on the coastal plain, the cacique and his principales *rrescatan* (literally, "recovered," "ransomed," or "secured"; here meant to convey the idea of exchange of one item for another) these metals, an early indication that they were forced to barter or trade with other indigenous groups to satisfy the demands of their Spanish master.[25]

Encomenderos regularly demanded gold and silver, often requiring native peoples to travel great distances to procure them. In his

TABLE 7
Tribute of Jayanca (1540)

Recipient	Loads of corn	Fowl	Sheep	Beds and mattresses	Blankets and ponchos	Other[a]
Lobo	600	600	36	36–42	120	24–30
Gutierrez	280	280	20	8	8	0
TOTAL	880	880	56	44–50	128	24–30

SOURCE: Gama, pp. 225–26.
[a] Loads of beans, fish, salt, and chili peppers.

will, Lorenco de Ulloa mentions sending 300 Indians from his encomienda of Guambos to pan gold in the Guayobamba River (see Map 1). If Andeans could not obtain gold or silver directly from the mines, they had to work for Spaniards to obtain it.[26]

During the civil wars of the 1540s, encomienda Indians provided many encomenderos with the labor needed to accumulate capital and begin ancillary economic enterprises, such as wheat mills and warehouses. They also produced goods that the encomenderos could sell—for instance, enough ham and biscuits to supply a fleet. Keith sums up the situation, stating that "one of the main functions of the encomienda . . . was to change what the traditional redistributive economies could provide—mainly agricultural produce, cloth and services of various kinds—into monetary income" so that the colonizers could acquire the foreign exchange needed to reproduce the European way of life in America.[27]

The system of production to fulfill these requests remained largely the same as before contact. The encomendero asked the curaca for what he wanted. The lord bargained over the commodities until the encomendero agreed on the amount. Then the lord divided the work among his subjects, either individually or by kin group (parcialidad). However, instead of delivering relatively small amounts of highly valued objects as they did under the Inca, community members carried large amounts of tribute goods to the Spanish on their own backs or on the backs of animals. Many commoners delivered goods to distant points, usually cities.[28]

If a community did not produce the required goods in one year, the outstanding amount was added to the quota for the next year. In the worst cases, the lords were sometimes blamed and punished. One well-informed critic, Fray Domingo de Santo Tomás, complained that caciques were burned, attacked by dogs, tortured, and abused for failure to deliver goods. Melchor Verdugo, to cite one specific local reference, allegedly commanded a dog to attack the young son of a lord of Cajamarca who had not delivered sufficient quantities of gold. In 1536 to 1537 on the coast, the encomendero of Pácora killed two to three of his lesser lords because they would not serve him. As noted in Chapter 2, lords sometimes lost their office for failing to live up to the expectations and demands of the encomendero. They were replaced by someone the encomendero deemed "would be a good executioner [*verdugo*] of the poor Indians, to carry out his will and unbounded greediness." Tribute, Santo Tomás concluded, was excessive and tantamount to stealing.[29]

The situation did not remain unregulated for long. Already the crown worried about the growing power of the encomenderos. State

policy-makers used the perhaps sincere royal concern for the natives' welfare and, less explicitly, the concern for the salvation of
the royal soul, as a pretext to restrict the vast powers of the encomenderos. Beginning in the 1530s, royal orders mandated that
tribute lists be made up and that the quantities prescribed therein
be set at less than what Andeans had given to Atahualpa. Specifically, a *real cédula* (royal decree) issued at Valladolid on July 19,
1536, directed to Pizarro, ordered that inspectors set tribute according to "what they [the natives] can and should easily and willingly
pay now." The reasoning was that if each community knew specifically what it had to produce, there would be fewer opportunities
for abuse. Although Pizarro was reluctant to implement the order
immediately, he eventually commissioned Diego de Verdejo to review the situation in the northern valleys from Chicama to Túcume in keeping with this and other directives. Verdejo was to count
local peoples and determine tribute based on what the natives had
given to the Inca. That these orders were carried out is certain from
the two extant records of this systematic regional inspection—
namely, of Jayanca and Cajamarca—that have been found to date.[30]
Other royal instructions (for example, to the governor Cristóbal
Vaca de Castro) and the New Laws of 1542 reiterated the order to review the tribute situation of the Andeans. But these orders were
rarely implemented.[31]

Regulation of the Encomienda: La Gasca's Tribute Lists, 1549–50

To end these notorious abuses, the president of the Supreme
Court, Licenciado Pedro de la Gasca, decided to enforce strictly
many previous royal decrees, ordering that the indigenous population be censused and detailed lists of tribute made for each community. This decision, coming right after the civil wars and pacifica-
tion, was part of the crown's attempt to regain control over the
rebellious encomenderos.[32]

To comply, several of the most prominent citizens of Trujillo—
Diego de Mora, encomendero of Chicama; Rodrigo Lozano, encomendero of Guañape and Chao; Francisco Perez de Lezcano, encomendero
of one-fourth of Pacasmayo; and Rodrigo de Paz, encomendero of
Saña—were called to testify on the value of the encomiendas in
their district. Their grants made them familiar with many of the
communities within the jurisdiction (*terminos*) of the city of Trujillo. Their estimations of the annual yield of their own encomiendas and those of their peers are summarized in Table 8.

TABLE 8
Estimates of Annual Value of Encomiendas of the North (1548–49)

Cajamarca	6,000 silver pesos (10,808 patacones 7 reales), tapestries (tapiceria), corn, meat, wheat, and abundant supplies for Melchior Verdugo's household from Cuismanco, Chuquimango, Cajamarca, and the mitimaes living in Cajamarca. The part of Cajamarca (Chondal, Bambamarca, and Pomamarca) belonging to Hernando de Alvarado yields about a third (3,603 patacones) of what Verdugo got.
Conchucos	3,000 pesos (5,404 patacones 3 reales) and wheat, meat, corn, and service for the encomendero. The other half of Conchucos gives the same to the successor of Luis Garcia Samanez.
Chicama	At this time, the Indians just worked on the encomendero's haciendas. They could give 1,500 pesos (2,768 patacones 3 reales) in cloth, wheat, corn, and service and supplies to maintain the encomendero's household. The other half of Chicama yields about half this amount.
Chimu	1,000 pesos (1,801 patacones 4 reales) in wheat, corn, cloth, and service for one household.
Chuspo	800 pesos (1,441 patacones 1 real) in cloth and other trifles (menudencias) each to Alcantara and the daughter of Miguel de Velasco and supplies to maintain two households "moderately."
Collique	1,500 pesos (2,702 patacones 2 reales) in cloth and very few supplies for one household.
Chepén	1,000 pesos (1,801 patacones 4 reales) in cloth, supplies, and service for one household.
Chérrepe	1,000 pesos (1,801 patacones 4 reales) in cloth, supplies, and service for the master's household.
Ferreñafe	(listed as Túcume, the part belonging to the children of J[uan] de Osorno); about 1,200 pesos (2,161 patacones 6 reales) in cloth and supplies to maintain a household well.
Guamachuco	5,000 to 6,000 pesos of silver (9,007 patacones 3 reales to 10,808 patacones 7 reales), tapestries, wheat, and corn.
Guambos	5,000 to 6,000 pesos (9,007 patacones 3 reales to 10,808 patacones 7 reales) and meat. The encomendero did not get corn, wheat, or personal service.
Illimo	(listed as Túcume, the part belonging to the children of J[uan] Roldan); 500 pesos (900 patacones 6 reales).
Jayanca	4,000 pesos (7,205 patacones 7 reales) in tribute, economic activities (grangerias), benefits (aprovechamiento), and service.
Jequetepeque	1,000 pesos (1,801 patacones 4 reales) in cloth, supplies, and service for one household.
Lambayeque	2,000 pesos (3,603 patacones) and supplies for one household.
Moro	1,000 pesos (1,801 patacones 4 reales) in cloth, supplies, and service for one household.
Olmos and Santo Velico	800 pesos (1,441 patacones 1 real) from the lords Penachi, Olmos, and Contailicoia.
Pacasmayo	Each of its four parts can give 1,000 pesos (1,801 patacones 4 reales) in cloth, service, and supplies for the household of each encomendero.
Reque	800 pesos (1,441 patacones 1 real) in cloth, trifles, and supplies to maintain a household moderately.
Saña	1,500 pesos (2,702 patacones 2 reales) in cloth and very few supplies to maintain a household.
Túcume	(listed as "de Zamudio"); 1,200 pesos (2,161 patacones 6 reales) in cloth and supplies to maintain a household well.

SOURCES: Loredo, Los repartos, pp. 255–57, 265, 269; Hampe Martínez, "Notas sobre población," p. 67.
NOTE: Pesos are assumed to be equal to 490 maravedís each. I used a conversion rate of 8.9 percent (Ramírez, Provincial Patriarchs, appendix 4, p. 388). Patacones are rounded to the nearest real.

These figures are approximations; one can only guess how accurate they are. Surely, the estimates were influenced by the individual personalities, friendships, and knowledge of the assessors and the consumption habits and reputations of the encomenderos and their households. On the whole, the figures probably reflect only a small fraction of the true worth. Labor services and household supplies were not given a value; only salable commodities, such as cloth, had a market price.[33] For purposes of comparison, these estimates are translated into pesos of 8 reales each (patacones) in Table 9. Despite their brevity, vagueness, and uncertain accuracy, these figures stand as a benchmark against which to contrast the detailed tribute lists (*tasas*) elaborated at La Gasca's request.

Rostworowski published about two dozen of La Gasca's actual tribute lists. Hampe Martínez studied and printed a somewhat later one for Cajamarca, dated 1550. Another for Pachacamac appears in the work of Escobedo Mansilla. A summary of the 1550 tasa of Reque is discussed by Zevallos Quiñones. Alejandro Malaga Medina offers a curious summary, based on Emilio Romero, of La Gasca's tribute by province.[34] A typical list for the community of Saña on the coast is summarized in Table 10. This list indicates that the 1,300–1,500 native tributaries were assessed in commodities (silver, gold, cotton, and animals) and agricultural and domestic services. Agricultural production took place both in the area of their community, perhaps on lands that had once been worked for the Inca, and in and around Trujillo. Some goods originated in the immediate area; others had to be brought from afar. The people of Saña did not have access to mines. Therefore, they either had to exchange some of their products for the metal, go to work for someone who would pay them in ore, or travel to Chilete and labor for the lord of Cajamarca in return for silver in a resource-sharing arrangement.[35] Some of the other products—such as cloth awnings or tents (*toldos*), thread, fish, salt, and mats—were items the natives may have produced for themselves before contact. Other items may have been made to order for the encomendero under his or his agents' direction—for example, mattresses, tablecloths, chairs, and beds. Pigs were not indigenous to America and therefore represent acquired knowledge and some degree of acculturation. Again, this list suggests that the commoners were quite mobile. According to the tasa, 85 Indians worked in Trujillo, either in the encomendero's fields, in his home, or guarding his cattle. Others labored for him in their own community or delivered products to the city.[36] More important, this list also reflects the institutionalization and elaboration of the evolving

TABLE 9
Value of Selected North Peruvian Encomiendas (to 1579)

Encomienda	Year[a]	Value[b] (in pesos[c])
Cajamarca	1536	12,812–15,374[d]
	1548	14,411
	c. 1549	110,000
Collique	1548	2,702[e, f]
	1559–63	7,279[e, f]
	1568	4,963[e]
	1572	1,894[g]
Chérrepe	1548	1,802[e, f]
	1556	4,674[h]
	1559–63	3,557[e, f]
	1566	1,760
	1569	1,324
Chuspo-Callanca	1548	1,441[e, f]
	1559–63	4,053[e, f]
	1572	2,262[g]
Ferreñafe	1548	2,162[e, f]
	1559–63	4,665[e, f]
	1572	1,831
Guambos	1548	9,007–10,809
	1556	8,273–9,347
	1561–64	5,427
	1572	2,747[g]
Illimo	1548	901[e, f]
	1559–63	1,357[e, f]
	1572	2,694[g]
Jayanca	1548	7,206[e, f]
	c. 1565–70	9,926[g]
	1572	3,985[g]
Jequetepeque	1548	1,802[e, f]
	1559–63	3,474[e, f]
	1572	3,047[g]
	1575	3,320[i]
	1576	6,618[h]
Lambayeque	1548	3,603[e, f]
	1559–63	5,542[e, f]
	1565	5,069[d, h]
	1566	1,318[h]
	1570	9,099[d, h]
	1572	9,265[d, h]
	1572	4,995
	1574	1,861[d]
	1574	11,374[d, h]
	c. 1575	2,554[d, h]
Pacasmayo	1548	1,802[e, f]
	1559–63	5,956[e, f]
Reque	1548	1,441[e, f]
	1559–63	3,640[e, f]
	c. 1565	3,309[d, h]
	1572	456[g]

TABLE 9 (*continued*)

Encomienda	Year[a]	Value[b] (in pesos[c])
Saña	1548	2,702[e, f]
	1559–63	5,790[e, f]
	1563	2,647[d, h]
	1572	937
	1572	608[i]
Sinto	1559–63	3,805[e, f]
	c. 1565	4,136[d, h]
	1572	2,180[g]
	1578	602[j, k]
Túcume	1548	2,162[e, f]
	1559–63	5,741[e, f]
	1566	9,529[d, h]
	1568	10,588[d, g]
	1568	4,235[l]
	1569	9,265[d, h]
	1569	3,706[l]
	1570	7,941[d, h]
	1570	3,176[l]
	1572	4,986[g]

SOURCES: BAH/ML, t. 82, 1548, 138–40; Múñoz, A 92, 1540, 66v–67; A 66, no. 211, 1591, 234–96v; ART/HO, 5-XI-1586; Mata, 26-VIII-1572; Vega, 3-X-1589; 1599 [1589]; CoO, 13-VII-1570, 112, 119v, 310v; MT, 1573 [sic 1587]; 1574; BUS/R IV, no. 60, 323; ANP/R, l. 2, c. 5, 1582, 129–35; l. 7, c. 16, 1590, 1163–64; SG, l. 2, c. 12, 1587; AGI/AL, 199, n.d. [1563], IV, 3; 203; 273, 168v; C, 1780b; E, 534A, 72, 375; J 418, 1573, 2v, 45; J 420, 1574, 2, 105v, 108v; J 459, 2653, 3030; P 97, r. 4, [1569], 10v, 16v–18, 45v; l. 108, r. 7, 1562, 51v–2; l. 113, r. 8, 63; l. 187, r. 20, 61; ASFL/Reg. 9, no. 2, ms. 21, n.d.; BNP/A157, 132, 135, 138; A538, 1580; Vargas Ugarte, "Fragmento," pp. 88–89; ACT, II, p. 102; Escobedo Mansilla, especially pp. 38–49; Loredo, *Los repartos,* especially pp. 250–58, 265; Hampe Martínez, "Notas sobre población," pp. 67–68; and Busto, p. 325.

[a]Unregulated prior to 1549. Note that when more than one estimate was found for any given year, all are shown.

[b]Net, unless otherwise specified.

[c]Rounded to nearest peso of 8 reales each. Conversion rates for various years are those published in Ramírez, *Provincial Patriarchs,* appendix 1, under prices for pesos corrientes and ensayados, and appendix 4, p. 388. If the type of peso is not indicated, the conversion rate of 450 maravedís to one is assumed.

[d]Estimate.

[e]These figures must be considered a minimum and are probably equal to only a fraction of the encomienda's true market value.

[f]The manuscript does not indicate the type of peso used. For conversion purposes, I assumed the pesos in 1548 equaled 490 maravedís each.

[g]Gross.

[h]Impossible to determine whether figures are gross or net.

[i]Total tribute less the sum of officials' salaries, the church construction fund, and the king's fifth.

[j]Not including the mitimaes (Indian colonists, living apart from the main community) of Saña. One encomendero held Saña and the mitimaes of Saña concurrently.

[k]Fixed pension paid from the tribute to the encomendero.

[l]Net for the year equals the total tribute less the king's fifth and 40 percent for the costs of collection and contributions. For 1591, I assumed that costs remained at the same average level as those of 1572.

TABLE 10

Tribute of Saña (1549)

---

200 silver or gold pesos (360 patacones 2 reales)

1,400 cotton suits of clothes

4 cotton mattresses

4 cotton awnings or tents (*toldos*)

8 tablecloths (*tablas de manteles*) and 80 cotton napkins (*panijuelos*)

16 *piernas* (literally, legs) of cotton cord (*cordonzillo*)

12 saddle blankets (*mantas*) for horses with 12 cotton aprons or cloths for grooming horses (*mandiles*)

60 pounds of cotton thread

2 cotton beds

Labor to plant, care for (*benefiçian*), and harvest on their own lands 25 fanegas (1.5 to 1.6 bushels) of seed corn and 10 of wheat. Of the harvest, 300 fanegas were to be delivered to the encomendero's house in Trujillo and the rest given out on their land. The corn had to be shucked and the wheat bundled (*encerrado en espiga*). The encomendero should thresh at his own cost and with the help of some Indians.

Labor to sow, care for, and harvest in the fields of the encomendero in Trujillo 10 fanegas of seed corn and wheat. The harvest—after the corn was shucked and the wheat bundled—had to be delivered to the encomendero's house. The encomendero had to thresh it at his own cost but with the help of some Indians. Sixty Indians had to come to plant, weed, and harvest these fields three times a year. Six Indians had to guard the fields from planting to harvest. After the harvest, the Indians were to return to their homes, but while they were in Trujillo, the encomendero was supposed to give them lands on which they could grow their own food.

The Indians were to plant, care for, and harvest on their lands 2 fanegas of beans. Thirty-six fanegas of the harvest were to be delivered to the encomendero's house; the rest were to be given (to the encomendero) in the field.

50 small baskets (*cestillos*) of chili peppers delivered to Trujillo

3 loads of sweet potatoes and squash (*calabaças*) in the field per week during their season

1,200 fowl, half of them females, delivered to Trujillo each year

100 eggs per month, delivered to Trujillo

12 pounds (three *arreldes* [4 pounds or 1.8 kilograms]) of fresh fish, delivered to Trujillo, and another 12 pounds in their community every Friday and meatless days

60 *arrobas* (25 pounds, or 11.5 kilograms) of salted fish each year: 28 to be delivered in Trujillo, 10 arrobas during Lent (*Quaresma*), and the rest in their lands

30 loads of salt, 18 placed in Trujillo and the rest in their community

25 pigs

600 loads of *algarrovo* (a hardwood tree that grows on the coast) pods for the encomendero's pigs

12 straw mats

12 chests or trunks (*petacas*), all in Trujillo

12 wooden poles of up to 25 feet in length

6 straight-backed chairs

15 wooden troughs (*bateas*)

100 large beds, 50 with all their wood, in Trujillo

15 Indians, male and female, for the service of the encomendero's house. They were to change with the mitas; three of them were to be skilled craftsmen.

4 Indians in Trujillo and 10 on their own lands to guard cattle and work the gardens of the encomendero

---

SOURCE: BAH/9-4664, 23v–24v.

NOTE: Each suit of clothes was an *anaco* (tunic or sarong), *liquilla* (shawl or cape) or *manta* (cloak), and *camiseta* (tunic or shirt) (ART/Mata, 11-II-1565). La Gasca set standard sizes for these garments before he left Peru (AGI/J 461, 1261v).

Spanish tribute system, representing another step away from the purely labor obligation system of the Incas. The commoners' tribute responsibilities had become personal service to the encomendero and his household—sometimes expressed in terms of labor and sometimes expressed as a certain quantity of various items, which were themselves an expression of labor, work, and energy expended.

The tribute list for the highland community of Huamachuco has a similar profile. The 1,900 Indians (and 398 *yungas*, or lowland Indians), perhaps because they were within ten leagues of mines, had to produce 3,000 pesos (5,404 patacones 3 reales) of pure (*de ley perfecta*) silver or gold. By this measure, the Sañas' bullion requirements were comparatively light. Besides gold, the Huamachucos provided the goods and services listed in Table 11. Every month (until tithing was instituted) they also had to give to the priest 2 fanegas of wheat, 4 fanegas of corn, 1 camelid, 2 deer, 4 pairs of sandals, 30 Spanish fowl (half of them female), and 1 fanega of potatoes. Each fish day, they were required to deliver 15 eggs, and 1 pig was due every four months. Every day they also had to deliver firewood and fodder for the priest's horse, together with 1 pitcher (*cantarillo*) holding a gallon (2 *acunbres*) of maize beer (presumably for the priest).[37]

In the cases of both Saña and Huamachuco, the product mix includes items from hot and cold climates. Coastal and highland communities alike had to produce corn and cotton (products of hot lands) and wheat and wool (products of temperate or cold climates). The tribute system did take location into account: the lowland community (Saña) produced mostly products from the hot lands, while its highland counterpart (Huamachuco) produced more products typical of the cooler climate of the mountains. However, the lists document that the natives worked a variety of lands, not just the ones near where they lived. If these tribute lists were indeed patterned on the pre-Hispanic obligations of local communities to the Cuzco overlords, then the necessity to travel to different fields to work on their own or for the Inca and the encomendero, to mine, or to deliver goods to an administrative center underscores the fact that the natives traveled a good deal, much more than previously realized and much more than the chroniclers suggest, both before 1532 and thereafter.[38]

La Gasca had to find a way to compromise between the demands and expectations of the encomenderos—some of whom had been involved in the civil wars and still either harbored suspicions of royal authority or felt their loyalty should be copiously rewarded—and the need to protect the native population from the unrealistic demands and, in some cases, brutality of the encomenderos. Although

TABLE 11

Tribute of Huamachuco (1549–50)

---

100 cotton suits of clothes

30 suits of fine wool (*cumbi*) clothes

1 bed of fine wool of 5 panels (*paños*), with its sleeves (*mangas*) and valance (*goteras*)

1 wool carpet or 2 wool ornamental flags, drapes, or hangings (decorated with a coat of arms [*reposteros*])

1 cotton awning or tent (*toldo*)

1 wool tablecloth (*sobremesa*)

2 *arrobas* (25 pounds) of wool

4 cotton tablecloths (*tablas de manteles*) and 50 napkins

Labor to make (with the encomendero's wool) 100 suits of clothes of fine wool. The weavers were to be paid 4 pesos (7 patacones 4 reales) for each suit.

Labor to make (with the encomendero's wool) 100 suits of clothes of coarse weave. These were to be delivered to the encomendero's house. The encomendero had to pay 3 pesos (5 patacones 3 reales) for each suit.

600 fanegas of corn

200 fanegas of wheat

100 fanegas of potatoes

300 of these fanegas had to be delivered to the encomendero's house. The rest were to be delivered to the encomendero in their community.

45 camelids (*ovejas*) and 35 more, which could be paid for instead of delivered at the rate of 3 pesos (5 patacones 3 reales) each

25 pigs

600 birds of Castilla, half of them female, half of which must be delivered to Trujillo

12 wooden chairs

12 medium and 3 large troughs (*bateas*)

50 wooden plates and mugs (*escudillas*)

60 pairs of hemp sandals (*alpargatas*)

30 pairs of cotton sandals

50 pairs of sandals (*oxotas*)

40 headstalls (*xaquimas*) with their halters (*cabestros*)

20 cinches with their straps

20 pairs of fetters (*sueltas*)

20 ropes for lassos (*lazos*) or packing straps (*sobrecargas*), each 5 fathoms (*braças*) long

20 bags (*costales*)

6 saddle blankets

50 hemp ropes to tie trunks or camelids (*ovejas* or *carneros*), each 5 fathoms long, delivered to Trujillo

40 eggs per week, except during Lent, when 80 eggs should be delivered to the encomendero's house

8 Indians to shepherd near their community

SOURCE: Rostworowski, "La tasa," pp. 93–94, or BAH/9-4664, 26–27.

NOTE: I used the second of two tribute lists for 1550, which taxes the natives at a much lower rate.

the complete records of La Gasca's review of tribute have never been found, most scholars agree that La Gasca proved generous to the encomenderos in specifying the amount of tribute, even though he had promised to alleviate the sometimes crushing tribute burden on the commoners. The facts that a subset of encomenderos were charged with adjusting and codifying the tribute exactions of their peers and that La Gasca rightly assessed that the encomenderos were the greater threat to stability moderated intentions to significantly lower tribute demands on the native communities. The tribute lists, to the natives, represented a hope of protection from impossible demands and brutality.[39]

Few were happy with this first effort to systematize tribute exactions. The encomenderos complained, not because they could command too few goods, but because the tasas infringed on their freedom to demand whatever they wanted from their charges. Still, they accepted the tribute lists, to avoid further conflict and the concomitant risk of losing control over the communities altogether.[40]

To impose the royal will, La Gasca probably threatened to totally outlaw personal service. A decree abolishing it, issued at Valladolid on March 28, 1549, arrived just as he prepared to leave Peru. It replaced such services with a system of rotative forced labor based on wages (the Spanish mita or repartimiento). We can speculate that La Gasca used the decree as an additional bargaining chip to douse the protests of the encomenderos. It remained unenforced, a dead letter that was implemented only later and gradually.[41]

The natives also protested La Gasca's "moderate tribute" exactions. La Gasca's efforts were largely ineffective, they claimed, and were not uniformly implemented. Some communities were asked to produce items they could not easily procure—a situation exacerbated by the division of the original communities into two, three, or four encomiendas and by the continued dismantling of the resource base under each curaca.[42]

Within two years, the king ordered the tribute to be reviewed and reductions made if necessary. As a result, native lords requested new inspections; the Real Audiencia in Lima obliged and reduced some tasas. The process continued throughout the decade. In 1557, for example, don Andrés Hurtado de Mendoza, the Marqués de Cañete (1556–61), ordered the 4,000 households of Cajamarca reviewed. The resulting tribute list, reflected in Table 12, required the Cajamarquinos to work less. Most of the table is stated in terms of goods, except for the labor the natives provided the encomendero for his home and for his cattle-raising and agricultural ventures. Although they had to deliver large amounts of agricultural products made from cotton, straw, wood, clay, and hemp, they no longer had to produce and transport large quantities of potatoes, barley (*cebada*), salt, chili peppers, and eggs.[43] All of the tribute exactions decreased except for the number of pigs the natives had to deliver.

TABLE 12

Comparative Tribute Assessments for Cajamarca (1550–57)

Items	1550	1557	Percentage change
Silver pesos	2,100[a]	2,000[a]	−5
Suits of cotton clothes	75	70[b]	−7
Suits of fine wool clothes	25	0	−100
Fanegas of corn	500	200	−60
Fanegas of wheat	200	80	−60
Birds	600	400	−33
Camelids or sheep	75	0	−100
Pigs	15	34	+127
Domestic servants	12	0	−100
Shepherds and farmers	12	12	0

SOURCE: Hampe Martínez, "Notas sobre población," p. 67.
NOTE: Other scholars have provided a macroeconomic picture of the hoard by establishing the amount of bullion officially shipped back to the royal coffers of Spain (TePaske and Klein).
[a]Unconverted pesos. Their equivalents are 3,783 patacones 1 real and 3,603 patacones, respectively.
[b]These were made of encomendero-provided thread.

Such kingdomwide reviews of tribute lists aimed at lowering the amount of goods demanded. For this reason, Carlos Sempat Assadourian labels the 1550s a decade of "alliance" between the state and the native lords, who spearheaded the reassessments (*retasas*) against the encomenderos.[44]

La Gasca's tribute lists and the subsequent, and usually infrequent, retasas remained the standard into the 1560s. In total, they showed the regional effect of Spanish colonization on the native population. La Gasca's census identified a population of almost 8.3 million, of whom 1.5 million were tribute payers. By the end of the Marqués de Cañete's stint as viceroy, Trujillo had a censused population of 215,000 people, of whom 42,000 (10.6 percent) were tribute payers. Their tribute yielded 63,800 pesos (119,273 patacones 1 real). This sum represented 5.2 percent of all tribute collected, showing that northern natives paid less than those in other areas, such as Cuzco (where 19.4 percent of the total tributary population paid 30.7 percent of the total collected tribute in the realm) or Guayaquil (where 0.6 percent of the tribute payers paid 1.0 percent of all tribute). One can only speculate on the reasons why. Was it because the population of the coast declined more rapidly than did that in the highlands, or because the coast did not have the mining resources the south had, or a combination of these and other factors?[45]

During the first half of the 1560s, although debate continued over the amount of tribute, little changed, despite subsequent royal mandates to review the tribute system.[46] The Conde de Nieva argued that tribute should increase because in the past the natives had paid more to the Incas. He judged that the retasas of the 1550s had done "great harm to the land because they reduced the income and tribute by half and more what they used to be worth." He probably exaggerated, according to the figures presented here, but the crown disagreed in any case. Two years later, a royal decree commanded the Spanish not to make the native population provide items they did not produce locally, thereby eliminating the Andeans' need to travel great distances and consequently risk sickness and death. The decree also ordered a further reduction of tribute to a point where the commoners would not have as much trouble producing it. Governor Lope García de Castro (1564–69) thought the retasas were already too low and therefore did not enforce the decree. Instead, he introduced the reducciones in an effort to concentrate the scattered native population into nucleated villages, and he created *corregimientos de indios*, Indian districts or jurisdictions under a bureaucrat or corregidor, ostensibly to protect and more effectively Christianize the native peoples, but clearly also to better administer (read, collect) the tribute and to control native labor.[47]

Meanwhile, the natives of northern Peru had to continue delivering goods and bullion and providing services to their encomenderos. In the late 1550s, two of the lords of Guambos, for example, paid 1,200 pesos (2,243 patacones 3 reales) of *plata ensayada* (assayed silver) to the encomendero. Because they had no access to mines, the natives of Guambos had to travel periodically to Trujillo to work for cash.[48] There they sold their cloth, built houses, and worked in the fields to earn the needed funds.[49] In other areas, native peoples were forced to work in the mines or on the increasingly numerous and constantly growing agricultural estates that dotted the landscape.[50]

Local documents indicate that for some communities, tribute had become so excessive that the natives could no longer deliver the prescribed amount of goods. In 1564, royal authorities investigated the inhabitants of Chérrepe because they had fallen far behind in their tribute deliveries. The community had been reevaluated once, in 1556, since La Gasca ordered the original tribute lists made, and their tribute was worth 2,500 pesos (4,673 patacones 6 reales). An indication of their arrears as of 1564 is shown in Table 13. In their defense, the natives stated that they could not produce as much as they had in the past because their numbers were so few. Likewise, the inhabitants of Pácora complained that their obliga-

TABLE 13

Chérrepe's Arrears (1564)

Assessed tribute	Actual tribute
900 pieces of cloth	Gave 600 pieces of cloth in each of the preceding two years.
2 cotton beds	Undelivered for the preceding three years. In one year before 1560, commuted tribute to cash and paid it.
Plant 36 fanegadas of wheat	Planted 12 fanegadas of seed, which yielded 200 fanegas.
Plant 2 fanegas of corn seed	Did not plant anything but beans and gave the encomendero 6 fanegas to eat.
1,000 fowl	Gave 1,000 fowl.
Eggs and fish (number unspecified)	Commuted tribute to cash at the rate of 4 pesos (6 patacones 5 reales) per month to avoid transporting eggs or stationing fishermen in Trujillo. Did not pay for four months because they had no money.
Salted fish	Had salted fish part of the year and gave it when they had it.
Salt	Gave all they had, but did not deliver it.
Pigs	Converted tribute to cash before 1562, but did not pay for two years because they had no money.
500 loads of algarrova wood	Gathered wood but did not deliver it.
10 beams or trunks (*maderos*)	Commuted tribute to cash before 1562, but did not pay for two years.
15 Indians de mita	Did not send or give Indians to the encomendero, who "rented" them at 10 Indians per peso (peso = 5.25 reales) to irrigate planted fields and clear land.
14 shepherds	The encomendero paid shepherds 4 pieces of cloth per year.

SOURCE: AGI/P 97, r. 4, 1569, 15–17v.

tion to produce 600 pieces of cloth was so heavy that workers were fleeing.[51]

Other coastal communities were still able to deliver to their encomenderos large amounts of cloth, one of the first indigenous items commodified by the growing forces of commercial capitalism. Table 14 shows the number of pieces of cotton cloth produced for the encomenderos of four communities north of Trujillo in the first half of the 1560s.[52] Thus, just one tribute item usually generated thousands of pesos of income for the Spanish each year, making the encomienda grant a highly prized holding and the source of much of the wealth of the encomenderos as a group. From the producers' perspective, this income represented surplus drained from their communities.

TABLE 14

Quantities and Prices of Tribute Cloth

Community	Date	Pieces of cotton cloth	Value (in pesos[a] of 8 reales)	Source
Ferreñafe	1565	1,145	n.a.	ART/Mata, 11-II-1565
Jequetepeque	1563	900[b]	1,800	ART/Mata, 8-II-1563[b]
	1564	900	1,800	ART/Mata, 28-VII-1563
	1565	900	1,800[c]	ART/Mata, 10-I-1565
Saña	1560	600	2,482	ART/LC, 2-XI-1560
	1563	1,200	n.a.	
	1564	380[d]	760[e]	ART/Mata, 18-IV-1564
Túcume	1564	1,520[f]	n.a.	ART/Mata, 22-II-1564

[a] Rounded to the nearest peso.

[b] All pieces were for females and all were dyed black.

[c] The encomendero maintained that the quality in 1563 was poor and therefore the price was low. His testimony, however, appears exaggerated when compared with selling prices of similar tribute goods in Jequetepeque in the same year (AGI/J 420, 1574, II, 105v, 108v, 117, 157).

[d] 300 pieces were from the natives of Saña on the coast, and 80 pieces were from the mitimaes of Saña living in the Cajamarca highlands.

[e] Paid in cash (as opposed to credit).

[f] A minimum of 200 of these were to be dyed black, and 560 were to be dyed other colors. The rest were white.

The Cuenca Visita of 1566

The volume of native complaints about excessive tribute demands continued to grow as their communities continued to shrink (see Table 1). Data for the highland communities are too fragmentary to identify trends, and the Spanish had only an imprecise idea of the size of the population of Cajamarca, even in the 1570s and 1580s (see Table 15). Native leaders alleged that authorities inflated the census figures, and in actuality these communities were vastly smaller than they had been during previous reviews because of disease, death, and flight. Yet the communities still had to produce the same amount of goods—that is, the living paid for those who were dead or had fled. Furthermore, native protesters declared that the authorities wrote the tribute lists without visiting the people in their towns and included items the commoners did not normally produce, thus requiring them to go outside their territories to obtain these goods, often "with much work and vexation."[53]

These complaints from the natives and concurrent complaints from the encomenderos that they were not receiving their due were some of the reasons why García de Castro ordered Dr. Cuenca to reform the tribute system on his inspection tour of the north in 1566.

TABLE 15

Population of Cajamarca and Guambos (1536–87)

Encomienda	Year	Tributaries	Total population
Cajamarca	1536		8,000–10,000
	1540	3,493	
	1567	5,169–5,229	
	1571–72	4,263–5,008	28,915
	c. 1581	4,768	24,674
Guambos	1572	668[a]	
	n.d.[b]	984[c]	
	c. 1587	1,005	4,717

SOURCES: Mogrovejo, p. 232; AGI/AL 320; J 418, 1573, 3, 115v, 203v, 256v, 301, 309, 312–14v, 315, 323, 339; J 420, 1574, II, 152v, 154v–55; J 455, 1317v; J 457, 701v; J 460, 486v; ART/CaO, l. 3, exp. 65, 15-X-1573; LC, 1558; Mata, 9-XII-1562; 28-VII-1565; 24-X-1565; and Hampe Martínez, "Notas sobre población," pp. 75–80.

[a]Excludes 28 tributaries "*de montaña*" (from the jungle), who pay half tribute.

[b]Between 1572 and 1587; exact year uncertain.

[c]Excludes 56 tributaries "*de montaña*," who pay half the tribute rate. The figure comes from the sixteenth-century visitation of Dr. Mendoza.

Cuenca's actions in the field contradict statements by Escobedo Mansilla and others that little significant change took place between the years 1556 and 1569.[54]

Cuenca abolished the old system and instituted a new one. Instead of assessment by community, tribute was now to be determined by individual tribute-paying married males between the ages of 17 and 47, although this rule was not always observed in practice. By 1568, unmarried males between these ages were paying tribute as if they were married, with the exception of tribute cloth, which they were assessed at half the married men's rate. What each individual had to give to his encomendero and to his cacique was clearly specified. Yanaconas serving native lords were added to the tribute list as regular community members, foreshadowing Viceroy Francisco de Toledo's similar move in the next decade. The curaca and his legitimate children, lords of *pachacas* (one hundred households), those persons who served on the native cabildos or in the church, and the sick were exempt from paying tribute and serving the mitas.[55]

The new tribute lists were much shorter and simpler than those elaborated under La Gasca's influence. The variety of goods was reduced to reflect more closely the possibility of local production. Each Guambos tributary, for example, had to provide 4 pesos (4 patacones 6 reales) *plata corriente* (peso worth 9 reales each after 1572), 1 fanega of corn, and 1 fowl. Cajamarca's married members had to produce the same commodities in the same quantities, but they only had to pay 2.5 pesos plata corriente (3 patacones) instead of 4 pesos (4 patacones 6 reales). According to Pilar Remy, Cuenca gave the natives the option of commuting some of the tribute goods into silver, so the total paid to the encomendero in 1567 was 14,780 pesos plata corriente (17,605 patacones 5 reales), 3,823 birds, and 2,584 fanegas of corn. On the coast, each tributary of Collique was responsible for 3 fanegas of corn, another 3 of wheat, and a piece and a half of cloth. Illimo had to provide these items plus firewood and fodder.[56]

Cuenca's actions in Lambayeque are unclear. One source states that Cuenca excused Lambayeque from producing wheat, reduced the number of fanegas of corn from 1,000 to 600, and reduced the cloth proportionately too. Another says that Cuenca increased the tribute of Lambayeque from 1,500 to 2,500 pieces of cloth plus 1,000 pesos in silver (1,191 patacones 1 real at 324 maravedís each and 2,117 patacones 5 reales at 576 maravedís each), 3,000 fanegas of corn, and about 4,000 fowl, which according to observers was "much more than they used to give."[57]

Globally, the community of Túcume had to produce for the encomendero 976 pesos 4 *granos plata ensayada* (2,067 patacones), 2,580.5 pieces of cloth, 2,406 fowl, 87 fanegas of wheat (from a communal field), and 875 fanegas of corn, according to Cuenca's tribute list. The tribute was worth between 7,000 and 8,000 pesos (14,823 patacones 4 reales to 16,941 patacones 1 real) per year.[58] The tributaries of Túcume, however, could rarely produce even this shortened list of goods in the quantities required. Table 16 shows the

TABLE 16

Tribute of Túcume (1570–73)

Year	Plata ensayada[a]	Suits of clothes	Fowl	Wheat[b]	Corn[b]
1566 (tasa)	976 pesos	2,580.5	2,406	87	875
30-IX-1570[c]	637 pesos	901[d]			
31-I-1571[c]	341 pesos	909	698	24	261
31-V-1571[c]	647 pesos	872[e]	698	24	265
V-1572[c]	292 pesos	700			
IX-1572[c]		700			
31-I-1573	290 pesos	694	660	50	194

SOURCE: ART/CoO: 13-VII-1570, 35v, 166, 190, 221, 244, 290, and 329–29v.
NOTE: Dates are in the form 30 (day)-V (month)-1571 (year).

[a]In unconverted pesos.
[b]In fanegas.
[c]One tercio.
[d]104 were paid for in cash rather than made and delivered.

[e]64 were paid for in cash at 2.5 pesos (almost 5 patacones) each.

quantities delivered in each of four years. These figures suggest a real struggle to meet quotas and constant shortfalls.[59]

The tribute records from other communities also show a difference between what the natives were supposed to produce and what they delivered. In 1568, for example, the corregidor collected 1,800 pieces of clothing, 300 fanegas of wheat and 700 of corn, and 1,000 fowl from the natives of Jequetepeque. By 1571, the encomendero of Jequetepeque received 14.3 percent less corn than he did in 1568, even though in theory the quotas remained unchanged.[60]

Cuenca further enforced the Marqués de Cañete's suspension of personal services. This meant that encomenderos could no longer take advantage of free labor, a valuable commodity. In the process, they lost all semblance of control over the labor of the charges of their encomienda. This change did not liberate the natives from working for government-favored enterprises, however. In conjunction with Cuenca's move, royal officials resurrected the mita system, with modifications, whereby the community members had to work on government projects or were allocated to "needy" citizens, according to the merits of their petitions, for agricultural labor, huaca exploitation, mining, and herding—a distribution of activities ranked in order of importance by the crown.[61]

Cuenca also set about correcting some of the most exploitative aspects of the tribute system. He disciplined and fined encomenderos who had cheated by collecting more goods than La Gasca and subsequent inspectors had intended. The best illustration of this was his stance on the collection of cloth (*ropa de tributo*). Weaving cloth had been a major tribute obligation before 1532 and had remained the most important marketable item in the north, given the relative paucity of sources for gold and silver. La Gasca had set the sizes of cloth before 1550, but the encomenderos had not been diligent in regulating the sizes. Judicial records clearly show that Cuenca found the encomenderos guilty of exacting more cloth than ordered. He prosecuted most of the north coast encomenderos for these excessive exactions.

The "perfect measure" for an *anaco* (tunic) was 2.5 varas long and 2 varas, or 10 *palmos* ("palms," about 20 centimeters), wide. A perfect *liquilla* (shawl) measured 1.5 varas by 1.5 varas. In Trujillo, the same measures were about 2 varas *escasas* ("scant") by 1.67 varas and 1.9 varas by 1.33 varas, respectively. The average piece was to total 7.5 varas (although it is not clear how this was calculated). The actual sizes of a sample of nine pieces of cloth were measured in 1566 at the time of the visita and are shown in Table 17. The com-

TABLE 17

Sizes of Tribute Clothing (1566)

Tunics (*anacos*)		Shawls (*liquillas*)	
Length	Width	Length	Width
2.83	1.83	2	1.83
3	2	2.125	2
2.875	1.83	2	1.875
3	2	2.08	1.875
2.5	1.75	1.75	1.75
2.83	2	2	1.75
2.83	2	2	1.75
2.5	1.67	1.75	1.67
2.5	1.67	1.75	1.67

SOURCE: AGI/J 459, 3026v-29.
NOTE: Length and width are in varas.

bined area was 83.42 square varas, or an average of 9.25 square varas each. Each piece on average, therefore, represented almost two extra square varas of cloth. Price was determined by quality, which took color, weight (by number of threads), and size into consideration. Thus, Cuenca prosecuted because the encomenderos had been exacting more than the tasa rightly allowed, even though the number of pieces had not exceeded those stated in the tribute list. With no evidence that the encomenderos denied the charges, we may conclude that Cuenca's actions were justified. It should be noted, however, that he did respond subsequently to a petition from the encomenderos requesting that the size of an anaco be increased statutorily. He granted their request and increased the size by one-fourth.[62]

Cuenca's visit and reform loosed a barrage of complaints to vice-regal authorities. Indigenous lords complained that natives who had left permanently had been included in the counts and that the labor assigned to support them was too little to maintain their respectability and power. Other natives complained that Cuenca had raised tribute too much. This last complaint was true in the case of Saña. Cuenca's motives for raising tribute were not clear. One charitable witness said it was a mistake; others believed it was because Cuenca was a friend of the encomendero. In the case of Guambos, the natives alleged that Cuenca set a high tasa to favor the encomendero Lorenzo de Ulloa because Cuenca wanted to arrange the marriage of his daughter to Ulloa's son. One contemporary generalized that under Cuenca all tasas had increased in favor of the encomenderos. Another claimed that the tasas were moderate and within the capabilities of the natives and their resource base, although he conceded that the amount of tribute cloth had indeed increased. Yet at least one encomendero, Francisco Perez de Lezcano, claimed that, after deducting the tithe and the priest's salary, his income fell by three-fourths as a result of Cuenca's actions.[63]

Because historically there were vast differences between what was assessed and what was produced and delivered, the commutation of goods to specie was extended to other goods produced by other communities. The natives of Túcume and the mitimaes of Saña, who could not produce cloth, were given an option to pay in silver at the market price for tribute cloth. Those of Saña, Reque, Chuspo, Sinto, Collique, Lambayeque, Ferreñafe, Túcume, Illimo, Jayanca, and Pácora were able to commute their tribute corn to silver in pesos de plata ensayada y marcada (silver assayed and stamped) of 12.5 reales (425 maravedís) each. Some natives welcomed the commutation alternative because it provided them with an option if floods, crop failures, and natural disasters resulted in tribute deficits.[64]

Tribute collection locally remained the responsibility of the curaca and his principales, who traveled to visit their subjects to gather the goods to meet their colonial obligations. These lords served as labor bosses, renting gangs of commoners to Spaniards for cash, which went toward meeting their tribute needs. In a concession that clearly favored the natives, Cuenca decided that they no longer had to deliver tribute goods to Trujillo but could present them to the encomendero or his agent in their own communities.[65]

The Toledo Visita

Cuenca's standardization of the tribute system, for all its faults, anticipated the efforts of Viceroy Francisco de Toledo six years later. Toledo's reforms had their greatest impact in the southern part of the viceroyalty, where no previous standardization had taken place. In the north, state officials merely increased the number of reducciones and again recounted and reappraised the tribute-paying potential of the indigenous population, with the aim of further reducing the power of the encomenderos.[66]

Toledo justified his actions in the north in part by correcting many of the irregularities of Cuenca's efforts. According to Joan de Hoçes, Toledo's corregidor and designated visitor in the north, Cuenca's practice of judging a native person's age by appearance or by the description of a father, mother, sibling, or encomendero, without actually seeing the person himself, was flawed. As a result,

Cuenca had inscribed on the taxpayer rolls boys as young as 6, 8, and 10 (when the youngest age prescribed by law was 17) and men as old as 50 and 60 (when the maximum age to pay tribute was 47). As a result, fathers and relatives had to work extra to make up the deficit in tribute for the young, old, and incapacitated erroneously included on the rolls. Hoçes claimed to have taken great care in determining ages, although he too often had to rely on appearance alone. Hoçes eventually exempted 1,000 elderly people and a large number of youths from paying. When Cuenca, who was still in Lima serving as a judge of the Real Audiencia, heard of these exemptions, he wrote to Hoçes asking him not to change the ages. Cuenca's objection is understandable. Hoçes's scrutiny exposed Cuenca's questionable methods, making Cuenca's work look less respectable. It also decreased the tribute to the encomenderos.[67]

Toledo justified his actions by saying that previous tribute regulations had not been carried out in an "orderly" and "uniform" manner (*ha habido desorden y variedad*). No one had implemented royal orders as written. The implication, of course, was that he, Toledo, would be more successful in carrying out the royal will. He reiterated that tribute obligations should be assessed by tributary, instead of by community, as this would better reflect constant demographic shifts. Otherwise, communities would be hurt if their population decreased, or encomenderos would suffer if it increased (not then a likely occurrence). No commoner was to pay more than one tribute, but lords, from this tasa on, were obliged to pay tribute for absent community members. Thus, in theory tribute was collected individual by individual, but in practice the community remained responsible for the number of tribute payers on the roll, regardless of demographic trends.[68]

At Toledo's instigation, Hoçes initiated some changes. He altered the definition of tributaries from males aged 17 through 47 to married, widowed, and single males aged 18 through 50. He also wanted most of the tribute paid in assayed silver (plata ensayada) to facilitate collection by the corregidor instead of by the encomendero's agent. To fix a just price for this commutation, fair to the crown and the natives, Toledo stated: "I ordered the values recorded in the auction books for the past five years be added together. And I declared that a fifth of that sum was to be the just price of the commutation and according to this rule all commutations were made of all the tribute goods." He made it clear, however, that encomenderos could not substitute one tribute good for another or accept personal service in lieu of goods.[69]

Toledo further argued that the encomenderos had corrupted the provisions designed to safeguard the natives. When the encomenderos lost the right to the personal services of their charges, the natives were reassigned to the mita, or *repartimiento de plaza* (theoretically a distribution of wage-earning commoners to Spaniards on the basis of Spanish need for labor). But he found that encomenderos continued to take the commoners they wanted from "their" encomiendas, bypassing the mita system and putting other entrepreneurial and productive Spanish citizens at a disadvantage. Moreover, the non-encomendero Spanish citizens often did not get their due share, because the encomendero often had influence over the person distributing the mita labor.[70] Furthermore, the corregidor allegedly favored the encomenderos and their enterprises, such as textile mills (*obrajes*) and sugar mills, to the detriment of the farming and herding interests of others. Toledo therefore reiterated the ban on all forms of personal service, whether to the encomenderos or the native lords. He also abolished the service to tambos and the previous requirement that commoners carry goods between one tambo and another.[71]

The encomenderos objected vociferously to these changes, which forced them to relinquish control of their communities to a royal official, the corregidor, who henceforth would serve as an intermediary between the encomendero and native peoples and would collect the tribute and pay certain costs, salaries, and subsidies from the proceeds before delivering the net to the encomendero.

Encomenderos and other Europeans also lost the free use of their yanaconas, natives who had broken contact with their communities and become personal retainers. Implementing an order from Philip II, Toledo ordered yanaconas to be concentrated in towns. He continued Cuenca's policy of assessing their tribute obligations, but guaranteed (at least in a juridical sense) that their labor would be paid.[72] Yanaconas initially were paid 1 peso per year; later, tribute was set at an annual rate of 5 pesos ensayados (9 patacones 7 reales). Toledo also ordered mitimaes to pay a head tax. Subsequently, by 1578, *sambos* (offspring of an Indian and a black) joined the tribute rolls. Encomenderos demanded compensation for the loss of personal services, but to no avail.[73]

More vociferous still were their frequent petitions against loss of income. Corregidors were to deduct the salaries of crown officials (such as their own and that of the protector of Indians—*defensor de indios*), local priests (although, at least theoretically, the encomenderos had been paying priests directly), and curacas from the native tribute, reducing the net encomienda income by 25 to 50 percent. In time, given continued population decline, some encomiendas did not yield enough to pay these costs, so encomenderos were left with nothing. Many others had much less than they had enjoyed previously (see Table 9). Thus, for the community of Callanca, the gross tribute collected in 1575 (1572?) was 2,262 pesos 6 reales. Of this, 548 pesos 6 reales paid the resident priests; 45 pesos were deducted to support church construction; 345 pesos paid royal authorities; and 98 pesos paid community officials. The encomendero received 1,226 pesos after the deductions, which amounted to almost 46 percent of the total.[74] In addition, tribute goods were valued arbitrarily, often at below their real value. To add insult to injury, Toledo established wage guidelines for mita laborers in the expectation that encomenderos would pay them.[75]

Such gross figures, like those of Callanca given above, mask the true impact of the revised Toledo-inspired tribute lists on the average tributary. Toledo's visit to the north institutionalized obligations imposed on the natives to support the priests, cacique, and lesser lords. The distribution in one particular valley is summarized in Table 18. It is interesting to note that money is given only to the Spanish priests. All other obligations are expressed as labor service,

TABLE 18

Partial Distribution of the Tribute of Chicama (1570s)

To priests (until the tithe is instituted):
    781 pesos ensayados (of 450 maravedís each) (1,292 patacones 1 real)
    2–3 mitayos to be paid by the priest for serving his household needs

To the cacique:
    10 old Indians (who no longer pay tribute) and 4 boys younger than 17 for his service and shepherding his cattle
    If he is married, 8 old female Indians (*yndias viejas sin sospecha*) for his wife's service and that of the household. All 8 must be given food, drink, and one suit of cotton clothes. They can only serve 6 months at a turn.

To 6 lesser lords who are exempt from paying tribute:
    4 old Indians who no longer pay tribute and 2 boys below the age of 17
    If married, 3 old Indian women for the service of his wife and household. They are subject to the same conditions and restrictions mentioned above.
    Their subjects must plant, care for, and harvest one chacara (planted field) of one fanega of seed corn each. The official must give the Indians the seed to plant and provide them with food and drink while they work.

To the pachacas (Indian officials in charge of 100 households), who are exempt from personal service (mita) and paying tribute:
    Their subjects must sow and harvest half a fanega of seed corn each. The pachacas must provide the seed and give the Indians food and drink while they work.
    1 old Indian and 1 boy for service
    For the wife, 1 old Indian woman, under the same conditions as above

SOURCE: ART/CoP, l. 281, exp. 3721, 20-X-1615, 1–IV, 4–6.

representing the Andean peoples' pre-Hispanic custom of personal service to superiors. The itemization of these obligations may also have represented the state's effort to restrict the lords' appropriations of unlimited amounts of their subjects' labor. Indeed, by granting lords' salaries, Toledo's reforms made them the equivalent of bureaucrats of the colonial state.

Toledo's tasas, most contemporaries agreed, were less than Cuenca's because they more closely represented the native reality (*sus posibilidades*). This was no accident. Toledo's underlying rationale was to protect the subsistence of the natives and guarantee their social reproduction while using the state apparatus to mediate among elite interests. Thus, in the short run, Toledo's tasas seem to have been somewhat more favorable to the average tributary.[76]

This finding is in sharp contrast to Toledo's reputation for having markedly increased the tax burden on the natives of Peru. In the long run, this reputation seems accurate. As the native population continued to fall, the amount of tribute remained unchanged as long as no new census was taken. The current population had to produce enough to cover the tribute obligations of the community at the time of the census, regardless of any intervening decrease in numbers. Since the population was in steep decline in almost every community, the impact on the typical tribute payer increased to the point where tribute became a real burden, in some instances threatening subsistence (and causing individuals and families to flee). Although population and summary tribute figures in the sixteenth century are far from complete, a rough approximation of this growing burden can be gained by contrasting the changes in population with those in tribute. Thus, as Table 19 shows, the tribute population of Jayanca declined 88.2 percent between 1536 and 1567–89, while tribute declined 44.7 percent between 1548 and 1572. The discrepancy meant that those still in the community were paying more. In Jequetepeque, the figures were even more dramatic. The population declined 75 percent between 1530 and 1572, while tribute increased between 84.3 and 267.5 percent between 1548 and 1575 or 1576, respectively. In these cases and those of Chérrepe, Saña, and Túcume, no matter which way the population and tribute figures of each community vary, the discrepancy means the tribute burden increased.[77] Only for Illimo, where the population increased faster than the tribute burden, do the trends favor the natives.

Thus, by the time of Viceroy Toledo, tribute from the natives was supporting the encomendero and his household as well as the growing Catholic church, the missions, the Spanish state, and the native

TABLE 19

Relative Tribute Burdens of Selected Northern Communities

Community	Change in tribute population		Change in tribute	
	%	Date span	%	Date span
Chérrepe	−34.5	1564 to 1576–83	−26.5	1548–69
Illimo	+178	1541–1572	+50.6	1548–72
Jayanca	−88.2	1536 to 1567–89	−44.7	1548–72
Jequetepeque	−75.0	1530–72	+84.3	1548–75
			+267.5	1548–76
Saña	−89.3	1532–72	−65.3–77.7	1548–72
Túcume	+30.6	1540–72	+130.6	1548–72

SOURCES: Tables 1, 9, and 16.

administrative hierarchies. The corregidor auctioned any produce the commoners still delivered; with the proceeds of the sale and the cash tribute, he paid the priest, the curaca and lesser lords, and royal officials like himself and contributed to the support of the hospital. Each encomendero received his due according to that stated in the tasa. If the natives delivered more or the auction of the commodities produced more than what was needed to meet the tasa quotas, the surplus was put into a community chest. If there was a shortfall, the curaca had to make up the difference.[78]

As previously, any natural disaster or climatic change caused the natives to fall behind. For example, Illimo and Túcume failed to meet their quotas in 1573 because the irrigation ditch called the Taymi was damaged. Only after they had repaired it could they replant their fields. Meanwhile, production was halted and tribute collection was suspended.[79]

The Depersonalization of Tribute

The Toledo visita established a benchmark in the evolution of the Spanish colonial tribute system in the sixteenth century. Only in the seventeenth century, when tribute was solely a monetary obligation, was this evolution complete. The timing of the evolution differed by a few years for different communities, but generally followed the pattern illustrated in Fig. 3, which shows that the native population's support of the colonial state and church had evolved from a purely labor obligation, which later was imposed on a rotative basis, through successive stages in which commodities and cash replaced labor.

Before 1549, the encomenderos could demand whatever services

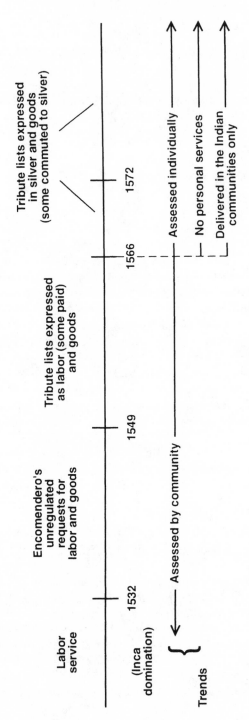

Fig. 3 Tribute in northern Peru

they wished. The risk of production of some items produced by tribute labor shifted abruptly from the beneficiaries to the native producers. President La Gasca, charged with reestablishing peace after the acrimonious civil wars of the 1540s, ordered officials to write the first tribute lists. Each community had to produce certain goods and provide specified amounts of personal services to their encomendero. Although designed to protect the natives, these first tasas did not alleviate their burden. As complaints mounted, another visitor, Cuenca, traveled north. Charged with reforming the system, he declared tribute to be an individual obligation and further simplified the tribute lists, reducing them to specific items and eliminating personal labor completely. He also allowed some commutation of goods to silver. Toledo and his agents extended this process in the early 1570s and made the type of tribute system imposed by Cuenca standard throughout the viceroyalty. Again, individuals were responsible for producing certain goods and paying a fixed amount in silver. More than ever before, however, officials encouraged natives to substitute silver for goods. Forthwith, tribute became akin to a poll tax, increasingly paid in cash rather than assessed in labor or produced in goods. That this evolution required 40 years and longer (in some areas) attests to the resistance of the Andean peoples.

To raise the increasing amount of cash needed, native lords often had to organize work crews for hire. In addition, more and more natives sold their produce in the marketplace. Thus, the evolving tribute system forced the indigenous population to participate in a market economy and adopt the implied values of this system—individualism, competition, and profit—that were anathema to people accustomed to reciprocity, redistribution, cooperation, and sharing. Finally, in this evolution, labor changed from being a personal obligation to an individual (the Inca, the native lord, or the encomo.endero) to an impersonal obligation to a faceless bureaucracy, the symbol and agent of a foreign colonial power.

Within a broader colonial context, this story epitomizes the policy changes and social repercussions occurring throughout the New World. The encomenderos as a class, too independent to suit royal pleasure, lost a solid and rich, though steadily declining, economic base. Those encomenderos able to recognize what was happening diversified and became miners, merchants, ship captains, or commercial farmers, or slipped into the relative archival obscurity of the nonelites. More efficient tribute collection and a more elaborate royal bureaucracy strengthened the crown's hand throughout the domain and made the state the mediator among elite groups, able to subsidize some favored economic activities, for example, through the mita for mining. These changes were aptly summarized by the author of an anonymous manuscript, who said that the Indians "are the feet and buttresses supporting and sustaining this [Spanish] republic and that it is growing and they [the Indians] are diminishing."[80]

CHAPTER 5

Huaca Looting on the Peruvian North Coast

A TALE FROM TWO PERSPECTIVES

And they [the natives] say that when that place [Yomayo-guan] is opened, they will all perish.

—AGI/J 404, 277–77v

God, Gold, and Glory; or, Gold, God, and Glory

Spanish motivations for the invasion and conquest of America are sometimes summarized as God, gold, and glory. Proselytizing became the driving force for the select few robed friars who first came to the New World. They braved largely uncharted seas and unimagined dangers to zealously preach their gospel to peoples who for years could not understand Spanish and who, even in their own language, could not fully grasp concepts such as the Trinity.

From the start, adventurers, some of whom survived to become "conquerors and first settlers," outnumbered these visionary, enthusiastic prelates. The conquerors definitely put gold ahead of God and glory, dreaming of riches and, to a lesser extent, the glory that gold could buy. For their daring and audacity, the crown rewarded these men with booty confiscated from the native elite they subjugated. Atahualpa, the Inca ruler that Francisco Pizarro first encountered in Cajamarca, had rooms filled with silver and gold. This treasure was hurriedly melted down and distributed to Pizarro's followers. Once such booty was exhausted, some of these same men and a few who arrived shortly thereafter were rewarded with encomiendas so they could direct the natives to mine gold and silver for them. Latecomers aspired to the same rewards, but often faced a lengthy petitioning process and then had to settle for pensions and sinecures.[1]

Spanish gold fever prompted encomenderos and others to prospect and mine. The native charges of Melchor Verdugo, the notoriously cruel encomendero of Cajamarca, worked the silver deposit of Chilete as early as 1540. Lorenco de Ulloa, the more benevolent encomendero of Guambos, immediately to the north of Cajamarca (see Map 3), detailed some of his wards to pan for gold in the Guayobamba River about the same time. Some Spaniards combined their knowledge of indigenous beliefs about the supernatural and of burial customs and practices to "mine," as they genteelly put it, sacred structures—or, more accurately, to rob graves and plunder temples. Most Spaniards looted indigenous pyramids and edifices with little regard to the significance of the structures. The Spanish did not consistently distinguish between temples and tombs, calling them all *huacas*, a generic term for sacred object or place.[2]

This chapter recounts the story of one incident of huaca looting on the north coast of Peru. The incident took place in Chan Chan, the ancient capital city of the Chimu people. On one level, it is a story of greed, official corruption and connivance, claim jumping, tax evasion, and deceit in the environs of the then (1558 to 1559) frontier town of Trujillo. The protagonists are some of the otherwise forgotten men (and women) who lived during this era, not members of the conqueror and encomendero elite whose exploits enliven most contemporary accounts and later histories. They are, for the most part, late-arriving Spaniards or first-generation mestizos of dubious status, people who sought their living in the service of the more influential or risked all to seek fame and fortune. Among them is a peripatetic prospector who brought suit against a loose coalition of men that included a former partner in grave robbing, the curaca principal (chieftain) of the Chimu Valley, a notary, and other royal officials all the way up the colonial administrative hierarchy to the district governor himself. To all of them, a rich strike at the "huaca" Yomayoguan[3] represented a chance to change their condition almost overnight and assume a respected place among the new monied elite on a frontier of this newly colonized and disordered land.

This story of pillaging and treasure hunting masks another story, which comes to light only in the testimonies of the Chimu. The natives tried to protect their ancestral legacy, both by force and eventually in the courts. Their paramount lord reluctantly joined the Spanish in partnership in the excavation. He never mentioned his motivations explicitly, but the subsequent use of his share of the treasure suggests he colluded with the colonizers to protect his subjects' communal values and way of life.

In their legal defense, the Chimu reiterated the principal of possession based on labor and work (as discussed in Chapter 3). They also insisted that the site in question was not a huaca, and their clear distinction between temples and tombs involved distinctly different rights concerning structures the Spanish considered similar in form and content. The hidden story, then, is that of the original inhabitants of a provincial area adjusting to a new and dominant culture whose use of indigenous words and concepts redefined them or simply misunderstood them. The natives tried to correct the misinterpretation, but the Spanish, for the most part, chose not to listen. The Chimu tried to assert their rights, but they were disregarded and eventually forced to accept Spanish precepts as the only way to avoid losing everything. For the Spanish, it was easier to use one term, "huaca," for any item or place the natives regarded as sacred. In this sense, the story epitomizes the culture clashes of the sixteenth century.

Of Grave Diggers and the Treasure They Sought and Found

The account unfolds in the approximately 1,700 pages of a manuscript of a court case (conserved in the Archivo General de las Indias in Seville, Justicia 404) over the partition of the gold, silver, pearls, precious stones, and other items the Spanish considered valuable[4] that were taken from a "huaca" near the Spanish provincial capital of Trujillo on the north coast of Peru. The "huaca" belonged to the group of structures identified as the pre-Inca Chimu capital of Chan Chan, whose ruins can still be seen today between the city limits of Trujillo and the Pacific seashore.

The sixteenth-century manuscript tells a story of one Alonso Zarco, who found a treasure in the "huaca" called Yomayoguan. Zarco, a poor urban outcast, was the laughingstock of the town—that is, until August 8, 1558. The respectable citizens of Trujillo described him as a bum with neither a house (and thus no citizen status or voice in town council deliberations) nor often food to eat. Before the trial, he relied on charity for food while incarcerated; during the trial, he was reduced to boarding with his lawyer. At one point, his case was almost lost because he could not pay the scribe who copied legal documents. His constant companion was a bastard mestizo boy named Gonçalo Suarez, whom he had raised from birth and whom the citizens variously described as Zarco's nephew, son, or servant. To add to his downtrodden image, he was deaf and probably had trouble speaking; witnesses claimed they could not understand him when he spoke.[5]

By his own admission, Zarco had been prospecting for treasure since 1556, both on the coast and in the highland hinterland of Trujillo as far as Huamachuco. Trujillanos ridiculed him for wasting his time, even though he had already found a significant amount of marketable cloth in one "huaca" in the Huamachuco highlands. In 1558, he was locally known as "the deaf man of the guacas." Around Trujillo people smirked and said he "wandered around lost in the clouds of the guacas." During the time he roamed the environs of Trujillo looking for buried treasure—perhaps eight months to a year—he became known as a "man who had nothing else to do," "a vagrant."[6]

Yet Zarco was literate and claimed he was an "honorable and noble man." Others admitted he was proud and serious. He knew something about the customs of the natives,[7] judging from his success in Huamachuco and several statements indicating that he knew in advance that the "huaca" of Yomayoguan was "very rich."[8]

People abruptly stopped laughing at Zarco in August 1558 when he recovered two large silver pitchers (*cántaros*) in a hole he dug two to three *estados* into a structure of Yomayoguan.[9] This "discovery" of what the Chimu knew to be there all along brought him instant notoriety and even grudging respect from the Spanish townspeople. His find triggered a gold rush that folk memory still celebrated, though with a few facts changed, over 200 years later. Many of his previous detractors (including the local notary, Antonio de Paz) and people who moved to Trujillo from elsewhere began prospecting for more treasure. But Zarco's good fortune proved to be short-lived, as savvy detractors quickly found an opportunity to jump his claim. August 8 of that year marked the beginning of a legal nightmare for Zarco that would last more than six years.[10]

The facts of the case are not entirely clear because of the often biased testimony of the witnesses. In broad outline, it appears that Zarco had already made more than one find: in addition to the one in Huamachuco, there was a second at a huaca "above the field of Pedro Ortiz, near the road that links Trujillo to Huamachuco." He worked and shared the latter strike with a partner, Miguel de Villalobos, who was one of the people involved in the claim jumping of the "huaca" Yomayoguan.[11]

After digging above the field of Ortiz, Zarco began prospecting at Yomayoguan between Trujillo and the sea. An attempt to get a license from the corregidor was denied, but he kept going to the "huaca" and therefore had de facto possession of it. The natives of the Chimu Valley watched him and on several occasions tried to physically impede his work. As he came closer to the prize, the native witnesses said, the Chimu became increasingly anxious. Once he began to dig down into a chamber of the actual structure of Yomayoguan, they tried to throw him off. According to the Chimu, they, under the direction of their curaca principal, don Antonio Chayguaca (or Chimu or Cheno), decided to preempt Zarco. At least eight days and perhaps as long as two months before Zarco's actual find, they began to dig through dirt and adobe themselves, with— according to the Spanish claim jumpers—the intention of removing the contents of the site to another location for safekeeping so that they could continue their traditional celebrations and religious practices.[12] Undoubtedly, the natives' reaction to Zarco's progress merely caused him to redouble his efforts. His testimony tells of a harrowing night on the structure just before he uncovered the first treasure, when he had to defend himself with his sword against Chimu assailants.[13]

On August 8, 1558, Zarco and the highland Indians he had hired to help him began digging at dawn. News of his activity spread, and several people walked from Trujillo to watch his progress. Before noon, Zarco and his assistants had dug "in the first of the chambers" and soon found two large silver pitchers. Over the next few hours, Zarco and his workers found another, smaller, gold pitcher (*cantarillo*), a gold *coco* (drinking cup or vessel) with the face of an Indian in relief (*medalla de rostro de yndio*), two Indian loads (*cargas de indios*) of small pitchers and silver platelets (*cantarillos y pedazos de chapas*), one little gold bar or plate (*tejuelo*), and several silver bars.[14]

Chimu witnesses had by this time gotten word to don Antonio, who was carried to the scene on his litter accompanied by a retinue of principales and commoners. Don Antonio protested. Atop the structure, a scuffle broke out in which Zarco pushed don Martín (a principal and don Antonio's brother) into the pit.[15] A stunned and breathless don Martín was carried away to Trujillo to the corregidor. The Chimu claimed that don Martín was mortally injured. The corregidor ordered Zarco arrested.[16]

Someone warned Zarco, who sought refuge in a monastery but was eventually arrested and jailed. Meanwhile, a consortium of Spaniards headed by Francisco Escobar asked the corregidor for a license to mine the structure. Their request was granted on the spot.. A *veedor* (an inspector, someone assigned to watch the treasure hunting and record the finds to ensure that the crown received its share)[17] was appointed that same day. By afternoon, Escobar had hurried to the "huaca" with Baltazar Castellanos, a notary who gave him legal possession of the site and later became his partner. Don Antonio protested this act, to no immediate avail. Zarco's claim had been jumped.[18]

Legal proceedings began almost immediately. Don Antonio sued Escobar and his partner, Pedro Núñez de Arraya, a lawyer, within ten days of Zarco's strike. Both parties eventually came to an understanding and became formal associates in the exploitation of the mound.[19] Meanwhile, the corregidor, suspicious of the Chimu claim that don Martín was dying, threatened to burn the principal's feet if he did not get up and walk. Don Martín stepped out of his hammock soon thereafter. The Chimu subsequently dropped their charges against Zarco, but the encomendero and lieutenant corregidor Pedro Gonzalez fined Zarco 10 pesos (18 patacones 6 reales) and sentenced him to five months of exile. The exile was suspended about two weeks later, but the evidence suggests that Zarco did not know of the suspension for several months. Zarco filed his own court case in Trujillo on November 14, 1558.[20]

The stakes were high. While Zarco was in exile, up to 90 Indian and black laborers dug at the site, and eventually Yomayoguan yielded its treasure. Eyewitnesses described some of the loot, as listed in Table 20.[21] The value of these items increased over time. Estimates that started at 60,000 pesos (112,169 patacones 1 real) jumped first to 80,000 pesos (149,558 patacones 7 reales) and then to 200,000 pesos (373,897 patacones). Finally, townspeople said that the treasure was worth 700,000 castellanos de oro (1,308,639 patacones 6 reales).

Table 21 lists the official royal treasury accounting of what was found in the "huaca" Yomayoguan during the first two years of looting. According to these figures, the silver amounted to roughly 144,612 patacones 6 reales and the gold to 21,859 patacones 3 reales. Thus, silver made up almost 87 percent of the total registered bullion of over 166,000 patacones; gold about 13 percent. The totals given in the popular accounts were wrong, and the estimate of 700,000 castellanos was astronomically high.[22]

But 166,000 patacones was a respectable fortune compared with Pizarro's distribution of precious metals at Cajamarca in 1532, where horsemen averaged almost 20,000 patacones (563.6 silver marks [4,512 patacones 7.5 reales] and 8,842.5 gold pesos [14,629 patacones 1 real]) and footmen averaged 6,900 patacones (144 silver marks [1,153 patacones] and 3,457 gold pesos [5,719 patacones 2.4 reales]). This find also rivaled some of the other most talked-about lootings in colonial memory. Cieza de Leon reports that a burial in the Ica Valley contained treasure worth 50,000 pesos (at 450 maravedís

TABLE 20
Partial List of the Contents of the Huaca Yomayoguan (c. 1558–59)

2 silver pitchers (which are variously described as knee high, as high as a
  person is tall, or at least as high as a man's breast; as big as the small jugs
  [*botijas*] of oil that were imported from Spain; or as large as a jug of Spanish
  wine); decorating the top of both the pitchers were hunchbacked men (*unos
  hombres de plata corcobados*) with painted faces
woolen figurines
cloth
precious stones or gems
1 small golden pitcher
1 drinking cup or vessel (*coco*) "with a low-relief figure of the face of an
  Indian made of gold"; more than one pair of silver cocos
2 loads of little silver pitchers or jars (*cantarillos* or *ollas*) and small silver
  plate(let)s (*chapas*)
silver and gold cups (*veveras* or *vasos*)
beads (*chaquira*) of bone and other materials (*de otras maneras*)
medallions and necklaces (*patenas*) and silver and gold crowns (*diademas*)
gold bars, wedges, or plates (*tejuelos*), one of which weighed as much as 550
  pesos (1,028 patacones 2 reales)
silver bars
turquoise
1 silver trumpet
1 silver spoon or ladle (*cuchara o mecedera*) for *chicha* (maize beer) (a *pac
  cha?—a mecedero de chicha de indios*)
silver pitchers (*cantaros* or *vasijas*)
1 copper idol (*pachacama*)
pearls[a]

SOURCE: AGI/J 404, 4, 26–28, 98–98v, 103, 104v, 107, 112, 113v, 129, 131, 133v, 151v, 153v,
160, 166v, 170, 186, 192, 227v, 229v, 232, 294, 309v–10v, 334v, 362, 365, 373–73v, 382, 386, 388,
390–92, 396v, 399, 404v, 427v, 446v, 451v, 453–54v, 552, 570, 598, 653, 831v.
[a]Evidence of exchange with the coast of present-day Ecuador. On the contents of a Cañari
tomb, see Salomon, "Ancestors," pp. 219–22.

each, 82,720 patacones 4.7 reales). Fray Reginaldo de Lizárraga describes the sacking of a "huaca" in Trujillo (which probably was not
Yomayoguan) from which the looters netted 170,000 pesos (assuming 450 maravedís each, 281,250 patacones) after paying the royal
fifth.[23] Feyjoo de Sousa cites royal accounts of a 1566 find by García
Gutierrez de Toledo—son of don Alonso Gutierrez Nieto, a prominent Trujillano—who delivered to the Spanish crown the sum of
56,527 castellanos of gold (93,518 patacones) from a "huaca" one
league from the city, next to the road that goes to the town of Guanchaco. Twenty-six years later, García Gutierrez de Toledo delivered
another 27,020 castellanos of gold (44,702 patacones) in the form of
fish and animal figures found in the same structure. Writing 200
years later, Feyjoo de Sousa adds, "According to tradition around
these parts . . . it [the treasure or take] was much greater [*excesiva-
mente mayor*] than that declared for tax purposes."[24]

TABLE 21

*Official Description and Value of the Treasure
from the Huaca Yomayoguan (1558–59)*

Date[a]	Description[b]	"In good money"[c]
Silver (in maravedís)		
31-XII-1558	10 bars, 2 tejuelos	1,094,577
	4 bars	472,516
12-I-1559	50 bars	3,629,027
17-I-1559	60 bars	3,177,317
18-I-1559	36 entries	2,466,569
21-I-1559	52 bars	3,371,411
23-I-1559	52 bars	2,777,236
24-I-1559	50 bars	3,021,308
26-I-1559	50 bars	2,789,788
27-I-1559	50 bars	3,072,017
28-I-1559	6 bars	202,512
24-III-1559	80 bars	4,994,553
1-IV-1559	3 bars	123,100
8-XI-1559	1 bar	27,520
5-III-1559	2 bars	36,695
SUBTOTAL		31,256,146
21-I-1559	3 bars[d]	300,155
	1 bar	58,315
	1 bar	11,581
4-II-1559	1.5 marco	3,375
	5 bars	320,925
	6 marcos, 3 ounces	11,794
22-II-1559	4 bars	192,825
	2 tejuelos	63,175
n.d.	2 bars	215,730
22-II-1559	1 bar	13,600
25-II-1559	5 bars, 2 tejuelos	342,185
28-II-1559	8 bars	584,160
	1 bar	93,488
n.d.	1 bar	37,463
6-III-1559	6 bars	532,940
6-III-1559	1 tejuelo	47,230
	1 bar	51,480
n.d.	1 bar	13,650
8-III-1559	3 bars	281,240
	21 marcos	44,520
	16 marcos	24,800
20-III-1559	2 bars	126,555
1-IV-1559	1 bar	40,500
	4 bars	284,000
	6 bars	385,505
	3 bars	168,230
	1 tejuelo	44,800
	6 bars	215,250
n.d.	3 marcos, 2 ounces	7,312
1-IV-1559	13.5 marcos	30,370
11-IV-1559	1 cantarrillo	4,780
	25 marcos	12,500
	5 bars	338,509

TABLE 21 (*continued*)

Date[a]	Description[b]	"In good money"[c]
	1 bar	80,940
	1 bar	46,725
	1 tejuelo	28,860
7-VII-1559	2 bars	88,980
9-VIII-1559	5 bars	205,755
	1 bar	35,460
18-VIII-1559	3 bars	70,670
25-VIII-1559	15 marcos	29,100
7-IX-1559	17 marcos	38,040
5-X-1559	3 marcos	6,750
9-X-1559	2 bars, 1 tejuelo	159,800
10-X-1559	13 marcos	29,040
	8 marcos	9,040
	1 bar	38,507
17-X-1559	8 bars	351,140
	4 bars	248,170
	2 bars	189,781
	1 bar	56,718
	3 bars	182,250
	1 bar	26,771
21-X-1559	17 marcos	36,550
	3 bars	167,250
8-XI-1559	1 bar	77,700
	8 marcos	14,980
	1 bar	12,000
15-XI-1559	2 bars	39,210
n.d.	various entries[d, e]	746,476
	1 bar	37,400
	2 bars	93,770
	37 marcos	73,250
	6 marcos, 5 ounces	14,906
	4.5 marcos	10,125
	6 marcos	13,500
	25 marcos	56,250
	1 bar	73,530
	1 bar	55,020
	1 bar	28,000
	1 bar	41,550
	2 bars	109,340
	1 bar, 1 tejuelo	82,265
	2 small bars	21,890
	2 pieces	40,250
	1 bar	55,120
	1 tejuelo	25,500
	1 bar	73,720
SUBTOTAL		8,078,515
TOTAL SILVER		39,334,661
		(or 77,354 gold pesos of 508.5 maravedís each, or 144,612 patacones 6 reales)

TABLE 21 (*continued*)

Date[a]	Description[b]	"In good money"[c]
Gold (in pesos)		
7-I-1559	28 bars	9,115p 6gr[g]
27-I-1559	1 bar	493p4t7gr
28-I-1559	8 bars	643p6t7gr
	1 tejuelo[d, f]	24p6t6gr
	1 tejuelo	140p2t
	2 tejuelos	238p7t
	1 tejuelo	113p6t2gr
	1 tejuelo	25p4t4gr
	1 tejuelo	235p2t8gr
	1 tejuelo	242p6t
	1 bar	240p3t7gr
	1 tejuelo	179p6t
	1 bar, 1 tejuelo	202p6t4gr
	2 cocos	11p3t
	2 cocos	39p6t2gr
	80 pesos de oro bajo	17p6t3gr
	701 pesos de oro bajo	225p7t6gr
	1 tejuelo	80p
	55 pesos de oro bajo	19p3t6gr
	1 tejuelo	253p
	1 bacinja, 2 vasos	102p3t7gr
	1 bar	205p4t5gr
	1 tejuelo	95p2t7gr
	18 pesos	14p3t3gr
	1 tejuelo	59p3t2gr
	657 pesos	151p2t
	1 tejuelo	40p2t8gr
TOTAL GOLD		13,212p6t4gr
		(or 264.26 gold marks, or 21,859 patacones 3 reales)

SOURCE: AGI/J 404, 524–532.

NOTE: Dates are in the form 25 (day)-II (month)-1559 (year). One must keep in mind that these values do not include the value of the pearls and jewels that were found but not assayed, or the value of clay pottery, cloth, copper implements, and beads, which were of less interest to the Spanish. That these items could be quite valuable is evident from the reports of the items taken from the "*guaca grande del rio*" (the huaca del Sol at the site of Moche on the south bank of the Moche River?) outside of Trujillo. Two emeralds of six that were found there were worth a thousand pesos (1,654 patacones 3 reales) in 1564 (ART/LC, 1564). Also note that "value" here refers to gross silver and gold delivered to the assayer for tax purposes.

[a] The date the metal was registered at the assayer's office.

[b] Each line represents a separate registration (*partida*).

[c] The manuscript did not specify the value of the pesos listed. I assumed that they used pesos ensayados of 508.5 maravedís each. Only the totals are converted.

[d] The person did not specifically declare from which "huaca" the metal was from. (The fact that the registrations were copied into the court case suggests that they were from Yomayoguan and were accepted as such.)

[e] These various entries add up to 905,386 maravedís, not 746,476 as noted in the manuscript.

[f] This and the following entries add up to 1,961.7917 pesos, not the 3,126 pesos 3 tomines noted in the manuscript.

[g] The units for assayed gold (pesos, tomines, granos) are here abbreviated p, t, and gr respectively.

Taxes were also evaded by the exploiters of Zarco's find. Various witnesses and principals charged that as much as 50 percent of the precious metals from Yomayoguan were hidden from the authorities. Zarco claimed that gold and silver were melted down in private homes and used to bribe witnesses, the scribe, and the judge.[25] Documents bound with the court case corroborate these charges. As Table 21 makes clear, the official accounts were divided into two categories: treasure specifically from Yomayoguan and treasure from unnamed "huacas." The local authorities, in copying the entries and submitting them as evidence in the dispute, presumed that all of the treasure was from Yomayoguan even though those who registered it could not or would not specify its provenance beyond stating that it was from an indigenous structure.

My analysis of the royal accounts shows that many of those who brought in treasure from unspecified "huacas" testified for Escobar and his partners. These individuals and others proved to be relatives or known friends and confidants of members of Escobar's partnership. Francisco de Villalobos, the brother of Escobar's partner Miguel de Villalobos, for example, registered 41,550 maravedís, or about 19 silver marks (or 152 patacones 6 reales), and 243 pesos 5 tomines 9 granos of buen oro (455 patacones 5 reales). Luis Sanches, whom Zarco identified as an intimate friend of Escobar's partners Villalobos and Castellanos, brought the assayer 205 pesos 4 tomines 5 granos of gold (384 patacones 2 reales) and over 350,000 maravedís, or 160.7 silver marks (1,286 patacones 6 reales). Zarco further charged that Alonso de Vargas, another intimate of Villalobos and Castellanos and inspector of the site, received six or seven loads of silver and gold, ostensibly in exchange for horseshoes and nails. The official record shows that Vargas registered 44,520 maravedís (20.4 silver marks, or 163 patacones 5 reales). Baltazar de Camora, a tailor by trade who owned a store with Pedro Gonzalez (the local representative of the crown treasury and lieutenant corregidor who heard part of Zarco's case), and Francisco de Rojas, the prelate (*comendador*) and sacristan of the main church, also had close ties to or testified in favor of Escobar's company and had delivered various amounts of treasure to be assayed. Such entries and the identities of the registrants provide circumstantial evidence supporting Zarco's and others' allegations of bribery.[26]

Bribery and unofficial leakage of treasure into the local economy were also charged by two yanaconas who complained to local authorities in a separate case that Escobar and his partner Baltazar Castellanos had promised them land and in addition had promised one of them a mare if they would agree to testify that Zarco was not the first Spaniard to dig at Yomayoguan. Such allegations of bribery were evidently true; trial proceedings state that Escobar later donated to each yanacona a house site in Trujillo. In addition, Pedro de Sigura, a merchant resident of Trujillo, actually admitted being bribed by Escobar and his partners and lying under oath the first time he was questioned. In addition, Zarco and his lawyer asserted that members of the claim-jumping company themselves used undeclared treasure to bribe other parties. Another native witness admitted that one of Escobar's partners offered him a *tómin* (less than 2 reales) after he testified but later claimed it was his daily wage. Besides bribery, Escobar and company threatened some witnesses with death by quartering.[27]

Failing to declare treasure and cheating the crown were not the only irregularities. Zarco's long court case strongly suggested that he had been framed to cheat him out of his find. Don Antonio, the leader and spokesman for the Chimu, dropped his suit against Francisco Escobar and Pedro Núñez de Arraya, who had joined in partnership to exploit the site. He did so, Zarco and his lawyer alleged, after Zarco and Núñez de Arraya paid Rodrigo Calvillo, an interpreter who lived in Escobar's house and slept with his maid, 500 pesos (934 patacones 6 reales) to persuade (or bribe) don Antonio to become a partner. Don Antonio agreed, in return for the promise to be given half the treasure, suggesting that the Spanish recognized indigenous rights to the site; Escobar and Núñez shared the other half. The Spanish half was eventually divided equally among Escobar, Bachiller Pedro Ortiz (as executor of the estate of the recently deceased Pedro Núñez de Arraya and mayor [*alcalde mayor*] of the city), Pedro de Prado, Baltazar Castellanos, Miguel de Villalobos, and the corregidor Licenciado Pineda—each of whom received a twelfth of the total take. The agreement dividing up the Spanish half, dated July 4, 1559, contains some damning language. The Spanish partners included the corregidor "because from today on you offer to solicit and favor our interests in the 'huaca' [quotes added] in the suit with Alonso Zarco and for other acts beneficial to us." The suggestion of illegalities—including graft, collusion, and favoritism—at the expense of justice is unmistakable.[28]

Less than a week later, don Antonio agreed to divide his portion into six equal parts (of one-twelfth of the whole), giving one each to corregidor Pineda and Pedro de Hojeda, the inspector and constable assigned to guard the "huaca,"[29] and keeping four parts for himself and his subjects. The next day, don Antonio signed another agreement giving Pineda another sixth of his share.[30] In return, the corregidor had to contribute to the costs (of excavating?) and to provide don Antonio with a lawyer (*letrado*) in Los Reyes if Zarco appealed the case to the supreme court.[31]

These partnership agreements show that Zarco faced the entire gamut of local society from the corregidor (the highest local royal authority) to the appointed inspector (who recorded the crown's share at the site) to the *alguacil* (the constable who arrested him and who distributed mita labor), as well as Br. Pedro Ortiz (a landowner and councilman), Baltazar Castellanos (a notary), and don Antonio and indigenous society—and all their friends, acquaintances, sympathizers, and partisans. With so powerful a coalition against him, Zarco fought a losing battle to secure justice.[32]

Zarco's case continued to be stymied by the network of his adversaries' personal ties all the way up to the high court in Los Reyes. When Zarco asked for a certification of his protest against the partnership, Antonio de Paz, the notary and a clear Escobar partisan, refused to give him one. The interpreter Rodrigo Calvillo, already identified as an Escobar partisan, did not translate faithfully. Finally, Zarco found out that the corregidor Licenciado Pineda's daughter had married a supreme court judge, Licenciado Sayavedra. In the end, Zarco and his lawyer thought their only hope for justice was to appeal to the Council of the Indies in Spain, where finally he was at least partially vindicated.[33]

At this level, the case seems one of a naive, impoverished prospector versus unscrupulous claim jumpers who were helped by greedy officials and others anxious to get a share of the loot. As mentioned above, the corregidor, lieutenant corregidor, notary, constable, and inspectors opposed Zarco, and the Chimu Indians resisted from the start. The authorities tried to discourage him by arresting and exiling him to get him out of the way. Their massive coverup was so transparent that at several points, in an attempt to keep the case local, Escobar and Castellanos offered to buy him out for 3,150 (5,888 patacones 7 reales) and 20,000 to 40,000 pesos (37,389 patacones 6 reales to 74,779 patacones 3 reales), respectively. Zarco tenaciously fought the odds for what he rightfully thought was his just due.[34]

Of Tombs and Temples: The Native Side of the Story

Almost lost in the manuscript of Zarco's case is a second, slightly different, version of the tale, one from the natives' point of view. It captures the Chimu at a time when they were only partially acculturated and were struggling to contend with competing value systems. It shows how the Spaniards virtually disregarded indigenous culture: the Chimu tried to explain themselves to the Spaniards, but their words went unheeded. The local Spanish were blinded by their quest for gold, their cultural myopia, and self-interest.

In 1558, 26 years after the conquest, the original inhabitants of the north coast (even those who lived in constant close contact with the Spanish in the Chimu Valley, where the Spanish provincial capital was located) could not be said to have been hispanicized. Few native officials—not even don Antonio, much less the commoners—knew enough Spanish to testify without an interpreter. Even if a particular Spanish word could be translated, natives could not always understand the concept. One Spaniard said, for instance, that "under oath they do not tell the truth because they do not understand what [the word] 'oath' means."[35] Native peoples who had adopted some aspects of Spanish material culture were rare and still provoked comment. Two natives, Diego de Paz and Hernando de Segovia, had adopted Spanish names and dress. They were described as very acculturated and understanding (*muy ladino y entendido*), but in the long procession of witnesses, they were the exception, not the rule.[36]

Furthermore, a significant number of the native witnesses had not yet accepted Christianity. They still had indigenous names and swore by their own "law" instead of on the cross when they were on the witness stand. Don Antonio himself admitted that his conversion to Catholicism was fairly new: "Only recently have I come to understand the teachings of our Holy Catholic faith and have I and the rest of the local inhabitants of this realm lost the dread and fear we used to have of the devil."[37] It is evident that don Antonio had incorporated into his belief system European ideas of devil worship and paganism. But his conversion and baptism were probably motivated more by political expediency than true devotion.[38] For most natives, conversion may have been equated with baptism, adopting a Christian name, and contributing to the maintenance of the church. For most, their conversion was no more than a shallow acknowledgment of another new god or power.[39]

Certainly, the reaction to the excavation at Yomayoguan suggests that the Chimu had not given up their pre-Columbian veneration of certain objects, structures, and places. According to Escobar (not an impartial observer),

> when the Indians of this city and its hinterland knew and saw us in possession of the said guaca they all mobilized crying and scandalized and

they rioted and shouted and made a great fuss which led us to understand, if one can say that, that they placed all their faith and hope in the idols, in the devil, in the conjurings and superstitions of that place . . . and they worshiped, honored, and adored the devil and so they say that after that place is discovered all the Indians will die, which is demonstrated more clearly to be as they say by the movement weeping and tumult that they universally made and even now [are making], after they found out that the Spanish were dismantling the said guaca and shrine; if what the said don Antonio meant to say [that the structure was the tomb of his ancestors] was true, which I deny, only he and those with him would protest and not all universally."[40]

Here Escobar is projecting the Spanish—and his own—individualistic perspective on the scene. He assumes that only an individual and his family would be upset if an ancestral tomb was disturbed. What Escobar does not understand is the significance of such a burial complex as a symbol of the origins, history, survival, and prosperity for all of don Antonio's followers. He fails to realize that the members of this community did not think in terms of nuclear or even extended families, as defined by Europeans; they believed that the living and the dead were all related and interdependent.[41]

Other witnesses described the natives' wailing and lamenting in much the same way. Some 50 years later, Guamán Poma de Ayala depicted a typical scene for a burial (*entierro*) among the peoples of the northern regions of the former Inca empire (Chinchaysuyo) (see Fig. 4). Note the weeping as the deceased is carried to the burial structure. A smug Escobar added that to dismantle (*sacar*) the huaca "is to uproot the great idolatrous and erroneous beliefs of these peoples and is of great help in their conversion to our Holy Catholic faith." In a sense, he portrayed huaca looting as an extirpating, quasi-religious, or devotional act.[42]

Spanish attribution of erroneous beliefs and superstitions to devil worship was a common way of distinguishing between "them" and "us." It reflected a European cosmic vision and belief system going back to the Middle Ages. In America in general, and on the north coast of Peru in particular, the Spanish used such language in petitions to royal authorities as a way of reminding officials to discriminate and of predisposing them toward favoring the European, civilized, Christian side of the story.[43]

The natives were not only devil worshipers, but in the eyes of the local Spanish they were also drunkards and liars (*borrachos*, *chicheros*, and *mentirosos*). Castas also perpetuated negative stereotypes of natives' character and behavior. According to Domingo de León, a mulatto *sillero* (chair maker or saddler) in his twenties,

Fig. 4 Guamán Poma de Ayala's drawing of a burial procession in northern Peru

"[The Indians] are customarily drunk, and they are liars because it is customary for all Indians to lie." Zarco and the partnership's lawyers used such statements, born of misunderstanding, mistrust, and fear, in an attempt to discredit native witnesses. This was a convenient way of denigrating Indians, undermining their credibility, and ultimately dismissing what they said.[44]

Despite the language problem, the great cultural gulf separating Europeans and natives, and the undeniable prejudice of the Spanish statements, the Chimu succeeded in establishing useful precedents in their ultimately unsuccessful efforts to save Yomayoguan. Their story is one of resistance.[45] In their legal defense, their version of the events starts with the assertion that they dug at Yomayoguan first— a claim the Spanish ignored but never denied. Curacas knew of the function and significance of many of the indigenous structures within their domains. Both don Antonio and don Juan of Collique knew where "treasure" was buried (see Chapter 2). Don Juan, in fact, offered to reveal the location of just such a site to Cuenca to save himself from being lynched in 1566. Don Antonio knew the location of the "treasure," and after watching Zarco prospect around the environs of Yomayoguan, he and his subjects resorted to violence and then decided to preempt Spanish efforts by digging at the site themselves,[46] perhaps disclosing in the process the exact location of the metal objects and other precious goods that had originally been left as offerings. Don Antonio even made a trip to Los Reyes to ask the viceroy for a license.[47]

The Spanish did not even consider these efforts. Zarco and Escobar lined up one witness after another to prove who between them had first dug at Yomayoguan, entirely dismissing the natives' effort. By Spanish law, the first person (meaning Spaniard) to excavate a site had the right to any treasure found there after paying the crown its share:

> After the Spanish came to this realm it has been and is the usual custom [*es uso y costumbre*] that the Spanish, with license of the Justice [and] with an inspector [*veedor*] present and appointed by royal officials, have, quietly, pacifically, and publicly and without contradiction, excavated and excavate many guacas and enjoyed and enjoy what they find except what belongs to His Majesty, and this has been and is customary, as it has been and is for more than 20 and 30 years [since 1529–39]."[48]

To further justify their rationale for possessing the "huaca" and disavowing native claims, Escobar said:

> What is in the said guaca are things that were there offered to the devil at various ancient times by various persons and what each person offered

there, after offering it, he assumed it a relic and he no longer was master of the offering and his will was to offer it and give it and make the devil the master of it and so like other relics belong to anyone who later finds and possesses them and so we possessed the said guaca legitimately, so we clearly are masters of it.

The Spanish imposed their will without much concern for the previous native traditions.[49]

In his claim, Don Antonio argued that, as heir to the jurisdiction and domain (as discussed in Chapter 3) of previous indigenous rulers,[50] by native tradition he "owned" the "huaca," and that by Spanish law he was also entitled to the treasure as the first person to have dug there. He implied that the tomb, or "house" (as he and other Chimu consistently referred to Yomayoguan), was a product of the natives' collective effort—that is, it was man-made and not naturally available or wild.[51] As such it could be claimed and possessed as private property in the Spanish sense. Later, on the same basis, the natives of Lambayeque stated that lords "owned" the "huacas" and lived on them. That don Antonio was willing to sue in court to uphold his beliefs and rights perhaps motivated the ensuing compromise and his partnership with the Spanish, signaling the Spaniards' implicit acceptance of his defense and its underlying principles.[52]

Nowhere in the transcribed testimony does don Antonio explicitly specify his motive for joining the partnership. At one point, he did state that his share of the items taken from Yomayoguan was to be used to alleviate his subjects' tribute-paying burden, so that they "might not be so bothered by paying [tribute]." Thus, we can conclude that this legacy was his motivation to join in partnership with the Spanish. Note that this conclusion is consistent with the Andean value of redistribution, which remained crucial to the continued legitimacy of don Antonio's leadership and is completely the opposite of the greed and individualism exhibited by the Spanish.[53] After don Antonio's death, his principales claimed over 24,000 pesos plata ensayada (39,705 patacones 7 reales) of his share. They used over 18,000 (29,779 patacones 3.3 reales) to invest in mortgages, the income from which was to be used to pay tribute to don Diego de Mora, their encomendero. (Feyjoo de Sousa reported a similar transfer two centuries later when 25,000 pesos ensayados of 13.5 reales each [which were equivalent to 42,187 patacones 4 reales] were invested in haciendas to provide a steady stream of income to pay the natives' tribute.)

Don Antonio also lent some of the money. Alonso de Avila recognized a debt of 400 to 500 pesos (plata corriente of 9 reales each or

450 to 562.5 patacones) in his will dated between October 6 and October 14, 1573. The money he owed don Antonio and his subjects and heirs was from their share of the treasure of the "huaca" Yomayoguan.[54]

Don Antonio furthermore claimed that there was a distinction between temples and tombs. The Chimu repeatedly insisted that Yomayoguan was not a "huaca." They argued that it was a house or tomb (*sepultura, enterramiento*) where don Antonio's father, grandparents, and other ancestors were buried. Yomayoguan "is not a guaca, it is instead a tomb of our grandfathers and ancestors."[55]

Nevertheless, the Spanish continued to call Yomayoguan a "huaca," referring to it as a temple or shrine, not a tomb.[56] For example, Escobar and his party described Yomayoguan as a

> shrine and guaca where anciently they worshiped, made offerings to, honored and adored him [the devil?] with their conjurings and ceremonies . . . and so the guaca and shrine appears, because although it is an ancient place there appears on the surface many bones of children, llamas and alpacas and wool and other evidences of sacrifice.[57]

To back up their claim, Escobar and Núñez de Arraya presented the corregidor with cloth and little woolen figures (*figurelas*) stained with blood, "which I [Escobar] exhibit before Your Honor to prove that these things were offered to the devil and the blood is a sacrifice that the Indians made to him and that shows that that place is a guaca and temple and not a tomb or burial."[58]

Testimony in the case is consistently divided on whether Yomayoguan was a temple or a tomb. At one juncture, the corregidor agreed that the "huaca" was a tomb, but after hearing the Spanish colonists, he hedged, admitting that he was unsure what the structure really was. He referred to it as a "guaca or tomb or whatever else it might be; . . . guaca or tomb or temple." His vacillation and the viceroy's reaction to don Antonio's appeal for a license indicate the Spanish authorities' equivocal acceptance of the native definition.[59]

The 'Huaca' That May Not Have Been a Huaca

The Chimu distinction between temples—huacas—and tombs is intriguing because it is seldom specifically made elsewhere in the chronicle literature. As we have seen, most Spanish contemporaries used *huaca* to refer to anything the natives considered sacred. Padre Anello Oliva defines *huacas* even more broadly as "impressive and notable things," including unusual objects, gods, spirits, or idols representing gods or natural forces. He adds that natives worshiped the "huacas" and also the places the huacas have been. Similarly, Cobo consistently defines *huaca* as "god" or "idol" or "sacred place" (such as a temple, burial place, or "whatever other revered place, where they offered sacrifices").[60] Miguel Cabello de Valboa, Betanzos, and Santillán also use or interpret the word loosely. In an anonymous account dated 1571, the word was used to refer to both temples and tombs.[61]

Many accounts use the term inconsistently. Thus, Padre Joseph de Acosta at one point specifically defines *huaca* as *adoratorio*, a temple or shrine. Yet he also uses the term to refer to the natural world (the sun, the moon, a spring, a tree, a river), man-made representations of natural forces or gods, extraordinary objects, and mummies—in short, anything the natives worshiped or respected as divine or sacred. Likewise, the Agustinos, describing primarily their experience in Huamachuco, define *huacas* as "shrines [oratorios] where [the natives'] idols and many shamans [hechiceros] are." In practice, they used it to refer to individual idols too.[62]

Other authors use the term more specifically, recognizing different types of huacas. An anonymous and undated account uses *huaca* to refer to both the devotional objects and the places where they were worshiped. Huacas could be natural things that had some peculiarity of note, such as mountain peaks (*cumbreras, apachitas*), forests (*montes, ocros*), springs (*fuentes, pucyu*), or caves (*huacas*), or they could be man-made, such as burial mounds (*huacas*). (For the anonymous author listing these usages, the term *huaca* translates several different concepts and names different things.)[63]

Likewise, the most comprehensive study of indigenous religious survivals, written by Padre Pablo José de Arriaga with the aim of uprooting what to his eyes were "pagan" practices, broke the broad category of *huaca* into various types. One type includes permanent, fixed huacas (such as the sun, the sea, the land, springs, rivers, hills, and snow-capped mountains); another type includes mobile huacas such as *conopas* (small stone or clay figures used for agricultural fertility rites), *mamazares* (mother corn, also known as *zara mama*), *compas, huancas* (stones), and mummies (called *malquis* in the highlands or *marcoyoc* and *munaos* on the coast).[64] He goes on to say that natives also worshiped the places where the huacas were. He mentions too that the Quechua word for ancient burials (of grandparents and ancestors) is *machay*, though he does not say whether such a tomb was a huaca. If, as he says, the places where natives worshiped were sacred, then tombs would fit the broad definition of huaca.[65]

In few contemporary works is the word defined and then used consistently. In the Segundo Concilio Provincial (1567–68), *huaca* refers to temple, or adoratorio. Polo de Ondegardo uses *huaca* to refer to gods or their idols. He does not use the term to refer to adoratorios. Cristóbal de Molina, in his "Relación de las fabulas y ritos de los Incas (1574)," refers to huacas, when used alone, as idols. In saying "huacas y adoratorios," he is thus referring to idols and the places or structures where they were adored. Likewise, Guamán Poma de Ayala talks of "guacas ydolos" when he traces the beginning of native religious beliefs and practices. He says that during the reign of the emperor Pachacuti Ynga Yupanqui, temples were built for gods, idols, and huacas; after discussing the Inca, Guamán Poma de Ayala usually makes a distinction between temples and huacas, with one exception. In these cases, he uses *huaca* to refer to idols and the places they were worshiped, not to tombs.[66]

That the natives originally made a distinction between temple and tomb is independently confirmed by Juan de Matienzo in his reliable (though not unbiased) and well-known compendium on early colonial law, *Gobierno del Perú*. In chapter 39, he clearly differentiates between tombs, which he says should properly be called *chulpa* or *aya*, and oracles or shrines, which technically are known as *huaca* or *vilca*.[67] He describes the indigenous burial practices and the distinction as follows:

> So, the Indians of this realm were accustomed to bury, with the bodies of the caciques and great lords, gold and silver drinking vessels, and much other silver and gold, and precious stones, and valuable clothes, and they even buried alive the women they loved the most, and their servants, because they thought that they would revive and those who were buried with the dead would serve them with the gourds and vessels that they put there . . . and these burials they called in Quechua *chulpa* or *aya*, although the populace commonly called them *huaca*.[68]

On the north coast (*los Llanos*), he continues,

> especially in the city of Truxillo, they have found many tombs such as these, as high as a great mountain or hill, all made by hand, and inside are constructed genteel vaulted apartments, and there are seated the dead corpses, and their servants buried with them, and much gold and silver. . . . Those [structures] that are the true huacas, and also known as *vilca*[s], are oracles and shrines.[69]

Cieza de León, an even earlier and usually credible eyewitness, uses *huaca* in the first part of his chronicle specifically to refer to burials in the coastal province of Chinchan (Chan Chan or Chincha?) and the north coast valley of Pacasmayo. In one place in the first part of his chronicle and consistently in the second and later parts, however, Cieza de León uses *huaca* solely to refer to temples. Does this indicate a change of meaning over time or just confusion and misunderstanding on his part? [70]

Local primary sources suggest a more consistent usage. In a court case before local Trujillo officials in 1563, a site is described as "the burial of *moyco*" (*el entierro de moyco*) and later identified as a "guaca burial hiding place." [71] Don Antonio describes Yomayoguan as "a burial or tomb inside the houses of my dead grandfather where in olden times my said grandfather and my father had buried and buried the gold and silver and jewels and clothes that they possessed and they themselves were buried there." More exactly Yomayoguan was described as "guacas hiding places or tombs where anciently the Indians of this realm often hid treasures and other things" or "guacas tombs or ancient hiding places." In the seventeenth century, licenses to excavate often described sites inexactly as "guaca tomb hiding place of silver, gold, gems or whatever," "a tomb hiding place or mine of treasure of gold, silver or other type of metal," "burial guaca of hidden silver and gold," or "burial or guaca tomb and hiding place." [72]

As these various citations suggest, there was no standard agreement on the meaning of the term among the Spanish, although in the long term usage became generic. The use of the term by Matienzo, Cieza de León, and local officials is consistent with what Francisco A. Loayza, annotating Molina's account, stated about changes in the meaning of the term. Under the Incas, Loayza states, basing himself on the Franciscan *Vocabulario políglota Incaico*, *huaca* originally meant burial: *sepulcro* or *tumba*. As the years passed, popular Spanish usage broadened its meaning to anything sacred or divine. Loayza notes:

> In the Inca Empire, the cult of the ancestors was so powerful that the dead were given sacred and divine attributes, as also everything that was related to them. Thus, for the ancient Peruvians, if their dead were sacred, so were their tombs, their *huacas*. And by a philological process of generalization, over time, the word *waka* was applied to all that was considered worthy of veneration, that is, to everything that was considered sacred and divine. Thus, indeed, *waka* was any shrine, any idol; *waka* was the ancestor's mummy and even offerings to it; and finally *waka* was all the material representation of the exuberant Inca mythology. [73]

Loayza's footnote is seconded by Cobo, a rather late writer who hints in one passage how burial places may in time have come to be regarded as temples:

From the veneration that they make to these corpses was born another prejudice and type of worship, that was to consider as shrines the tombs and some places where the lords, when they were alive, used to sit and visit frequently; and for that reason such shrines became a great number, in all of which, besides adoring them [the lords], they routinely made [them] offerings.[74]

What all these references make clear is that the Spanish imputed much meaning to the word *guaca* (or *huaca*) based on their own cultural beliefs. They also used the word generically to refer to all manner of indigenous devotional objects and places, despite what may have been an original indigenous distinction between temples and shrines and other sacred precincts, such as tombs. Thus, very quickly original meanings of *huaca* (as well as *chacra*, as described in Chapter 3) were lost or confused by the Spaniards (and eventually by the natives as well). A notary, referring to a mound ("huaca") on the corner of the plaza of the town of Saña next to the Camino Real two years after the official founding of the Spanish settlement, defined the term as an "altar" (literally, "offering place [*ofresedero*] of the Indians"). During the term of Viceroy Principe de Esquilache (1615–21), the Spanish recognized the following as huacas both on the coast and in the highlands: *idolos dios penates, adoratorios, idolos guancas, idolos compas, cuerpos gentiles, madres del maiz,* and *cuerpos hurtados de la iglesia* (literally, "corpses stolen from the church," mummies?). In a register of huaca licenses from Cuzco for the years 1612 to 1614, the wording of four entries mentioned "huaca" alone; two entries regard "huaca and tomb" as a single entity (i.e., huaca and tomb refer to the same structure); and only one makes a distinction between huaca and tomb (i.e., "one guaca and one tomb"). The officials charged with eradicating idolatry in Concepción de Chupas in 1614 also used *huaca* generically as an idol representing gods or as something sacred. The same was true in Carampoma during colonial times. In 1763, Feyjoo de Sousa wrote of buried treasures: "These regularly have been found in some indigenous shrines and tombs of Indian lords, that in Quechua are called Huacas." Church authorities still used the term generically in 1782.[75]

That the Spanish were ignorant of the nuances of indigenous words drew the contempt of the mestizo and bilingual chronicler Garcilaso de la Vega, who commented that the Spanish misinterpreted and corrupted the language. Using the term *huaca* as an example, he wrote that the Spanish were confused about the religious beliefs of the Indians because they did not know the exact meaning of the language to know how to ask for and receive the account from the Indians; from whose ignorance has been born the belief that the Incas had many gods, or as many as they took from the Indians. . . . Particularly, this falsehood was born because the Spanish did not know the many and diverse meanings of the term Huaca; which pronounced with the last syllable high on the palate means idol, like Jupiter, Mars or Venus. . . . Besides this first and most important meaning, it has many others. . . . It means sacred object, like where all those through which the devil spoke to them: that is, the idols, the rocks [peñas], the large stones and trees. . . . Likewise, they call *huaca* to the objects they had offered to the sun, like figures of humans, birds and animals . . . and whatever other offerings.[76]

Garcilaso de la Vega noted too that the term *huaca* was used to refer to a temple, burial (*sepulcro*), or anything unusual or extraordinary, whether beautiful, ugly, or defective (e.g., twins or breech-born or malformed babies). He continued:

All these and similar things [the natives] call huaca, not because they consider them gods, nor because they adore them, but because of the particular good [*ventaja*] that they brought to the communities: for this reason they looked upon them and treated them with veneration and respect.

He commented (wrongly, as my previous discussion shows) that the Spanish believed that *huaca* referred only to an idol, and therefore they assumed all things called huacas were gods, which he asserts was untrue. The Spanish thought the word *apacita*, for instance, applied to the peaks of very high hills (*cuestas*). The correct interpretation of the word, he declared, was to give thanks and offerings to the power that gave individuals the strength to climb such heights. Thus, the original meaning of *huaca* appears to have been lost once the Spanish began using the word to cover a whole Spanish category of objects. As with their misapplication of the Caribbean term *cacique* to all headmen of a certain rank and the term *principal* to an entire administrative hierarchy, the misuse of *huaca* obscured the indigenous view of society and the world.[77]

Given the confusion, one might ask if there was an architectural difference between a tomb and a temple. One word the Chimu used to describe Yomayoguan was "house," as mentioned above. Don Antonio said that within the houses ("*cassas*") "of my dead grandfather there is a burial and a tomb." This description may be the closest Spanish translation for the Yunga word and concept to which he referred.[78] Burying a north coast native in his house is a tradition that goes back to the legendary times of Naymlap, the mythical founder of a Lambayecan dynasty. When Naymlap felt it was time to die, he went to his house and died there.[79]

A few chroniclers too use "house" to describe huacas. The Agustinos use the phrase "sumptuous house" as a synonym for "devil-infested [*endemoniada*] guaca." Acosta says that major huacas were "house[s] of worship [*adoracion*]." Cobo mentions that mummies had "their own houses, according to their rank." Santillán recognized that each idol had a "house." He describes the burial place of the kings and great lords as houses, with a receiving room (*sala*), hall (*cámara*), bedroom (*recámara*), kitchen, patio, and storage chambers. The sealed chamber became the tomb of the mummy. In an antechamber his survivors left his treasures, dishes, clothes, and food. Volunteers committed suicide and were placed in the antechamber, if men, and in the treasure cove, if women. Other rooms were kept open so that the living could enter and pray to the gods for the dead.[80] Sometime later, after wars and floods, the tombs were completely sealed and buried, "making sepulchral monuments [*túmulos*] and mounds [*terraplenes*] like hills over them."[81]

Aside from this general description, Santillán provides precious little information on characteristics of the structure that might provide a practical, empirical way to identify Yomayoguan as a temple or a tomb. Although most witnesses had worked at Yomayoguan, few described it in detail. They said that the looters dug through two to three estados of adobes and dirt in "the building of the guaca" in the "first of the chambers," noting that there were several chambers in the edifice, probably of various sizes. They mentioned that Yomayoguan lay within high adobe walls and next to another "huaca" that itself was among others. And there were surface indications—described as *rastros* (vestiges), *insignias*,[82] or *buenas muestras* (good material evidence)—that something of import was buried there. This physical description suggests that Yomayoguan was a burial platform that was itself part of a compound, or *ciudadela*, and that it was one of many; but this description is not detailed enough to serve as a diagnostic test for distinguishing between structures.[83]

Neither do the physical description and inventory of the treasure and other articles quarried from the site help evaluate Yomayoguan as a temple or tomb. Besides the gold and silver (detailed in Tables 20 and 21), precious stones, beads, and bones were found. The Spanish, arguing that Yomayoguan was a temple, described the bones as evidence of sacrifices. Escobar uses the bones to refute the claim that Yomayoguan was a tomb, saying, "It is clear from what has been discovered that the said guaca is not a tomb but a shrine where they offered to the devil and sacrificed children." Elsewhere, he claims that besides children, the Chimu also interred "llamas and alpacas."[84]

In contrast, native witnesses like Francisco Cunquinan, who was don Antonio's subject, servant, and litter bearer (*hamaquero*), claimed the bones were evidence that Yomayoguan was a burial site. Don Antonio insisted that the uncovered bones were the remains of his ancestors, "and not of children sacrificed as claimed [by the Spanish]." That don Antonio and his followers started to dig at the site themselves gives credence to Escobar's allegation that they wanted to remove the contents for reburial elsewhere. Natives often stole the bodies of deceased family and community members from Christian churches, where they had been buried, to reinter them in "indigenous tombs from [the time of] their infidelity where they had certain guacas and idols."[85]

Can the treasure listed in Table 20 tell us whether Yomayoguan was a temple or tomb? Escobar says such items were "things that were there offered to the devil at different ancient times by various persons." According to the corregidor Pineda, the same items found at the principal burial sites were related to ancestor worship:

> In the principal tombs Indians customarily held ceremonies and other rites and . . . the gold and silver and other things that they placed in the burials were to perpetually be in conformity to established or conventional standards of proper behavior [*estarse a ley*] with the dead and to make offerings to them.

Don Antonio did not say anything about these items except that all belonged to him and his ancestors, implying that such offerings were grave goods.[86]

When chroniclers mention sacrifices with regard to huacas, they mention presents and services but do not generally distinguish between the goods offered at a temple and those offered at or buried in a tomb. Cieza de León and Cabello de Valboa claim that natives sacrificed animals and humans and offered the gods their blood.[87] Cieza de León also states that in and around such famous temples as Pachacama (also written Pachacamac), Curicancha, and Guanacaure, great treasures—described as "silver and gold jars and emeralds, cups, jars, and other types of vessels, all of fine gold"[88]—were buried. In addition to these items, Guamán Poma de Ayala mentions sacrifices and offerings of Spondylus shell (*mullo*), guinea pigs, cloth, dishes (*baxillas*), finger- or toenails (*uñas*), eyelashes, hair, cotton, coca, fruit, and chicha. Padre Antonio de la Calancha, speaking specifically about moon worship in the northern valley of Pacasmayo, stated that food, chicha, animals, birds, and five-year-old children were sacrificed.[89]

These same chroniclers mention identical items as grave goods. Lords, as founders of a lineage, were regarded as gods and were crowned and dressed and offered sacrifices. They and other high-status individuals were buried with various amounts of their possessions (gold and silver dishes), women, children, servants (pages and personal attendants), and cattle, in a manner roughly analogous to their earthly status. In the coastal valleys, the dead were buried with these accompaniments and with cloth, food, jugs (*cántaros*) of chicha, and llamas. Their tombs remained open so that the living could periodically bring more cloth and food and continue to bury others there.[90]

In the Chimu capital of Chan Chan, archaeologists excavated the ciudadelas, palaces or walled compounds containing platforms built presumably in honor of one person (the king or ruler), who was interred in the main chamber upon his death. High-ranking individuals were buried with vast quantities of grave goods or offertory ware, including fine pottery, fancy textiles, ceremonial or ritual paraphernalia, carved wood, weaving implements, metal objects, and Spondylus shell. These compounds also contained many human and animal bones, perhaps indicating ritual sacrifice. In the compound called Laberinto, Geoffrey Conrad found the remains of 93 individuals in 25 cells. The smallest cell (and the only one to be completely excavated) contained 13 complete skeletons. Conrad estimated that one platform contained 200 to 300 burials, many of them adolescent and young adult females. Many of the same grave goods, as well as bones, some of which were identified as human, are mentioned in the records of the excavation of Yomayoguan. Again the material record is of little help in determining whether there was a practical difference between temples and tombs.[91]

Given these considerations, one might hypothesize that there were no structural differences between temples and tombs, that, in fact, they were one and the same, but not both simultaneously. A structure may have begun as a house or palace or a ceremonial structure and precinct with a burial platform in it. If a dead ruler was "great" and he was remembered after several generations, his house and tomb may have become a temple or shrine, a monument to him where subsequent generations left offerings or were themselves buried. Cobo's comment, quoted above, regarding mummies being buried according to rank rings true.[92]

Regardless of the word used to describe the structure, what escaped clear articulation in the Spanish court records was its symbolic meaning and value to the Chimu. This was what they struggled to communicate and what the Spanish neglected or refused to acknowledge: To the natives, Yomayoguan was a ritual center and monument memorializing the ancestors of don Antonio and his line, their "good government" and their wealth, measured not by the accumulation of material goods as much as by numbers of their subjects. Yomayoguan, then, represented kinship, the blood ties that bound society together from the present to the cosmological past. It was an ancient place (probably predating the grandfather of don Antonio), described as a house (the physical representation of a lineage, house, or dynasty in the European usage) with many chambers of various sizes, built behind walls where the remembered and revered ancestors dwelled with their servants and goods. It was a place of devotion and ritual that the living frequented to make offerings and sacrifices to their ancient mothers and fathers, believing that the dead affected the fate of the living. The monument served to remind the living of their relationship to and dependence on their ancestors and to make them ever aware that don Antonio, the present paramount lord, came from a group of rulers responsible for their well-being. In this sense the site embodied the legitimizing ideology that guaranteed order, prosperity, and the smooth functioning of society. Thus, the wailing and crying of the natives, characteristic of funerary practices elsewhere in the Andes, and their defense of Yomayoguan were natural, given their belief that if the structure and the ancestors were destroyed, the reciprocity between living and honored dead would be broken; as a consequence, all the Indians—and, by extension, their society—would perish.[93] Guamán Poma de Ayala captures the importance of these beliefs in his portrayal of a procession during the month of November and the Festival of the Dead, shown in Fig. 5.

Yomayoguan Within the Context of the Encounter

Both the Spanish and the native views of the search for, discovery, and excavation of the structure called Yomayoguan are significant. The Spanish side of the story gives a fair indication of the relative importance of the motivations for the discovery and conquest. Gold came before God and glory, at least for some individuals. This story

Fig. 5 Guamán Poma de Ayala's drawing of a procession during the Festival of the Dead

also reveals how the early power structure was skewed, not only against the natives, but also against poor and powerless Spaniards, at least at the local level. In such a small arena, where almost everyone knew each other, personal contacts could easily bias the outcome of a trial to the point where the powerless could not get a fair hearing. Also, the discussion of the value of the treasure as documented in the royal treasury accounts reminds scholars to be wary of official figures. The numerous lengthy testimonies of many witnesses on both sides of this case agree that as much as half the treasure went unreported and therefore was not included in the accounts of the royal coffers. Likewise, the history of the reporting of the Yomayoguan finds also indicates the inaccuracy of local oral history. (Recall the discrepancies between contemporary accounts and Feyjoo de Sousa's eighteenth-century recollections.)

The Chimu side of the story is certainly more interesting here, given the perspective the native claims provide of pre-Colombian beliefs and practices. The use to which don Antonio put the treasure testifies to the survival of his culture and the redistributive ethic, even though he "sold out" to the Spanish, in a sense, by becoming a partner with the likes of Escobar. Perhaps this was a pragmatic decision, given the overwhelming odds against his being able to win in the local courts. Unlike the Spanish, he was covetous not out of personal greed, but out of concern for the survival and well-being of his community. This attitude reinforces the image of the curaca as not only conservator of information passed on from generation to generation but also as caretaker and guardian of his ancestors and his followers (see Chapter 2). Noteworthy too are the parallels between these beliefs and better-known, better-studied highland beliefs. Like their high-altitude counterparts, coastal inhabitants revered their ancestors as representatives of their past and of the present viability of their communities. Various witnesses refer to ceremonies and burial rituals that conjure up Guamán Poma de Ayala's visual images of such practices. A second similarity is the concept of ownership. Don Antonio claimed ownership because the tomb was handmade (cocido), rather than natural (crudo), to use the categorization first discussed for the Andes by Murra (based on work by Claude Lévi-Strauss) in his analysis of a quipu.[94]

Of most interest to the debate set forth in this chapter is the Chimu definition of the term *huaca*. The Chimu claimed that burials are not huacas. Only temples and shrines and, by implication, idols and supernatural forces were huacas. Matienzo, Cieza de León, and the local corregidor provide early evidence that the natives' claims in this regard are valid, but the varied use by chroniclers, royal officials, and others indicates that the distinction was quickly and summarily lost. After the first phase of the conquest, most Spanish, including most chroniclers and royal officials, did not make this distinction. This semantic debate epitomizes the encounter between two peoples with radically different traditions and goals.

CHAPTER 6

Spanish Influence on the Indigenous Polities of Northern Peru

No good can come from the lack of understanding, at first,
of the functioning [orden] of these native communities.
—Polo de Ondegardo, "Del linage de los ingas"

The hundred years or so following the Inca conquest of the north in about 1470 were extraordinary times for the inhabitants of the region. Twice they were unwillingly implicated in a struggle to maintain their independence and their way of life. First they became subjects of the Incas, whom the coastal Chimu considered their technological, if not social, inferiors. About sixty years later, the Chimu, Cajamarcas, Guambos, and Incas alike faced a new menace from the sea, Spanish imperialism. The chapters of this book are meant to explore the impact and meaning of the latter event on the inhabitants of a region stretching from the coastal center of Trujillo, on the south, to Motupe, on the north, and inland from the Pacific Ocean into the Andes Mountains of Guambos and Cajamarca.

Relatively little can be said about the Inca conquest of the north, given the lack of written sources describing those times. More can be said about the Spanish conquest of the area, but the task of writing about it has not been proportionately easier. To determine what really happened and to ascertain the true impact of events has meant months of excavating, removing layer after layer of the European ethnocentric veneer, bias, misdepiction and misunderstanding of indigenous ideas and concepts about themselves and their environment. It has meant reading and rereading indigenous statements to try to understand what the natives were trying to say in a language that was not their own. It has meant reading what the Spanish said the natives said and comparing this with what the Indians said and did to better interpret the significance of the contact and clash of cultures that was taking place, with the ultimate aim of recreating, even only in an outline form, the precontact indigenous culture.

The Precontact North

Just prior to the Spanish invasion in 1532, the north of Peru was still a rather unsettled place. Innovations began soon after the Inca breakup of a defensive alliance between the people of coastal Chimor and highland Cajamarca in the 1460s or 1470s. After the Chimu's valiant but abortive attempt to thwart Inca expansion, the Inca dismantled the coastal Chimu empire into several separate polities to keep the peace. Perhaps to limit the disruption this balkanization caused, the Cuzqueños confirmed, at least on the coast, the traditional extent of the irrigation network and long-established customary jurisdictional limits of traditional lords. Both on the coast and in the highlands, the Inca allowed local native authorities to wield power as long as they were willing to accommodate the new order by providing labor services that would produce a surplus to support the imperial state and religious hierarchies. Finally, the Inca imposed his empire's supreme god, the sun, on the local religious pantheon and mandated the adoption of the Quechua language. Both efforts were meant to incorporate the various northern ethnic groups into what the victors hoped would become, in time, a unified and homogeneous Inca empire.[1]

Although Inca propaganda stressed the benefits of joining the dominant union, the northern peoples resisted. Even after the "conquest," individual polities resented the Inca's northern onslaughts and sometimes rebelled, as in the known examples of the communities of Túcume and Saña.[2] Given such resistance, by about the end of the second decade of the sixteenth century the Inca's influence extended only as deep as the top administration. Commoners continued traditional religious practices in their own language. Many political boundaries were unchanged. Labor service to high-ranking lords and the state antedated the Inca's rule; only the destination of the labor and the resulting surplus were different. Groups were moved to locations far from their home territory to work for the Inca. Likewise, the surplus goods of coastal peoples were no longer carried to the Chimu capital of Chan Chan (outside modern Trujillo), but instead to storage in the Cajamarca hinterland, presumably to better supply Inca forces still pursuing imperial expansion.[3]

The paramount lords of the various Inca provinces directed this traffic and most of the other activities within their administrative domain. The size of their provinces was of less importance, however, than the number of their subject populations. Native informants report that a curaca's subjects lived in hundreds of population clusters scattered at resource sites within his administrative territory.[4] On periodic surveys of these hamlets, the paramount lord oversaw exploitation of such diverse ecological niches as salt pans, reed beds (for mat and basket making), and clay deposits (for pottery making). He also probably received reports on crop production, the upkeep of irrigation canals, and related matters. He often persuaded his subjects to work on special projects, such as repairing, cleaning, building, or extending an irrigation canal. Or he might dispatch laborers to plant, weed, or harvest crops on land assigned to support the state or religious hierarchies. Still others might be instructed to make adobes at a construction site. Commoners accepted this duty to work for their recognized lords; their labor service was their tribute.[5]

The greater the work force he could muster, the greater a lord's success at maximizing production and surpluses and the greater his people's well-being. Extending the irrigation system opened up more land to potential cultivation. Even the construction of a new temple or palace could be justified by a metaphysical argument that such work would please the deities, spirits, or ancestors, thus guaranteeing the future well-being of society. A large surplus of food and other necessary goods (such as salt, corn, pottery, and cloth) could be distributed by the curaca to maintain and possibly improve the living standards of his people. The higher the quality of life of his people, the larger the population might grow—either naturally or by inward migration and voluntary subjugation or indentureship. This win-win relationship between what the natives described as an "old-style" paramount lord and his subjects was memorialized in song and epitomizes what Guamán Poma de Ayala and others called *buen gobierno* (good government)—a phrase that meant one thing to the natives and quite another to the Spanish.[6]

Building irrigation ditches on the coast to reclaim desert land for agriculture may have been the original means of establishing the administrative jurisdiction of a lord or his predecessors. The building of an irrigation canal to bring water to a field conferred on the responsible person, or more likely his entire kin group, a claim to the use of the land and the produce resulting from their labor thereon for as long as he or they continued to occupy and maintain it. At least one archaeologist has confirmed the conjunction between the limits of the irrigation network and a polity's outermost boundaries.[7]

Reports from as early as 1540 show that, although the curaca did not claim ownership of the land in the Western sense, he did have some say over who could exploit resources within his administrative limits. This control explains, at least partially, how and why the subjects of one paramount lord lived and worked among subjects of another. It was in a paramount lord's interest to allow subjects of another lord to exploit resources within his jurisdiction. The other lord benefited by gaining access to the resource, and the host lord also benefited by getting part of the production of the guest subjects. This arrangement added to the supply of goods both lords could distribute to their people. Such resource sharing explains, for example, why natives of coastal Jayanca lived and worked in the highlands within the traditional domain of the lord of Guambos, why subjects of the lord of coastal Saña lived and worked in nine villages in Cajamarca, and why, in 1540, subjects of an unnamed coastal lord worked in the silver mines of Chilete under the lord of Cajamarca.[8]

Petitions and testimony in court cases to which native communities were party reveal that such relationships might be formalized by gift giving and marriage. They might also have been the first step in a process by which guest subjects loosened their allegiance to their own lord and eventually allied with and sought protection from their host. Consequently, there was competition for subjects among lords, and though ties of kinship proved a strong cement binding subjects to their original ruler, in times of crisis subjects often left one lord to seek resources from another in order to live. They might well have sought to join a prosperous, growing community under a curaca with a reputation for institutionalized generosity and good government. Or they might have heard his subjects praise his good works in song, the key to immortality in a culture without writing.

If a respected and generous lord was celebrated for several generations after his death, he could join the ranks of the community's honored ancestors. His tomb, which perhaps was in the same structure as that of his forebears if he came from a distinguished line, would become a shrine to be visited by the community. Certainly, his memory, if not his mummy or worldly remains, would be invoked in the ritual observances of the community (as shown in Fig. 5). Offerings fed his spirit in a reciprocal exchange between the living and the dead. This exchange symbolized the interdependence between those present and those past—the earth and heaven, the people and their lords—to nourish and be nourished, to feed and be fed. The ancestral house, or tomb, and shrine represented the cooperation necessary for survival, continuity, and prosperity. The structure represented the basis of legitimacy on which the lords exercised power before the Spanish invasion. As we have seen, the emphasis was on reciprocity and regulation, not hierarchy and control.[9]

The Spanish Impact

This interdependent world of shared resources began to crumble soon after Pizarro's arrival in 1532. One of the first assaults on the organization of the indigenous society was the granting of encomiendas as early as 1534 and 1535.[10] From the conquerors' point of view, this institution was well suited to the circumstances. The Spanish had no idea how large an area they had "discovered" and were largely ignorant of its geography. They neither spoke the native languages nor understood the rationale on which indigenous society was established. Therefore, granting a Spaniard the stewardship of a lord and his subjects became a convenient means of establishing the Spanish imperial presence and domination. The encomendero dealt with the commoners through their traditional lord and so did not have to worry about the geographical extent of his dominion. In return for "protection" and instruction in Spanish culture and Catholicism, the natives through their labor supported their encomendero, his household, and the empire he represented.

From the Native American point of view, the encomienda system built on indigenous foundations, leaving traditional lords in place as intermediaries between the imperial power and the commoners. Furthermore, commoners' obligations could still be satisfied through labor and service, but now instead of benefiting the Inca, the surplus supported and eventually enriched a small percentage of the growing Spanish population in the New World.

In granting lords and their subjects to different Spaniards, Pizarro, out of ignorance or arrogance, often split the original polities into as many as four encomiendas. The paramount lord might be given to one Spaniard and his second-in-command to another. Mitimaes, who lived as far as several days' walk from their lord's administrative center, were often assigned by the Spanish to the control of a lord closer to where they lived. This piecemeal dismantling robbed lords of subjects, their labor, and the ability to exploit enough ecological niches to guarantee polities some measure of self-sufficiency.

The granting of encomiendas also substantially disrupted the native hierarchy. Lesser lords given in encomienda to a Spaniard rose to equal status with their own paramount lords, and indigenous ranks collapsed. At the same time, the decline in population due to disease, migration, and overwork increased competition among lords for subjects to maintain their status and power. A growing portion of forasteros (outsiders, natives who had cut ties or lost contact with their home community) either sought protection from another indigenous lord or flocked to urban centers and worked for the Spanish. As an agrarian commercial economy became established, some natives fled to the questionable sanctuary of the estates and became personal retainers, or yanaconas, of the owners, or hacendados.[11]

Another major factor that changed the indigenous political economy was the gradual revision of the tribute system (see Chapter 4). Tribute obligations evolved from uncompensated service to specific quantities of goods; later, increasingly, goods were commuted to silver. As the tribute system was modified, so too was the role and status of the paramount lord. The once respected and sometimes beloved "old-style" curacas were fast disappearing in the 1560s and 1570s, dying in office or being removed from their position and replaced by men chosen by the encomendero or corregidor. Paramount lords were no longer charged with the well-being, safe keeping, and growth in numbers of their subjects. They were no longer the terrestrial guardians of their communities, chosen by their peers for their ability to manage, provide, and intercede with the ancestors and the forces of sun, thunder, moon, and sea to forestall natural disaster and maintain balance in the universe. After the Spanish conquest, the curacas became mere tribute collectors for the colonial power, siphoning ever-increasing amounts of surplus out of indigenous communities to support ever-increasing numbers of Europeans rather than investing that surplus in their own people. In their new role as cultural brokers and servants of colonialism, the curacas became impoverished, not so much in material wealth, but by the indigenous standard of numbers of subjects, so many of whom died or fled to escape the increasing demands of the Spanish. The delicate equilibrium between the curaca's obligations to his subjects and their obligations to him was destroyed. Commoners who remained in their communities had to work harder to keep up with Spanish demands. Communities sank into poverty, lost respect for their leaders, and watched the whole fabric of their collective well-being unravel.[12]

The reformulation of the curaca's role was accelerated by forced resettlement (see Chapter 3). In the north, this did not begin, as it

did farther south, during the Toledan era. In fact, it began informally
as early as 1540. As lords and their subjects died, remnants of a population usually became subjects of another lord. While it is not always clear whether this was voluntary or not, this aggregation took
place without Spanish direction and continued sporadically until
the early 1560s, when the first systematic, Spanish-directed efforts
at concentration took place.

The resettlement push and the increasingly permanent settlement of the Spanish in the north weakened the paramount lord's
control over his administrative jurisdiction. Newly founded Spanish
towns had administrative domains of their own, superimposed on
the indigenous landscape, which might or might not correspond to
the traditional jurisdictional boundaries of native units. So paramount lords no longer controlled all those who entered their administrative realms. This coincided with the increasing interest on
the part of the Spaniards in acquiring land for their own purposes.

Chroniclers were divided on whether or not the Inca owned the
land. When the chroniclers claims are compared to what individual
natives actually said about land and their earliest practices, the ethnocentric myopia of the Europeans clears, and we can see that the
natives did not understand the concept of ownership in the European, Western sense. They thought of undeveloped land as "raw," a
good free in nature, open to community members to occupy and
use. This understanding is evident in what the indigenous witnesses
said and did during the first years of contact with the Spanish. Natives admitted only to occupying land. This understanding of land
and tenure explains why the natives did not immediately protest
the Spanish use of land.

The lords, as early as 1537, allowed the Spanish to use land in return for gifts (e.g., of cattle and European cloth or clothes). This
practice was consistent with the cultural norms of resource sharing
that native peoples had practiced prior to 1532. Over time, gifts in
kind from the Spanish to the native lords, which they interpreted
according to their standards of reciprocity and resource-sharing,
were commuted to periodic cash payments by the Spanish. Many
native lords did not understand fully the significance of the relationship. Indeed, many undoubtedly assumed such gifts, in kind or in
specie, were their just due for allowing the Spanish to remain among
their subjects. Some probably welcomed the payments, since they
increasingly needed cash to make up the deficit in the tribute exactions of the Spanish.

The Spanish interpreted this relationship from their own cultural viewpoint. Indeed, it is from this era, if we accept Spanish claims at face value, that the first evidence exists that a few curacas grasped the basic idea of private property. If this was the case, it was likely because the Spanish themselves always attributed "ownership" to the natives, not because the concept was part of the indigenous culture. The gifts, as concessions or acknowledgment of reciprocity, became, according to the Spanish, rental fees or even payments for the sale of property. Thus, according to Spanish colonial sources, a few curacas "sold" land to the encomenderos and other settlers at the time, although in my extensive research of the local, regional, national, and international archives I have yet to find a single legal bill of sale from this early period. The Spanish, with increasing investments in the area, wanted better guarantees. They began to claim before Spanish authorities that the periodic cash payments and "gifts" they had given to the local lords for grazing privileges were not rent but actually an early colonial version of installment payments for the sale of the land that they had previously only used. In the 1590s, some of these "sales" were legalized (from the Spanish point of view). Thus, these gifts (from the native point of view) or payments (from the Spanish viewpoint) were the proverbial foot in the door. Years later, some natives still expressed astonishment and disbelief that these symbols of mutual dependence were used by the Spanish to claim permanent and exclusive possession of land and other resources, used or not.

The same kind of misunderstanding is seen in the looting of Yomayoguan, which is just one example of a systematic attack on native culture and belief systems throughout the early period of contact. The encomenderos were obliged to hire priests as they arrived from Spain to minister to the natives. As Christianity became entrenched, Spanish morality dictated that traditional lords with many wives choose just one. Don Juan of Collique, an old-style traditional lord, the epitome of the *dueño de indios*, was hanged, ostensibly because he refused to give up his favorite mistress. All over the north, polygyny was outlawed.[13] The priests, furthermore, told the natives to worship one god; their traditional gods were denounced as evil. The Spanish ridiculed the natives' ancestor cults; their rites were outlawed and their tombs and temples sacked and destroyed, sometimes adobe brick by adobe brick, as the Spanish hunted treasure.

Yomayoguan and its contents represented one thing to the Spanish and another to the natives. To both, Yomayoguan was important. The Spanish sought wealth measured in gold, silver, gems, and pearls. The local peoples fought to maintain the site because the wealth of their community, measured in the health and well-being of their kin group, was at stake. Don Antonio's reluctant submission to the Spanish effective takeover represented perhaps a pragmatic compromise to reap at least some benefit from the sacrilege. The proceeds from the investment of his share of the recovered bullion were meant to alleviate his subjects' tribute burden, thereby lessening their work and suffering and thus providing for a measure of well-being.

The Yomayoguan incident provides a more intimate glimpse of the religious beliefs and practices of the Chimu Indians than that gleaned from most records of the extirpation of idolatry, where only the names of gods occasionally surface. The natives' remarks help us understand their relationship with the dead and their value system of reciprocity; they also throw light on the role and duties of the curaca and the basis of his legitimacy. The descriptions of ancestor worship found in the records of huaca looting provide rare details of Chimu cosmology, which has often puzzled scholars.[14]

Taken together, these changes turned the natives' way of life upside down. With the legitimacy of the paramount lords undermined, they could no longer mobilize a labor force large enough to build and maintain the infrastructure, make best use of the local resource base, and produce a surplus to improve the lives of their subjects and attract others. "Institutionalized generosity" was replaced with extraction to benefit the Spanish—in other words, exploitation.

As the shared redistributive and subsistence system crumbled, native needs were increasingly supplied by a growing market for labor and resources that benefited the strongest and most capable. Here the Spanish held the advantage, since few natives understood the market system and therefore could only weakly exploit or protest it. Well-intentioned royal protective legislation was unevenly enforced because it was not in the best interests of the enforcers to implement it. Thus, over time, the native communal ethos for collective well-being and even survival was replaced by a foreign ideology characterized by greed, self-interest, and individual gain. As we have seen, community members survived by withdrawing, fleeing, and adapting their culture to outside pressures.

All of these changes were well under way before Toledo set foot in northern Peru in the late 1560s. Thus, this tale of the north puts what happened in other regions, notably the better-studied southern highlands, in perspective. Scholars of the southern Andes consider the visita of Viceroy Toledo in the first half of the 1570s a turning point in the history of highland indigenous life. In that region, they contend, Toledo made the first systematic attempts to rationalize Spanish colonial rule by censusing the population for tribute reform, consolidating the population into towns (the reducción policy) and regulating land, water, and labor distribution and mining.

As the preceding chapters show, much of Toledo's efforts in the south had already been accomplished in the north by 1570. Although often implemented piecemeal, informally, or indirectly, Spanish colonial policy accomplished the censusing and reduction of the northern indigenous communities as early as 1540. Regulation and reform continued to the eve of Toledo's arrival in 1569. Thus, although Toledo's visita had some significant effects, it merely furthered previous efforts to bend indigenous culture to Spanish imperial ends. The present-day scholarly emphasis on Toledo and his times has obscured the type and extent of cultural change that had already taken place in the north.

The apparent preservation of the indigenous political structure in the north has led many commentators to overlook the deep and lasting political changes that followed the conquest. The personnel changed, often at the whim or insistence of a foreigner; the lord's function changed; and with it the basis of legitimacy of his role. In precontact Peru, each community was semi-autonomous under the Inca. The duty of the curaca, as head of the community, was to use his power to manage and control people, who used the resources that had been occupied and improved by the ancestors and bequeathed by them to them all. It was his ability to use human and natural resources efficiently that proved the favorable disposition of the ancestors, thereby underpinning the curaca's authority, as shown diagrammatically in Fig. 6. Under the traditional system, the curaca was the link between the inhabitants of this world and those of the next. Temples and tombs were the locales where the curaca facilitated communication between his subjects' realm and the spiritual one. At these sacred structures the lords, through propitiation and service, harnessed the supernatural powers of the ancestors, whose favor gave lords the wisdom and power to organize society to work the resource base productively, thus guaranteeing subsistence and fertility. Part of the surplus resulting from managed labor and resources was offered to the ancestors through rite and ritual; the remaining, greater, part went to the community. To work for the lord, then, was also to work for oneself, one's family and lineage, and one's ancestors for the good of all. By sponsoring the production of artisans and influencing the designs and iconography on ceramics and textiles, lords controlled and spread these ideas of reciprocity between the living and the dead, thus reinforcing native society's

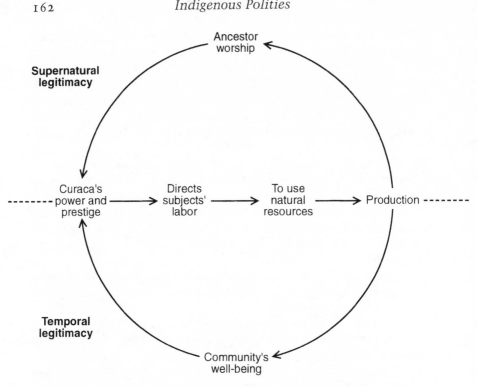

Fig. 6 The curaca's role, according to local cosmological beliefs

legitimizing philosophical and political myth. In exchange for "good government," the communities worshiped their curacas. Such communities resemble a lower-level version of Sahlins's "heroic polities," where societies vest the fate of an entire people in the person and actions of a divine leader, thus blurring the line between sacred and secular. Politics was indivisibly linked to religion (as McCormack has shown) and, I would add, to economics. Indeed, such Western categories are arbitrary divisions of the Andean understanding of the world.[15]

After contact, the paramount lord changed from being an intermediary among the Inca state apparatus, his people, and the ancestors to being the intermediary between his subjects and the Spanish. Simultaneously, his economic base eroded. As the basis of his community's wealth disappeared, the dispersed population was concentrated in reconfigured settlements, often losing access to resources, especially land, with a subsequent loss in the community's ability to provide for its own subsistence. The evolving Spanish tribute system changed the meaning of service and eventually forced the Andean peoples to work for the money they needed to satisfy state demands while learning to raise European cattle and plant new crops. Furthermore, the representatives of the dominant culture supplanted the natives' customs, beliefs, and language in favor of their own. Monogamy replaced polygyny, at least in theory. Likewise, Andeans were asked to revere one god instead of many, forsake their ancestors, and even help dismantle their sacred precincts. The link between living and dead that defined and reinforced traditional indigenous society was weakened and in some cases severed.

If the story in fact begins earlier and the degree of change is already great in 1570, then scholars of continuity and change in the south have a new context and perspective against which to assess what happened there. Structures continued, but their meaning changed. The implications for those who start their histories in the 1570s with Toledo's reorganization are great; they cannot always assume that they are starting with a preserved reflection of the Andean pre-Hispanic past. They cannot assume that there was little or no change in the forty or fifty years since Atahualpa met Pizarro.

In addition, this story suggests that at first the Spanish built their system atop indigenous institutions, just as they built their churches on top of sacred structures, and only gradually modified them to suit their needs. Thus, curacas remained in charge of native labor. Only with time did Spanish exactions increase and the role of curacas change accordingly. Paramount lords were not all replaced at once for inability to measure up or recalcitrance in fulfilling Spanish expectations. Land was not appropriated in a wholesale manner. At first the Spanish needed only sites for their cities and suburban gardens. Five years later they were grazing herds of imported domestic animals on the natural pastures. Curacas allowed them to come into their districts (*terminos*) and gladly accepted the gifts proffered. Only with the passage of time did the Spanish seek ownership and title to still relatively small tracts of land for cultivation. Only then did these gifts, which the native lords accepted under the guise of custom surrounding resource sharing, turn into payments, according to the Spanish, for the right to exclusive control of the resource. Tribute, too, began as a labor obligation, in keeping with customary indigenous understandings.

The period under consideration is one of tremendous transition, born as much of misunderstanding as of intent. The Andeans judged Spanish actions by indigenous standards of reciprocity and redistribution, and the Spanish, judging natives on the basis of European cultural assumptions, made no attempt to explain themselves in indigenous terms. Cultural friction roused the natives to acts of defiance and resistance, both outright and covert, which the Spanish mustered their copious resources to suppress.

But as the interactions continued, the Andean peoples reacted. In the face of Spanish ignorance, they took advantage. More commonly, they tried to explain to the Spanish the wrong they were doing. But the Spanish either did not listen or heard only what they wanted to hear, so native resistance increased. The fishermen of Chérrepe appealed to authorities to remain settled by the sea. Lords protested against restrictions on riding horses and serving chicha, explaining that without the latter their subjects would not work. They defiantly protested cuts in support and spoke out against increasing tribute; with each increase, the volume of their complaints soared. Sometimes protests took on the guise of mourning; others involved shouting and physical defense. Sometimes, the dispute ended up in the courts. Many commoners, who were less able to sue or stand up for their rights, simply fled to seek a better situation. In this way, they played one lord or master off against another.

Finally, the history of the coast suggests a good deal of cultural overlap between Andean peoples there and in the highlands. In contrast to those who argue that the socioeconomic structure of the highlands was fundamentally different from that of the coast, I find strong evidence that the basis of legitimacy of the curacas, the view of natural resources and the rules for their use, the idea and system of tribute, and the beliefs and practices of ancestor worship were common to all Andean communities. Furthermore, highland and coastal peoples shared the values of reciprocity and redistribution, which upheld the basic self-sufficiency of communities throughout the old Inca empire. Other significant commonalities also link the societies of the coast with those of the highlands: lords competed for their subjects' loyalty; precontact northern peoples all defined wealth in the same way; and populations from all regions dispersed over wide areas, with coastal peoples living in the mountains, and highland peoples on the coast. These facts imply a significant degree of contact and interdependence, a coincidence of cultures, between the two geographical areas in the years immediately before the Spanish invasion, a point Murra has made previously. Thus, the evidence given here suggests, in broad outline and with allowances for time lags for specific areas, that similarities between Andean peoples of the coast and highlands, in the north and in the south, were more numerous and more significant than previously thought.[16]

Reference Matter

Abbreviations

AAL/	Archivo Arzobispal de Lima
	Apelaciones de Trujillo (Apel Truj)
AAT/	Archivo Arzobispal de Trujillo
	Causas
	Diezmos
ACMS/	Archivo de don Augusto Castillo Muro Sime (Lambayeque)
ACT	*Actas del Cabildo de Trujillo*
AFA/	Archivo del Fuero Agrario (Lima)
	Mocupe
	San Luis
AGI/	Archivo General de las Indias (Seville)
	AL Audiencia de Lima
	C Contaduria
	E Escribania
	IG Indiferente General
	J Justicia
	P Patronato
ANCR/	Archivo Notarial de Carlos Rivadeneira (Lambayeque)
	Alvarez
	Herrera
	Mendoça
	Polo
	Tumán

ANP/	Archivo Nacional del Perú (Lima)		
	Aguas		
	DI	Derecho Indígena	
	Histórico		
	R	Residencia	
	RA	Real Audiencia	
	SG	Superior Gobierno	
	Tierras		
	Títulos		
	Tributos		
ART/	Archivo Regional de Trujillo (now Archivo del Departamento de La Libertad)		
	Alvarez		
	CaO	Cabildo Ordinario	
	Co	Corregimiento	
		AG	Asuntos de Gobierno
		Aguas	
		Compa	Compulsa
		HS	Hojas Sueltas
		JR	Juez de Residencia
		O	Ordinario
		P	Pedimento
		R	Residencia
	H	Hacienda	
		Compa	Compulsa
		O	Ordinario
	I	Intendencia	
		AG	Asuntos de Gobierno
		Compa	Compulsa
		O	Ordinario
	LC	Lopez de Cordova	
	Martinez de Escobar		
	Mata		
	MT	Muñoz Ternero	
	Notarial		
	Palacios		
	Reyes		

RH Real Hacienda

   Compa Compulsa

   JComp Juez de Compocisión

   O Ordinario

Salinas

Vega

ASFL/ Archivo de San Francisco de Lima

ASFT/ Archivo de San Francisco de Trujillo

   B Libro de Bautismo

BAH/ Biblioteca de la Real Academia de la Historia (Madrid)

   ML Mata Linares

   Muñoz

BCH/ Museo de Volkerkunde, Hamburg, Brüning Collection

BM/ British Museum

BNMadrid/ Biblioteca Nacional de España (Madrid)

BNP/ Biblioteca Nacional del Perú

BP/ Biblioteca del Palacio Real (Madrid)

BUS/ Biblioteca de la Universidad de Sevilla

   R Colecció

Notes

Chapter 1

1. León-Portilla; and Guillén Guillén.

2. Lockhart, *Men of Cajamarca*, *Nahuas and Spaniards*, and *The Nahuas After the Conquest*; Schroeder; Horn; Wood; and Haskett.

3. Murra, "El control vertical"; Netherly, "Local Level Lords"; Zuidema, *The Ceque System*, "Kinship," "Hierarchy and Space," "The Lion in the City," and *Inca Civilization*; and Salomon, *Ethnic Lords* and *Native Lords*.

4. Rostworowski, *Curacas y sucesiones*, "Dos manuscritos," *Etnía y sociedad*, and *Historia del Tahuantinsuyu*; Spalding, *Huarochirí*; MacCormack; Stern, *Peru's Indian Peoples*; and Wachtel.

5. Guamán Poma de Ayala, *El primer nueva corónica*, vol. 1, p. 220 [222]. (The alternate spelling, not used in this text, is Huamán.)

6. Andrien, p. 141.

7. On the date of the Inca conquest of the Peruvian north coast, see J. H. Rowe, "The Kingdom of Chimor."

8. MacCormack. See also Salomon, *Ethnic Lords*, *Native Lords*, and "Vertical Politics"; Stern, *Peru's Indian Peoples*; and Ramírez, "The Inca Conquest."

9. Porras Barrenechea, *Fuentes* and *los cronistas*; Pagden; and Mac-Cormack.

10. See Andrien, and Adorno.

11. This latter example, as will be shown in more detail in Chapter 5, is another illustration of what Sahlins describes as "cultural change, externally induced yet indigenously orchestrated" (p. viii).

12. Ramírez, *Provincial Patriarchs*. For a more detailed description of the coast, see Ramírez, "Land Tenure," especially pp. 33–36.

13. No one definition of the boundary between the highlands and the coast exists. Indigenous highland lords controlled mines and other resources

at 1,000 meters above sea level, while colonies of coastal Sañas lived in the mountains of Cajamarca. See Ramírez, "The Cajamarca Connection." Lechtman (p. 9) uses 2,000 meters as the division between highlands and coast.

14. The descriptions of Pedro Cieza de León, Felipe Guamán Poma de Ayala, Antonio Vasquez de Espinoza, Andrés García de Zurita, Joseph Garcia de la Concepción, Cosme Bueno, José Ignacio de Lecuanda, Tadeo Haenke, and Alejandro de Humboldt are conveniently extracted and presented by Ravines.

15. J. H. Rowe, "The Kingdom of Chimor"; Urteaga, p. 32; Salomon, *Native Lords*, p. 194; Ramírez, "The Inca Conquest"; and Pease, "Los Incas."

16. Betanzos, pp. 96, 123, 231, 233; Cabello de Valboa, pp. 331–32; and Rostworowski, "El señorio de Changuco," pp. 16, 18. Note that several different versions of the Inca conquest of the north are given in various chronicles. The one presented here is the one most accepted by scholars.

17. See also Stern, *Peru's Indian Peoples* and "The Rise and Fall"; Betanzos, pp. 295–96; Salomon, "Ancestors, Grave Robbers," p. 212; Assadourian, "Dominio colonial," especially pp. 8–9; and Cabello de Valboa, p. 319. Guilmartin explains the Incas' defeat by the Spanish in terms of technology, political fragmentation, Indian allies, and disease. Assadourian, in his article "Dominio colonial," states that the Incas may not have wanted to destroy local ruling hierarchies or ethnic identities.

18. I am indebted to the late Martha Anders and to Helaine Silverman, Izumi Shimada, Michael E. Moseley, Tom Abercrombie, Catherine Julien, Peter Burghi, Kent Day, Herb Eling, Richard Schaedel, R. Tom Zuidema, Enrique Mayer, Franklin Pease, Gary Urton, Frances Hayashida, Guillermo Cock, Frank Salomon, Lyn Lowry, Hector Noejovich, Cristóbal Aljovín, Alan Kolata, and many others who shared their knowledge (and, sometimes, unpublished work) with me in this effort. I, of course, take full responsibility for any errors, interpretive or otherwise.

19. As a postscript to Chapter 3, I trace, for a better perspective, the evolving tenure system and the transfer of resources from the natives to the Spanish well beyond the end of the sixteenth century. This was necessary to show the imposition of the idea of private property and the long process of appropriation.

20. Farriss.

21. MacCormack, and Larson.

22. Murra, "El control vertical"; Rostworowski, "Breves notas."

23. Ricard.

24. Duviols, *Cultura Andina*.

Chapter 2

1. *Cacique*, a term for chieftain, was imported by the Spanish from the Caribbean and is a synonym for *curaca*, the word used in the Andes for paramount lord.

2. All spellings of indigenous words and names are modernized, except in direct quotes. I have transcribed and translated all of the quotations from Spanish sources.

3. AGI/J 459, 3084–86; AL 167, 1648; Rostworowski, *Curacas y sucesiones*, p. 104. Note that references to manuscripts follow this general form: Archive/section, *legajo* (l.) number and/or identifying date (day, month, or year), *cuaderno* (c.) number or expediente (exp.) (if used), folio or page. Sanz Tapia also found two categories of Mexican caciques (see p. 280).

4. Sahlins, p. 138.

5. See, for example, Farriss; and Taylor, *Landlord and Peasant*, especially chap. 2.

6. The north coast is specifically defined here as including the area from the Jequetepeque Valley on the south to the Motupe Valley on the north and inland to the altitude of approximately 2,000 meters above sea level in the Andes Mountains.

7. *Dueño*, though it literally means "owner," should not be interpreted in a Western "slavery" sense. A better translation that takes into consideration the temporal and institutional context is "leader" or "commander" of Indians. See also note 41 below and the corresponding text. Díaz Rementería (especially in the introduction and chaps. 1 and 2) also discusses the problems of using Spanish terms to describe indigenous phenomena.

8. See Moore, especially the appendix, "Forbidden Acts and Their Penalties," pp. 165–74, for a summary of crime and punishment under the Inca. Closer to the Inca heartland, curacas were supposed to seek permission from the Inca to take a subject's life. This was not the case in areas, like the north, incorporated late into the Inca domains. See Melo, p. 273; and Wachtel, p. 80.

9. For a sketch of Cuenca's life, see González de San Segundo, "El Doctor."

10. AGI/J 461, 857v; J 459, 3085v–86, 3090v; and AL 92, 1566. Another sixteenth-century document describing Chincha on the south central coast of Peru also states that curacas had power over life and death: "It is understood that [the curacas] had enough power to punish and kill Indian commoners because it has been ascertained that they had authority to punish and kill in all the valleys" (Castro and Ortega Morejón, pp. 482, 485). The same document states that one of the worst offenses was to seduce a woman of one of the Incas (p. 482).

11. Guamán Poma de Ayala, *El primer nueva corónica*, vol. 2, pp. 455 [457], 456 [458]; Cobo, vol. 2, p. 121. Note that the above edition of Guamán Poma de Ayala uses two types of pagination: the number of the original version (written in c. 1615) and, in brackets, the actual consecutive page number. Duplication and omission of page numbers in the original version explain the discrepancies. Spalding ("La red desintegrante") and Díaz Rementería (especially p. 56) also show this.

12. Gama, especially pp. 252 and 254; and Wachtel, p. 80; AGI/J 418, 1573, 209; and E 502A [1607–11], 7 and 54. See also Ramírez, "The Inca Conquest."

13. J. H. Rowe, "The Kingdom of Chimor," p. 40.

14. Guamán Poma de Ayala, *La primer nueva corónica*, vol. 1, pp. 111 [111], vol. 2, p. 852 [856], vol. 3, p. 1074 [1084]. See also Murúa, p. 233. A cacicazgo can be defined in territorial terms only after the Spanish conquest. See Rossel Castro, p. 242. For an interesting discussion on curacas and land tenure in Mexico, see Taylor, "Cacicazgos coloniales," especially pp. 10 and 11; see also Chapter 3.

15. AGI/J 458, 2041v–42. Also see Guamán Poma de Ayala, *La primera nueva corónica*, vol. 1, p. 353 [355], on boundaries.

16. ART/CoR, 30-IV-1576. See also Ramírez, "The Inca Conquest," and Chapter 3 for my fuller discussion of the archaeological confirmation of this division by Eling.

17. Guamán Poma de Ayala, *La primer nueva corónica*, vol. 3, p. 1074 [1084]. I believe that these boundaries had been established long before the Incas took control of the north. The Cuzqueños merely reconfirmed the order that already existed.

18. Netherly, "The Management," p. 247; and Murra, "El control vertical." See also Chapter 3.

19. AGI/J 461, 1395v; and Chapter 3. The Indians of Canta that Rostworowski studied said that land on the coast was theirs because it was irrigated with their water. Rostworowski, "Las etnías del Valle de Chillón," p. 82. Note also that the boundary between Pacasmayo and Saña corresponds to the reach of the respective irrigation networks (Ramírez, "The Inca Conquest"). The land was "theirs" only as long as they used it.

20. Gama, p. 271; and León Barandiarán, *Mitos*, pp. 139–43. A copy of the original document from which León Barandiarán probably transcribed the story almost verbatim exists in the private archives of the late don Augusto Castillo Muro Sime and gives the "legend" a basis in fact. ACMS/1654–1765, especially pp. 7–7v. See also Ramírez, "'Myth' or 'Legend.'" The same story appears in the proceedings of a court case in ANP/RA, l. 27, c. 95, 1610, 141; and Brüning, *Estudios monográficos*, Facsículo III, p. 59; and AGI/J 460, 483; and AL 92. It is possible that the water was withheld by diverting it to others. See, for example, Cieza de León, *The Travels*, chap. 66 and 67, pp. 236, 240.

21. AGI/J 418, 1573, 465. This confirms Farrington's archaeological evidence for decentralized water control. Also see the discussion of water rights in the Jayanca visita by Gama, p. 271. The term "*camayo[c]s*" is also used there as officials who "are in charge of caring for the water."

22. ANCR/1586–1611, 12.

23. Ibid., 23v–24v.

24. AGI/J 461, 1563 and 1566–66v; and ANCR/1586–1611, especially 12, 14–14v, 18–18v, 24.

25. AGI/J 418, 1573, 459v–60; ANP/DI, l. 6, c. 122, 1649, 39v. Cieza de León, *The Travels*, chap. 66, p. 236, states that it was well within the technological capability of the Andeans to divert water and thereby deprive some of its use. See AGI/J 418, 1573, 465, for a specific example.

26. Rostworowski, *Curacas y sucesiones*, pp. 15–16. See also, AGI/J 461, 1521 and 1525.

27. AGI/J 418, 1573, 312 and 459–60. During Gama's visit to Jayanca, the paramount lord sent his subjects into the interior to acquire gold for the encomendero (p. 270).

28. BAH/A109, 112.

29. Gama, p. 270. There were several other circumstances under which subjects of one lord would go to live with subjects of another, marriage being one. When a male subject of one lord took a wife from among the subjects of another, he had to pay tribute to the lord of his wife as well as to his own lord. Cuenca prohibited this in 1566–67. AGI/P 189, Ramo (hereafter r.) 11, 1566. Should a man have several wives, he would owe tribute and therefore be subject to several different lords (AGI/J 455, 1700v). See also Fray Domingo de Santo Tomás on the same subject in CVU/1-1, VII-1550. See also Ramírez, "Social Frontiers."

30. ART/Mata, 25-IV-1565; and Cobo, vol. 2, pp. 120–21.

31. AGI/J 461, 866v; and J 458, 1778v–79 and 1829v; and AL 92, 1566; CVU/1-4, 1564; and Gama, "Visita de Jayanca."

32. Loredo, *Los repartos*, pp. 269–71; and AGI/J 458, 1749 and 1830; J 460, 377v and 385–85v; and J 462, 1860v.

33. Rostworowski, *Curacas y sucesiones*, p. 16. See also Cieza de León, *The Travels*, chap. 61, p. 219; and *La crónica*, especially p. 205; and Zevallos Quiñones, *Los cacicazgos*, p. 47.

34. Las Casas cited by Rostworowski, *Curacas y sucesiones*, pp. 16, 27; AGI/J 458, 1779v–80; J 461, 1469v–71; and AL 28A; Guamán Poma de Ayala, *La primera nueva corónica*, vol. 1, pp. 66 [66], vol. 2, 898 [912–13]; Salinas y Cordova, p. 54. See also Cieza de León, *The Travels*, chap. 61, p. 219; and Melo, p. 275.

35. AGI/J 458, 1801–1v.

36. AGI/J 461, 1469v–71.

37. Spalding, "La red desintegrante," p. 105.

38. AGI/AL 28A, 6. See also note 26.

39. Rostworowski, *Curacas y sucesiones*, pp. 18, 28, 38.

40. Santillán, p. 23. All references are to the 1927 edition, except where the 1968 one is specifically mentioned.

41. Murúa, p. 155; and AGI/J 458, 1802.

42. Probably, few individuals ever accomplished much mobility in practice, except perhaps in times of war and expansion, when rewards of women were frequent. Guamán Poma de Ayala, *La primer nueva corónica*, vol. 1, p. 189 [191]; and Espinoza Soriano, "La poliginia." Spalding, in "Los escaladores sociales," notes that the resource base of a community could expand through donations of additional natural resources from the Inca. She does not address the possible growth in numbers of a community. See especially p. 71.

43. Rostworowski, *Curacas y sucesiones*, p. 55; Murra, "Andean Societies," p. 85; and Castro and Ortega Morejón, p. 484.

44. Spalding, "Los escaladores sociales," p. 44; Murúa, pp. xxi, 213 (also in Moore, p. 167); and Levillier, *Gobernantes*, vol. 9, p. 275 (also in Moore, p. 167). It is also possible that the idol's removal may have occurred in a year marked by the arrival of the Niño current and the resulting ecological consequences, implying that the climatic conditions may not have been a reflection of supernatural ire.

45. See AGI/J 459, 2845; and Cieza de León, *The Travels*, chap. 68, p. 242, for references to curacas as rich men. Wills of Andean lords are found in the following: AGI/J 461, 868v; ART/CoO, 6-XII-1560 and 11-VIII-1582; CoR, 30-VI-1576; and CaO, 24-I-1587. It is interesting to note that the earliest of the four wills makes no mention of land per se. A field of corn is the only item mentioned that has to do with land tenure. This will be discussed in greater detail in Chapter 3.

46. AGI/AL 92, 1566; and Cieza de León, *The Travels*, chap. 63, p. 229, who states that "they had, and still have, the custom of mourning for the dead before the body is placed in the tomb; during four, five or six days, or ten, according to the importance of the deceased, for the greater the lord the more honour do they show him, lamenting with much sighing and groaning and playing sad music. They also repeat all that the dead man had done while living, in their songs; and if he was valiant they recount his deeds in the midst of their lamentations." Melo states that "the Indians had no writing whatsoever but they passed the knowledge of their rights and customs from one to another and for this reason as has been said they were accustomed to sing of the things [happenings or achievements] of his rule to remember them" (p. 276). See also Spalding, *Huarochirí*, p. 61.

47. Gama, pp. 266–68.

48. Cieza de León, *The Travels*, chap. 67, p. 238; and Cook, "La visita," pp. 24, 36.

49. AGI/J 457, 1144v–45; and CVU/1-1, 1-VII-1550. See also Murra, "El control vertical," p. 74; and González de San Segundo, "Pervivencia," especially pp. 65–67.

50. ART/CoCompa, 9-VII-1568; Santillán, p. 27. See my efforts to define the original cacicazgos in Ramírez, "La organización económica," especially pp. 285–88. On the usurpation of curacazgos, see Levillier, *Don Francisco de Toledo*, vol. 1, p. 262.

51. AFA/l. 1, c. 19, 94–95; and Ramírez, *Provincial Patriarchs*, chap. 4.

52. The reductions had started earlier still, almost naturally. The principal of Túcume testified that there were five principales of Pácora in the 1530s. Only one survived in 1570, "for which reason the communities have been combined into only one that is called Pacora of which he is now cacique." AGI/J 418, 1573, 219–19v; J 456, 419; J 459, 3062–62v; and J 460, 376. See also Ramírez, "Chérrepe en 1572."

53. Ramírez, "Chérrepe en 1572"; ANP/DI, l. 19, c. 483, 1793, 41v–42; and AFA/l. 1, c. 19, 94v–96. See also Ramírez, *Provincial Patriarchs*.

54. AGI/J 457, 1163; and J 460, 461.

55. Ramírez, "La organización económica," p. 286.

56. AGI/J 458, 1778v–79v, and 1830v; J 461, 1453v and 1469v–71; and P 189, r. 11, 1566. See also Assadourian, "Dominio colonial," p. 13.

57. AGI/J 457, 701v. For a fuller discussion of tribute, see Chapter 4.

58. AGI/J 457, 776v; J 458, 1261; and J 461, 1407, and 1521v. The year before, curacas of the valleys complained that they could not support three new *corregidores* (district administrators) because the corregidor of Trujillo had assigned them very little tribute, without regard for the available natural resources and number of subjects (ART/Mata, 16-V-1565). For a more complete definition of *fanega*, see Ramírez, *Provincial Patriarchs*, appendix 2. Another factor that subsequently limited a curaca's power was the establishment of a native cabildo, or municipal council. I do not discuss it here because it did not become a significant functioning institution until after Toledo's visit.

59. AGI/J 459, especially 3068v.

60. Santillán, p. 26; Guamán Poma de Ayala, *La primer nueva corónica*, vol. 2, p. 452 [454]; and Rostworowski, *Curacas y sucesiones*, p. 104. See also AGI/AL 123; and González de San Segundo, "Pervivencia," pp. 68–69.

61. AGI/J 418, 1573, 329v.

62. Assadourian ("Dominio colonial," p. 15) cites a colonial observer (without naming the source) as follows: "And what the caciques take from the Indians is not so hurtful because almost all is redistributed back to them, because they eat and use it up together, and finally[,] the caciques do not hoard[,] instead they use it with the Indians."

63. There are a few examples of curacas who remained staunch defenders of their communities. See Rossel Castro, p. 244. Otherwise, for a general statement on curacas who allied with the Spanish, see Nuñez Anavitarte, especially pp. 9–11.

64. Rostworowski, *Curacas y sucesiones*, p. 14.

65. Ibid., p. 15. Spalding, in an article entitled "Resistencia," shows how this tradition continued. As late as 1723, a curaca had to help preserve ancestor worship or he was deposed or killed by his subjects. Another instance comes from Ferreñafe, where Zevallos Quiñones found that people rejected the cacique as late as the middle of the eighteenth century because he lacked legitimacy in their eyes (*Los cacicazgos*, p. 40).

66. On the death sentence of don Juan as an exemplary punishment, see Levillier, *Don Francisco de Toledo*, vol. 1, p. 263.

67. AGI/J 461, 923v–24v and 935; and ANP/DI, l. 4, c. 72, 1622, 120v. On the connection between generosity and legitimacy, see the description of Guamán Poma de Ayala of the third *colla* (queen), Mama Cora Ocllo: "And because of pure miserliness she was not on good terms with her vassals. And for this reason, the great lords and principales paid little attention to her. She hoarded riches and food in the storage areas; here they rotted and ended" (*La primer nueva corónica*, vol. 1, p. 125 [125]). This contrasts sharply with the praise he allowed to the sixth and seventh coyas (the Anglicized spelling of *colla*), each of whom was a "friend of singing and music and playing the drum, having parties and banquets" and a "very generous

person who helped the poor," respectively (*La primer nueva corónica*, vol. 1, pp. 131 [131], 133 [133]). See also Wachtel, who alludes to the same phenomenon, especially p. 130.

68. AGI/J 461, 923v–24v, 1427v, and 1490–92v, for a series of such petitions; J 457, 1063v–64v and 1156; J 458, 1827v; and J 418, 1573, 210 and 327v.

69. ART/CoJuez de Comisión, 29-III-1558. The same phenomenon occurred in the southern highlands. The encomendero Lucas Martinez Vegazo had people in Arequipa from Huamachuco, Cuzco, Ubinas, Andaguaylas, Cañaris, Chuquito, Chunbibilca, Condorcanas, and Yungas. See Assadourian, "Dominio colonial," p. 17; and Trelles Aréstegui.

70. ART/CoJuez de Comisión, 29-III-1558. The Villamarins' research on the Chibchas near Bogota shows that caciques there started lawsuits to recover Indians who had migrated to other jurisdictions only in 1575.

71. ART/CoJuez de Comisión, 29-III-1558; and AGI/J 458, 1455; and J 461, 1123v–24.

72. Santillán, p. 17.

73. AGI/J 418, 1573, 459–60 and 123; J 455, 1691; J 458, 1888v–89; J 461, 948v, 1432v–33, 1491, and 1522v; ART/CoR, 3-VI-1564. This was also happening in the adjacent Cajamarca highlands; see ART/Mata, 20-VII-1565. Spalding also mentions competition among communities for lands and service. See "La red desintegrante," p. 115.

74. AGI/P 189, r. 11, 1566; Santillán, p. 78. Indians were also recruited, sometimes by Spaniards, "because of the chaos when they did not have a paramount lord to obey" (AGI/J 418, 1573, 325).

75. AGI/J 461, 845–46 and 935.

76. AGI/J 461, 1120v; and J 418, 1573, 315–15v; BNP/A538, 1580; and ART/CoJuez de Aguas, 31-VII-1583.

77. AGI/J 461, 935, 951, and 1395. They were, therefore, censused in more than one place.

78. Guamán Poma de Ayala, *La primer nueva corónica*, vol. 2, p. 872 [886]; Powers, "Resilient Lords"; and Stern, *Peru's Indian Peoples*, p. 174. On recent research on migration, see the book edited by Robinson; also see Wightman.

79. Guamán Poma de Ayala, *La primer nueva corónica*, vol. 2, pp. 819 [833], 860 [874], 864 [878], 872 [886].

80. Santillán, pp. 77–78; Murúa, pp. 211–12, 229. See also Mellafe, "La significación histórica," p. 73. There were some exceptions to the immobility rule: procurement of raw materials in neighboring provinces needed for tribute purposes, state business, etc. See Ramírez, "The Inca Conquest," especially p. 37; and my discussion of La Gasca's tribute lists of Saña and Huamachuco in Chapter 4.

81. AGI/J 461, 1515–15v; and P 97, r. 4, 1569, 15.

82. AGI/AL 92.

83. Santillán, pp. 36–37, 79. See also Murra, "Nueva información."

84. In Chincha, those who fled became yanaconas: "And because they

wander about as lazy rogues they become yanaconas" (Castro and Ortega Morejón, p. 485). See also Mellafe, "The Importance of Migration," pp. 306–7, 310–11.

85. Farriss, especially pp. 96–99, 229, 231–232, 255; Taylor, *Landlord and Peasant*, especially p. 83. Gibson discusses the rapid decline of a cacique's power and status in colonial times in the central valley of Mexico. See especially pp. 80, 90, 112, 155, 163, 165–166.

86. Wachtel agrees on the rapidity of "destructuration." See p. 138.

87. Burga, in a personal communication dated January 8, 1987, cites Castro and Ortega Morejón to the effect that the Inca state used less than 1 percent of the land and therefore probably exacted a proportionally small amount of labor service. Santillán also states that only one of a hundred Indians worked in the mines for the Inca (p. 39).

88. Spalding, "Los escaladores sociales," pp. 73, 81; Archivo Jara (Trujillo)/Juan de Mata, 1562, 12–14, as cited by Netherly, "Los señores tardíos," pp. 13, 18; and AGI/P 189, r. 11, 1566; J 461, 868v; ART/CoO, 6-XII-1560 and 11-VIII-1582; and CoR, 30-VI-1576; and LC, 29-III-1563.

Chapter 3

I thank Mario Pastore, John V. Murra, Robert Jackson, Nils Jacobsen, Hector Noejovich, and Robert G. Keith for their thoughtful comments on earlier versions of this chapter.

1. Notable studies of land tenure include Murra, *Economic Organization*, chap. 2, especially pp. 34–40; Rostworowski, "Dos manuscritos inéditos," and "Las tierras reales"; Conrad, "The Inca Imperial Expansion"; Wachtel, pp. 66–67; Moore, especially p. 46; Latcham, pp. 6, 32; J. H. Rowe, "Inca Culture", pp. 272–73; and a late synthesis by Espinoza Soriano, *Los Incas*, especially chap. 6.

2. See Chapter 5 on the meaning of *huaca*, for example.

3. Rostworowski, "Testamento," p. 507; and "Relación de Piura," pp. 91–92.

4. AGI/J 404, 405 and 428v.

5. Betanzos, p. 7. See also Valdez de la Torre, p. 50, and Friede, p. 28, on the Indian ignorance of the Spanish language, law, and practice. In ART/CoR, 30-VI-1576, the *escribano* (scribe) admits that the Indians still do not understand the judicial system. See also Chapter 5.

6. Mannheim, especially chap. 3 and pp. 134–35; Polo de Ondegardo, "Del linage," pp. 74, 81.

7. Santillán, pp. 44–45; Latcham, pp. 6, 51–52; Ossio, p. 42; J. H. Rowe, "Inca Culture," p. 273; Valera, pp. 56, 115–16. See also AGI/AL 101; Betanzos, p. 36; and Noejovich, p. 36. In "Poder y riqueza," p. 149, Cock bases a coastal curaca's power on his ownership of lands. I believe his interpretation is a result of reading late sixteenth-century documentation and ascribing the patterns found then to a pre-Spanish contact time.

8. Santillán, p. 45; AGI/P 188, r. 22, 1561, 3; Latcham, p. 10; Acosta,

pp. xv, 299; Polo de Ondegardo, "Informe," p. 133; Cobo, vol. 2, pp. 120–21; Rostworowski, "Dos manuscritos inéditos," pp. 223–24, 229; Betanzos, p. 51. Scholars have found evidence of this tripartite division all over Peru— in the Chillón Valley (Rostworowski, "Plantaciones prehispánicas," p. 181), in Jauja, in Vilcas, in Ica, and near the former Chimu capital of Chan Chan on the north coast (*ACT*, I, 11). But their studies show that the size of these allocations was unequal. The Inca's portion was in some districts as little as 1 percent (Moore, p. 37; Parkerson, p. 114).

9. Murúa, p. 231; and Melo, pp. 275, 285.

10. BAH/Muñoz, A-92, 6; and BM/Add. 13992, 412.

11. Falcón, p. 149. Note that the chroniclers are here referring to the boundaries of administrative domains, not to individual plots that were periodically reassigned.

12. Santillán, p. 17; and Melo, p. 272.

13. Morales; and note 8.

14. Bandera, pp. 494–95, 500–501, 509; BAH/Muñoz, A-92, 7; and Acosta, p. 300.

15. Castro and Ortega Morejón, p. 486. See also BM/Add. 13992, 413v; Baudin, pp. 103–4; Cunow, p. 96; and Trimborn, pp. 579–606, 978–1001. Rostworowski says señores gave personal lands to the Inca ("Plantaciones prehispánicas," p. 181).

16. Polo de Ondegardo, "Del linage," p. 54, and also his statements on pp. 63, 67–68; and "Informe," pp. 133, 141; Castro and Ortega Morejón, p. 488.

17. Falcón, 148–49.

18. On yanaconas, see Chapter 2; on mitimaes, see Ramírez, "Retainers of the Lords," especially table 2, p. 127.

19. Don Pedro Rocxa (or Ocxa) was *ladino*, meaning that he spoke Spanish.

20. AGI/J 461, 1031v.

21. ART/CoP, 31-VIII-1563.

22. ART/CoJR, 3-VI-1564.

23. ANP/DI, l. 6, c. 122, 1649, 28v; AGI/J 461, 1031v; and AL 33. See also Polo de Ondegardo, "Del linage," p. 63. When the Spanish put words in the mouths of natives, words implying ownership (in the Western sense) are used. A Spanish source dating from 1566 states that both curacas and commoners have "their own private lands ["*tierras propias suyas*"]," but I believe in this instance that these were formerly community lands that hispanized Andeans claimed or that the Spanish attributed to them as their own. In the same document, a Spanish bureaucrat said that the curacas were selling and renting community lands *as if* they belonged to themselves (AGI/P 189, r. 11, 1566). Elsewhere, the cacique of Túcume claimed that he had private lands that he inherited from his father and grandfather (AGI/J 461, 1525). I believe his claim is apocryphal and stated in those terms for the benefit of the Spanish visitor and to enhance his chances of having his petition granted.

24. A hanega, or fanega, was a dry measure equal to 2.58 bushels (see Davies, "The Rural Domain," p. 25; see also Ramírez, *Provincial Patriarchs*, appendix 2). The phrase refers to the quantity of seed (5 × 2.58 bushels = 12.9 bushels) that was planted on the land. Note that land was thus measured by the amount of seed needed to plant it.

25. ART/CoO, 6-XII-1560. Wills of commoners make no mention of land either, but this may have been because they had since moved into an urban context. See ART/LC, l. 4, 29-III-1563; and Mata, l. 7, 17-VIII-1563.

26. See Ramírez, "Social Frontiers," on the population bases of a lord's authority and further discussion of this point below.

27. ART/Mata, 22-VI-1565. Note also that lords left subjects to their successors, not lands. The widow of a cacique named don Francisco stated in 1566 that "because of the end and death of her said husband, don Francisco, her son who succeeded to the chiefdomship succeeded in the Indians who he had in his parcialidad [among whom he had kin and Indians] and their service" (AGI/J 461, 1524).

28. ART/CoR, l. 313, 30-VI-1576.

29. But don Garcia Pilco Guaman of Moro may have been one of the few remaining lords not to claim private property. Other wills, the first to mention lands in and of themselves, date from the 1570s. These belong to the lords—those who, as cultural brokers, are most in contact with the European invaders and are first to learn Spanish and to become Christian. In these wills, the lords began to claim specific parcels that were sometimes named, but whose boundaries were usually not designated. See also ART/Notarial, l. 31, 1-VI-1573, 263v, for the will of the cacique of the community of Guaman, as opposed to the wills of commoners and females in 12-VI-1573 and 6-VII-1573. As late as 1617, land was left with retainers. For example, Joan Pololo, principal of Pololo, left "two acequias of corn accompanied by Sebastian," a native born in the community of Lambayeque (ANP/DI, l. 6, c. 122, 1649, 23). Also, Cuneo-Vidal reports that the curaca of Tacna legalized the possession (*compuso*) of lands in 1568, which he probably passed on to his heirs (p. 316). That the natives begin to grasp the idea of exclusive, long-term rights to land as an object about this date is probably due to the increased Spanish presence in the area, as discussed below.

30. ART/CoO, l. 154, exp. 208, 11-VIII-1582.

31. Gama.

32. Rostworowki, "Plantaciones prehispánicas," p. 180.

33. Rostworowski, *Historia del Tahuantinsuyu*, p. 239.

34. Rostworowski, *Curacas y sucesiones*. See also her article, "Testamento," p. 521; and Castro and Ortega Morejón, p. 478.

35. AGI/J 418, 1573, 311v–313. Note that Bandera writes that this was a pre-Inca practice: "It was custom that the subjects of the one who subjugated them had to plant a chacra of corn, coca, and chili peppers and deliver it [the harvest] to him; and in this way there were many who conquered, like the lord [señor] of the Valley of Truxillo, who was called Chimo Capac" (p. 494). This was also true under the Inca. Upon the Inca conquest, as a

sign of submission, the curaca, as the chief executive and representative of the community, agreed to work lands for the imperial state and religion. Castro and Ortega Morejón declare that lords assigned (*señalaron*) lands to the Inca:

> The tribute that they gave to the Ynga in this [Chincha] and the surrounding valleys is this that they called them up by their units [guarangas] and parcialidades each guaranga a chacara . . . and this the commoners worked [*benefiziavan*] . . . and the fruit of these was harvested and was put in storage and from this [part] was carried to Cusco, to Xauxa, or to Pachacama. . . . The chacaras that these [coastal peoples] gave to the Ynga in which they made these fields . . . were given by the lords of each valley from their own. (pp. 479, 486–87)

Thus, as principales and their subjects worked part of their lands for a curaca as a sign of obedience, so the curacas and their subjects (which included those of the principales) worked part of the lands for the state to show reverence and obedience. These indigenous representatives of their communities were allocating the work of their people in recognition of their subordinate status and allegiance. However, implicitly it was expected that should the Inca ever stop being their ruler, the obligation to work (be it on parcels of land or digging irrigation ditches) would end, and the use of the lands and the enjoyment of their products would revert to the community. That some communities hoped to regain independence is indicated by the reports of revolts. See Betanzos, p. 233, on a regional revolt in Saña.

36. AGI/P 188, r. 22, 1561, 4.

37. AGI/J 461, 1524–1524v. For an alternate view, see the introductory statement to Castro and Ortega Morejón, pp. 476–77, 486; and Cock, "Power and Wealth," p. 178. For a situation analogous to that of Peru, see Taylor, on Mexico, "Cacicazgos coloniales," p. 10.

38. Castro and Ortega Morejón, p. 477.

39. Murra, *The Economic Organization*, pp. 29–30; and Guamán Poma de Ayala, *El primer nueva corónica*, vol. 1, pp. 249 [251], and vol. 3, p. 1149 [1159].

40. Later, in colonial times, native peasants based claims to "ownership" on this basis (ANCR/1586–1611, 2–2v). Assuming a generation is 25 years, continual ownership according to this source goes back to 1532. One witness listed ten individuals who had held land before him (14–14v).

41. ANP/DI, l. 6, c. 122, 1649, 6v–8 (for 1631), 19–19v, and 30v; ANCR/1586–1611, 12 and 16v. Barriga (p. 117) says that Indians were leaving land to lords when they died. Here the curacas were representatives and custodians of the community. Torres (May 18, 1959, p. 1) reported an instance when a cacique (curaca) took the land of dead Indians. He probably took land as a trustee and in the name of the community.

42. See Bastein, p. 110, for a late sixteenth-century example of resource sharing in Bolivia.

43. AGI/J 1063, no. 3, 1570, 5v; and Polo de Ondegardo, "Del linage," p. 56. In AGI/AL 28, 6v, the Spanish regulate this relationship. See also

Cock, "Power and Wealth," pp. 174–75, regarding lands of Hiço shared by two polities; AGI/AL 92; and ANCR/1586–1611, 24, on resource sharing and the establishment of encomiendas, which split communities. Reducciones may explain land disputes between native communities (e.g., AGI/J 457, 829; between Chuspo and Sinto, 1566). Resource sharing was called "customary" by the middle of the seventeenth century (ANP/DI, l. 6, c. 122, 1649, 19–19v).

44. ACMS/1654–1765, 17–17v; AGI/J 461, 1521. Indian renters of land still paid rents in kind to other natives in the eighteenth century (ANP/Tributos, l. 2, c. 25, 1734, 2).

45. See Chapter 2; Ramírez, "Social Frontiers," on resource sharing; ANP/Aguas, 3.3.18.68; and Golte, mentioned by Rostworowski, "Plantaciones prehispánicas," p. 186.

46. Murra, "Las etnocategorías." For the original discussion of "raw" and "cooked," see Lévi-Strauss.

47. Latcham, pp. 31, 38–39. Crudo and cocido also underlie the distinction between ore and metal (silver) money discussed by Harris.

48. Salomon, *Native Lords*, p. 161; see also Chapter 5.

49. Topic, p. 155; Moseley, "Introduction," pp. 11, 22; AAT/Causas, 1737; Salomon, "Ancestor Cults," p. 161. Irrigation had not reached its potential, because rivers in the sixteenth century, unlike today, still discharged to the sea year round, meaning that excess water was available that was not being used for irrigation purposes.

50. Domain as used here refers to the administrative or population unit the curaca governed, which on the coast was confirmed by the Inca at the time of this conquest. See Ramírez, "The Inca Conquest."

51. Murra, *The Economic Organization*, p. 29, on *llacta* and the identity of land with kinship; also Ossio, on the same.

52. AGI/P 97, r. 4, [1569], 16v, for Chérrepe in 1564; Rostworowski, "Nuevos aportes," p. 32; and *Historia del Tahuantinsuyu*, p. 241.

53. Angulo, p. 286.

54. ANP/Títulos, l. 23, c. 611, 1783; Keith, "Origins of the Hacienda System," pp. 60, 67; Rostworowski, "Mercaderes," p. 151; "Ruinas de Concón," pp. 315–26; and "Las etnías," p. 52; also AGI/AL 100, [1646], 30; and ACMS/1778.

55. Garcilaso de la Vega, vol. 2, p. 8; Cobo, vol. 2, p. 268; Valencia Espinoza, pp. 7, 70; ART/ICompa, 11-XII-1787; ANCR/1787-1788; Davies, "The Rural Domain," p. 57; Rostworowski, "Nuevos aportes," pp. 31–32; *Historia del Tahuantinsuyu*, p. 246; and Reyeros, p. 831. Latcham, p. 12, equates a topu with a fanega of land for corn planting, "although the hanega is reckoned as one and a half times those of Spain." See also Murra, "Derechos a las tierras," pp. 280–81, on the measurement of potato lands.

56. ANCR/Polo, 5-III-1748; and 1756, 2 and 4v; ART/Palacios, 6-III-1611; and ANP/DI, l. 6, c. 122, 1649. In Tacna, lands were also described by the number of grape vines planted on them (Cuneo-Vidal, p. 317).

57. Trimborn, p. 52, quoting Kosok; Morales; and Ramírez, "The Inca Conquest."

58. Ramírez, "The Inca Conquest"; Cieza de León, *The Travels*, pp. 135, 220, 210, 409, and "El señorio," pp. 83–84; Castro and Ortega Morejón, p. 478; Polo de Ondegardo, "Informe," p. 131; and "Del linage," pp. 56, 79; Bandera, p. 500; Betanzos, p. 150; Guamán Poma de Ayala, *El primer nueva corónica*, vol. 3, p. 1074 [1024]; Falcón, pp. 148; Murúa, p. 231 and "Relación de Piura," p. 96. Rostworowski, "El señorio de Changuco," p. 103, shows that water (rivers and ocean) served as boundaries of the community of Guaman. She also mentions that the same is true for Huanuco ("Mercaderes," p. 124). See also Murúa, p. 231, who says that jurisdiction is established "according to the course of the rivers," and Netherly, "The Management."

59. Betanzos, p. 33.

60. Polo de Ondegardo, "Del linage," pp. 61, 66; Cobo, vol. 2, pp. 122; Guamán Poma de Ayala, *El primer nueva corónica*, vol. 1, p. 189 [191]; and Valdes de la Torre, p. 77. See the 1579 will in Rostworowski, "Dos manuscritos inéditos," p. 225, where lands are not chacaras. It is also interesting to note that most lists of mercedes from the Inca do not mention land conspicuously, e.g., Bandera, pp. 494, 501, 504; "Relación anónima," p. 295; Betanzos, pp. 57, 159, 179; and Murúa, p. 172. See also Murra's discussion of "Incas by privilege" in *The Economic Organization*, p. 36. Moore (pp. 23–24) states that lands were enjoyed by a grantee and his descendants in perpetuity. The same point is made in 1561 by Polo de Ondegardo in "Informe," p. 141, and AGI/P 188, r. 22, 1561, 4.

61. Guamán Poma de Ayala, *El primer nueva corónica*, vol. 2, p. 852 [866]; Melo, p. 272; and Betanzos, p. 90. See also Julien, p. 198.

62. Jiménez de las Espada, "Relación de Piura," vol. 2, p. 240; Wachtel, p. 68; Rostworowski, "Breves notas," pp. 209–10, and "Las etnías," p. 39. See also Moore, p. 18. For a different view based on unpublished material, see footnote 20 of Polo de Ondegardo, "Del linage," p. 92. Rostworowski also alludes to this fact in *Curacas y sucesiones*, p. 8. Pease ("La noción de propiedad," pp. 5–6) and I are not convinced that the highland and coastal economic systems, especially in regard to rights to land, are entirely different.

63. Jiménez de la Espada, vol. 1, p. lxvii.

64. AGI/P 189, r. 11, 1566.

65. Betanzos (p. 60) and Polo de Ondegardo ("Del linage," p. 49) use the word *alquiler* (to rent) to refer to soldiers in the Inca armies. Guamán Poma de Ayala hints at the precontact meaning of *alquiler* when he reports that Indians "eat and drink instead of [receiving] payment" (*El primer nueva corónica*, vol. 1, p. 251 [253]).

66. Sahlins, especially p. 125. See Betanzos, pp. 60 and 72–73, on chicha and ceremonial visiting. Another source that clearly refutes private ownership of property in the northern valleys is Cuenca's ordinances of 1566, which in part read:

> Item, because the lands and waters of the communities belong to their indigenous members and not to the cacique or lords who cannot and should

not have asked for nor taken from individual Indians from ayllus and parcialidades tribute [*terrasgo*] for [use of] the lands that the individual Indians work for themselves and pay to be given water . . . it is ordered and commanded that from this moment on the said caciques and lords cannot ask for anything. (AGI/P 189, r. 11, 1566, 13–13v)

If the curaca did not own the lands, he could neither "sell" them (which would have been impossible in a nonmarket economy such as the one that existed before 1532) nor "rent" them (in the Western sense). Another primary source that says much the same thing deals with Collique (near Lima) (see BNP/A185, 12).

67. Gama, pp. 268–70; Polo de Ondegardo, "Del linage," pp. 70–71; AGI/J 460, 377v; and "Relación anónima," p. 292.

68. This phrase is taken from the title of a chapter by Neale on the meaning of land in precolonial India. I am indebted to my colleague and friend Gregory Kozlowski for bringing it to my attention.

69. Díaz Rementería, pp. 19, 54; and Betanzos, pp. 93, 96.

70. Díaz Rementería, pp. 19, 54; and Ramírez, "Social Frontiers."

71. Betanzos, p. 288; AGI/P 188, r. 22, 1561, 6; and Cobo, vol. 2, p. 121. See the description by Castro and Ortega Morejón, pp. 478–79.

72. Betanzos, pp. 72–73. Regardless of the term or terms used to describe the results, what is evident here is an operating system of lifelong mutual obligations and responsibilities between the lords and their peoples.

73. Ulloa Sotomayor, p. 406. See also Noejovich, p. 39.

74. Latcham, pp. 40, 64; Pease, "La noción de propiedad," p. 11; AGI/J 461, 1395v; ANP/DI, l. 19, c. 483, 1793, 3v; and l. 6, c. 122, 1649, 9v, for a will dated 1629 of a commoner of Lambayeque. See also Freidel, p. 127, for a similar practice among the Maya; Rostworowski, "Las etnías," p. 82, for Canta; and Millon, p. 698, regarding a Mexican community where trees were owned.

75. ANCR/1586–1611; ANP/DI, l. 6, c. 122, 1649, 13v, for 1629; and Rostworowski, "Plantaciones prehispánicas," p. 182. Later and elsewhere, this was held among natives of colonial times (ANP/DI, l. 6, c. 122, 1649, 14v). See also Chapter 5.

76. AGI/J 1063, no. 3, 1570, 2v–3; P 108, r. 7, 40; and AL 201, 1633.

77. AGI/J 418, 1573, 252.

78. See note 39.

79. Recall that *chacaras* referred to planted crops, not the land, according to the Indians' understanding. The plants were cocido. Estancias on unplanted, naturally occurring pastures were crudo, and open to all. Ramírez, "Land Tenure," chap. 1.

80. There is no general agreement on the exact date of the founding of Trujillo. See Cabero, and also Vargas Ugarte, "Fragmento," for example.

81. ART/Salinas, 1539, 28; and Betanzos, pp. 74, 169, 296.

82. ASFL/Reg. 9, no. 2, ms. 26, 1647, for 1595.

83. BAH/9-4664; and Zurkalowski, p. 256.

84. Borah.

85. ART/Salinas, 1539, 28; AGI/J 418, 1573, 462, for 1539; Busto, pp. 327–64.

86. AFA/l. 1, c. 18, for Ucupe *"por ser tierras de pastoreo no tienen limites precisos,"* in 1688.

87. ART/LC, 21-IV-1559, 50–53v; Mata, 25-IX-1562.

88. AFA/l. 1, c. 2.

89. ASFL/Reg. 9, no. 2, ms. 26, 1647, 43.

90. As I show in "The Inca Conquest," the lord often took the name of his administrative jurisdiction and domain, so the lord's name and the toponym that was associated with his administrative center were often one and the same. See also ANCR/1586–1611, 18–18v.

91. AGI/J 459, 3031; ART/LC, 1591 [1561].

92. ART/Mata, 29-IV-1565.

93. ASFL/Reg. 9, no. 2, ms. 26, 1647, for 1595.

94. ART/Mata, 29-IV-1565.

95. AGI/J 460, 336–336v; ART/CoP, l. 280, exp. 3611, 31-VII-1583, 3.

96. ART/CaO, 1557–1566; and AGI/J 457, 1149.

97. AGI/J 461, 1441–41v, 1528, 1559; BCH/1555; and ART/Reyes, 1561; Mata, 19-II-1562; and CoO, 30-I-1564.

98. ART/Mata, 9-II-1562 and 2-V-1562; See also ART/CoP, l. 280, c. 3611, 31-VII-1583; and Mata, 29-IV-1565.

99. Vassberg, "Concerning Pigs," pp. 51–52; *La venta de tierras baldías*; and Lockhart, *Men of Cajamarca*, pp. 27–31, especially table 3, p. 28.

100. Weeks, p. 62; BAH/ML, t. 21, 191–92; ANP/RA, l. 27, c. 95, 1610, 17v; AFA/l. 1, c. 8 and c. 18, 1v.

101. ANP/RA, l. 27, c. 95, 1610, 17v–18.

102. Polo de Ondegardo, "Del linage," pp. 69–70.

103. AGI/J 461, 1441–41v; P 189, r. 11, 1566.

104. AGI/AL 92; ANCR/1586–1611; See also ANP/Tributos, l. 2, c. 25, 1734, for a later example.

105. AGI/J 461, 1528, 1554, and 1559.

106. ART/CoO, l. 156, c. 65, 12-VI-1566.

107. ART/Mata, 1592; ANCR/Alvarez, 2-V-1663; Cabero, vol. 1, no. 2, pp. 345, 372.

108. ART/LC, 1560.

109. ART/1595, 258v–59, 265. Note that nothing is said about land.

110. ART/CoO, 27-VII-1580.

111. Arroyo, p. 24.

112. ART/LC, 7-X-1560.

113. Mellafe reaches the same conclusions in "The Importance of Migration," p. 25, for the first century. See also *ACT*, III, 1602, 174.

114. BAH/Muñoz, A110, 62–62v, for 1541; *ACT*, II, 277–78, for 1570; Lissón y Chaves, p. 76.

115. *ACT*, I, 202–3; ART/CoO, l. 147, exp. 21, 11-IX-1562.

116. This is a clear case where Spanish-attributed ownership of the land

is repudiated or contradicted by the natives (AGI/J 460, 458; see also BCH, 1555, on land grants by the Audiencia in Chérrepe).

117. AFA/l. 1, c. 19, 94v–96; Angulo, pp. 297–98.

118. See, for example, ART/Mata, 29-II-1564 and 17-II-1565.

119. AGI/J 457, 1253; P 189, r. 11, 1566; ART/Mata, no. 897, 1595, 228v–30v; ANP/R, l. 22, c. 57, 1611, 118–118v.

120. ART/LC, 16-V-1564; Mata, 4-V-1565; see also Keith, "Origins of the Hacienda System," p. 124; and ART/LC, 1559.

121. A condition to the 1576 encomienda grant of Lambayeque reads: "And with the condition that within the domain and limits of the said encomienda [the grantee] cannot have land holdings or mills[;] they can raise cattle as long as [the animals] do no harm to the Indians." Note that the Spanish were giving a grant of the right to labor and to collect tribute a territorial dimension (such as occurred in Spain during the reconquest of the peninsula). AGI/P 113, r. 8, 1565, 28–28v.

122. See also AAL/Apel Truj, 2-III, 1632; ART/Palacios, 1579; ASFL/Reg. 9, no. 2, ms. 8, 1591; ART/Mata, 5-IX-1562; 1565; 1588.

123. ART/Mata, 1580; CoO, 30-IX-1582.

124. Don Pedro also allowed Pedro de Morales to establish an estancia on this land (ART/CoR, 30-VI-1576).

125. ART/CoP, l. 280, exp. 3612, 30-X-1583, 1–2.

126. AAT/Diezmos, 1588, 9.

127. Polo de Ondegardo, "Informe," p. 144; Rostworowski, "Las etnías," p. 39.

128. *ACT*, II, 16–17.

129. BCH, 1555.

130. Some Indians learned faster than others (AGI/J 461, 1525).

131. ANP/DI, l. 6, c. 122, 1649, 28v; AGI/J 461, 1031v; AL 33. See also Polo de Ondegardo, "Del linage," p. 63.

132. AGI/J 418, 1573, 459–459v, for 1539; AL 92.

133. AGI/J 461, 1395v.

134. AGI/J 461, 1395v, 1529, 1531, 1558v–59, 1562v–63, and 1570v–71.

135. AGI/J 461, 1528, 1571v, and 1581.

136. AGI/J 461, 1553–53v. Or it may be because of Cuenca's reduction; see also J 457, 829, for another case; and J 458, 1898, over lands.

137. AGI/J 461, 1399v.

138. ART/CoR, 30-VI-1576.

139. ART/CoO, 30-IX-1582; see also AGI/P 189, r. 11, 1566; *ACT*, II, 3–7.

140. AGI/J 461, 1399v.

141. AGI/J 460, 429v.

142. AGI/J 456, 419.

143. AGI/J 461, 1563v–64.

144. AGI/J 461, 1515–15v.

145. Ramírez, "Chérrepe en 1572"; AGI/J 455, 1148; and Chapter 2.

146. Ramírez, *Provincial Patriarchs*, p. 74.

147. A decree issued in 1573 (although probably implemented much

later) granted Indian communities an *"exido"* of one league radius around their new settlements (Valdez de la Torre, p. 67).

148. See also ART/CoO, l. 157, c. 301, 14-XII-1595, on the effect of the reducción on communities at higher elevations. Also Ramírez, "Chérrepe en 1572."

149. ANCR/1586–1611, and 1756, 8.

150. Ramírez, *Provincial Patriarchs*, pp. 30–32.

151. AGI/P 189, r. 11, 1566. See, for example, OCIL/Monsefú, P. 110, 5345. Such sales were later annulled because commoners had no legal right to sell land. See also OCIL/Reque, p. 89, and ANCR/Mendoça, 1633, where one Spaniard sold another the usufruct and "benefit that I have of a plot of alfalfa that I have planted on lands of the Indians and cacique of Mocupe." Other examples of Indians selling the dominio util are in AFA/l. 2, c. 4, 1712; and ANP/Histórico, 1075, 1790, 45v.

152. Sales of estancias show that the price included the cattle and the right to mitayo shepherds. Sometimes corrals and buildings are included; land is not. See ART/CoO, l. 154, exp. 208, 11-VIII-1582, 9; 4-XII-1596; ANP/RA, l. 123, c. 443, 1642, 106v–107.

153. AGI/P 187, r. 20, 67v, for 1556.

154. Ramírez, *Provincial Patriarchs*; ART/IO, 18-X-1788, especially 1–9; AGI/AL 100 [1646]; ASFL/Reg. 9, no. 2, ms. 26, 1647, 114. In contrast, a few officials supported the natives' claims. See, for example, BNP/C2195, 1756, 66 and 104; ANCR/1766; and ANP/DI, l. 19, c. 483, 1793, 5, 10, and 22. On the Spanish precedent on this occupation or "squatting," see Herr, especially p. 19.

155. AGI/J 461, 1528; ART/CoO, l. 157, c. 301, 14-XII-1595, 10; Mata, 1580.

156. AFA/l. 1, c. 2; ART/CoAG, 20-VII-1607.

157. See also Guamán Poma de Ayala, who condemns this practice in general (*El primer nueva corónica*, vol. 3, p. 944 [958]).

158. *ACT*, II, 112, for 31-III-1568.

159. ANP/RA, l. 194, 1676, 139.

160. AGI/J 457, 1147v–48; ANP/Aguas, 3-3-6-17, 1767, 8v; Sevilla Exebio, 2–3.

161. ANP/Tributos, l. 2, c. 25, 1734.

162. ANP/RA, l. 148, c. 1222, 176, 3.

163. AGI/E 511A, 1648, 7; AAT/Causa, 1789, 1 and 3v.

164. ART/RHJComp, 1-IX-1787; ANP/DI, l. 17, c. 417, 1786, 3v–4.

165. AGI/P 189, r. 11, 1566.

166. OCIL/Reque, p. 99. On the regulations on such sales, see Valdez de la Torre, p. 81.

167. AGI/E 534A, 768v; ANP/DI, l. 24, c. 687, 1606.

168. BAH/ML, t. 97, 66.

169. Ibid., 679–84.

170. English corsairs were an effective threat to the north coast as early as 1586.

171. For a detailed and more complete discussion of the *visitas* and their socioeconomic consequences, see Ramírez, *Provincial Patriarchs*.

172. Brüning, Facsículo 3, p. 16.

173. ASFL/Reg. 9, no. 2, ms. 26, 1647, 43–44; AGI/IG 1660; Torres, 20-V-1959, pp. 6, 8; AFA/l. 1, c. 2; l. 19, 91v.

174. AAL/Apel Truj, 2-III, 1663; ASFT/B, 4-VIII-1595, 30-X-1596, 20-VII-1600, 30-X-1600, 26-IV-1609, 2-I-1613.

175. ART/Martinez de Escobar, 1609; Palacios, 1579.

176. ANP/Histórico 1075, 1790, 45v; RA, l. 44, 1619, 109, for the 1590s.

177. Ramírez, *Provincial Patriarchs*, appendix 3.

178. AGI/AL 132, l-IV, 3, for 1594.

179. ANCR/1595.

180. McBride, p. iv.

181. Valdez de la Torre, p. 50; Friede, p. 28; Gibson, p. 296.

182. He was subsequently acquitted in Spain of wrongdoing (AGI/E 511 and 1199).

183. ART/ICompa, 16-II-1785; according to the Conde de Chichon, in Los Reyes 25-IX-1634.

184. Torres, 20-V-1959, p. 1.

185. AGI/AL 100, [1646], 32.

186. AGI/AL 100, [1646], 30–31 and 33v.

187. ASFL/Reg. 9, no. 2, ms. 19; AGI/IG 1660.

188. Torres, 12-V-1959, p. 3.

189. AGI/AL 100, [1646].

190. ANP/DI, l. 6, c. 122, 1649, 5.

191. AGI/IG 1662; ANP/RA, l. 194, 1676, 138.

192. AGI/AL 100, [1646], 68.

193. ART/CoAguas, 26-IV-1768.

194. AGI/AL 100, [1646], 67–69.

195. Brüning, Facsículo III, pp. 24–27.

196. AGI/AL 100, [1646], 15; León Barandiarán, *Tradiciones Lambayecanos*, p. 228.

197. AGI/AL 100, [1646] 13–15v.

198. ART/I, l. 1, 22-II-1785; AGI/IG 1660; AL 100.

199. Torres, 11-V-1959, p. 1; 14-V-1959, p. 1; 16-V-1959, p. 1.

200. ART/ICompa, 24-V-1795; Torres, 11-V-1959, p. 3.

201. ASFL/Reg. 9, no. 2, ms. 24; ANCR/1727; 1787-1788, 149. See also ANP/Tributos, l. 2, c. 25, 1734, 4–4v.

202. ACMS/1813, 13v; AFA/l. 2, c. 11, 14v; ANCR/Herrera, 11-X-1718; 1740, 45; Comisión del estatuto, pp. 90, 96, 101.

203. ANP/DI, l. 12, c. 295, 1756–58, 1–2v.

204. ART/IO, 18-X-1788, 62v. Slaves became increasingly expensive after the Porto Belo fair ceased to be a major entrepôt and after the development of the sugar industry in the Caribbean offered a more convenient and ready market for the recent African arrivals.

205. Brüning, Facsículo III, p. 16; Ramírez, *Provincial Patriarchs*.

206. ANCR/Tumán, 1782–83 and 1812; AFA/Mocupe, 13–14; ART/CoAG, 28-IV-1768.

207. ASFL/Reg. 9, no. 2, ms. 26, 1647.

208. ANCR/1782–1783.

209. ANP/Títulos, l. 23, c. 611, 1783, 44.

210. BAH/ML, t. 112, 280v–281; ART/IAG, 22-II-1765.

211. BAH/ML, t. 112, 280v–281.

212. Ecclesiastical censuses taken for another purpose were more complete; they counted all "souls."

213. BP/2817, 5.

214. BP/2717, 7.

215. Vollmer, p. 252. Some of the increase may have been due to Indians and blacks passing as mestizos and castas.

216. This was not the first land reform in the area. A previous one was effected by Corregidor O'Kelly. In 1775 he gave the parcialidad de yanaconas land (a parcel called "La Pampilla" on the road between Chiclayo and Lambayeque) belonging to Collique (ART/RHJComp, 20-I-1788; OCIL/Reque, p. 21).

217. ART/IAG, 22-II-1785.

218. This may have been 445 fanegadas de sembradura de indios.

219. ANP/Títulos, l. 23, c. 611, 1783, 37–45.

220. AFA/San Luis, 190–190v and 200.

221. OCIL/Reque, 30v; AGI/AL 996, 1780, 16–18v.

222. AFA/San Luis, 190.

223. ANP/RA, l. 148, c. 1222, 1763, 28; SG, 1782–1792, 11v.

224. ANCR/1787–1788, 145v.

225. These reforms reflected the state's move to free and rationalize the economy and encourage individuals to pursue their own self-interest. See MacLachlan, pp. 75–80, 115. MacLachlan states that Bernardo Ward and José del Campillo y Cossío had advocated providing natives with land and assistance and liberating them from negative and initiative-stifling supervision. The Ordenance of Intendants, article 61, authorized the compensated expropriation of uncultivated private holdings and distribution of royal land to Indians and others "for their own profit." This likewise parallels the on-again-off-again trend in Spain to sell the *tierras baldías* (common pastures) and reform the country according to liberal principles. See Herr, in general, and especially pp. 3, 19–21, 42–44, and 72–77.

226. ANP/Tierras, l. 5, c. 37, 1811–1819, 65–66v.

227. ANP/RA, l. 283, c. 2511, 1789, 8v; DI, l. 19, c. 483, 1793; OCIL/Ferreñafe, 1970, 79–80; AAT/Causa, 1664.

Chapter 4

1. Lockhart, *Men of Cajamarca*, pp. 80–81. TePaske and Klein provide a macroeconomic picture of the hoarde by establishing the amount of bullion officially shipped back to the royal coffers of Spain. On early encomendero investment, see Varón Gabai and Pieter Jacobs.

2. Escobedo Mansilla; Keith, "The Encomienda"; Zurkalowski; Rostworowski, "La tasa ordenada" and "La tasa Toledana"; Hampe Martínez, "Notas sobre población"; Zevallos Quiñones, "La ropa de tributo"; and Rio.

3. On negotiated tribute, see Assadourian, "La renta," pp. 111–12, 133.

4. AGI/AL 167, 1648; Murra, "The Mit'a Obligations," pp. 237–39, 257; and *ACT*, I, 11. Note that "raw" items also included hunted creatures or items neither cultivated nor manufactured by human labor. See also Chapter 3.

5. For the classic article on the importance of cloth in the precontact Inca state, see Murra, "Cloth."

6. Murra, "The Mit'a Obligations," p. 240–43; Cieza de León, *The Travels*, p. 241; AGI/P 188, r. 22, 1561, 5v, 6v; BAH/Muñoz, A92, 5v, 9v, and 17–18; Falcón, pp. 151–53, 159, 162; Polo de Ondegardo, "Del linage," pp. 60, 64; BM/Add. 13992, 413v; Betanzos, pp. 96, 164–65; Keatinge; *ACT*, I, 11; AGI/J 1063, no. 3, 1570, 10. In "La organización económica," I differ from the chroniclers who make the relationship between craftsmen and the Inca sound as if it was direct. Note that Assadourian ("Dominio colonial," p. 7) does not believe that the Inca made efforts to overcome ethnic identities. This may have been partially due to lack of time rather than lack of will. The Inca often established ties of kinship by marrying local women. See Ramírez, "De pescadores."

7. The term "guancabamba" was probably meant to refer to Guayna Capac ("Guaynacaba" in text) (Gama, p. 226).

8. My reading of the document makes me believe that this cacique principal was originally subordinate to the curaca of Jayanca. He assumed that title when Jayanca was split into two encomiendas, which therefore made him a cacique in his own right—at least in the Spanish untrained, unknowing, and misunderstanding eyes.

9. AGI/J 1063, no. 3, 1570, 9–9v. This section of the original document is published; see Gama (pp. 34–35) for a version with slightly different wording.

10. BAH/Muñoz, A92, 5v and 7. See also Murra, "The Mit'a Obligations," pp. 240–41.

11. Polo de Ondegardo, "Del linage," pp. 54, 60, 63, 66, 89; AGI/P 188, r. 22, 1561, 4 and 10; Santillán, p. 66; Falcón, pp. 154–56; BM/Add. 13992, 413v; and BAH/Muñoz, A92, 7v.

12. Santillán, p. 38; AGI/J 460, 377v; J 461, 1256; and J 462, 1860v; Ramírez, "The Cajamarca Connection"; and Rostworowski, "Patronyms." Carrera also mentions many more Mochica-speaking groups in these same northern highlands that presumably existed before the Spanish invasion. I have a hunch that chroniclers' statements regarding restricted travel may have reflected better the conditions at the time they wrote than the precontact reality. Perhaps the Spanish did more to restrict indigenous travel by the 1570s than the Incas had before 1532.

13. Falcón, p. 162; Cieza de León, "El señorio," p. 65, and *The Travels*, p. 241; AGI/P 188, r. 22, 1561, 21v; AGI/J 1063, no. 3, 1570, 9–9v; and Parkerson, p. 116.

14. BM/Add. 13992, 413v; Castro and Ortega Morejón, p. 486; BAH/ Muñoz, A92, 7v; AGI/P 188, r. 22, 1561, 3, 4, and 11v; Falcón, pp. 154–56, 159; and Santillán, p. 38.

15. *ACT*, I, 11; AGI/P 188, r. 22, 1561, 3, 10–11v and 13–13v; BAH/ Muñoz, A92, 7–7v; Ramírez, "Ethnohistorical"; and Santillán, p. 41.

16. Betanzos, p. 97; Guamán Poma de Ayala, *El primer nueva corónica*, vol. 1, p. 338 [340]; Santillán, p. 41; BP/2846, 262; BAH/Muñoz, A92, 5v, 7 and 9–10. There were other authors who for political or personal reasons said the tribute exactions of the Spanish were less than under the Inca (AGI/P 188, r. 22, 1561, 8).

17. AGI/P 188, r. 22, 1561, 5–6 and 8; BP/2846, 262; Falcón, pp. 154, 161; BAH/Muñoz, A92, 5v, 9v, and 17–17v; and Santillán, p. 41.

18. BAH/Muñoz, A92, 9v; and Santillán, 1927, p. 39. For other examples, see Murra on the Chupaychu, where service is not so light ("The Mit'a Obligations," pp. 240–41); Cock, "The Lord's Control"; and Zuidema, "Inca Cosmos."

19. Falcón, pp. 155, 162; Keith, "The Encomienda," p. 144; BAH/Muñoz, A92, 7–7v and 9; AGI/J 1063, no. 3, 1570, 10; and Santillán, p. 39.

20. Keith, "The Encomienda," p. 237. For examples of Spaniards who understood the principals of reciprocity and redistribution, see Trelles Aséstegui; Platt; and Stern, "The Rise and Fall."

21. There were exceptions, as in the case of Martínez Vegazo mentioned above. Zurkalowski, p. 267; Santillán, p. 66; BAH/Muñoz, A112, no. 132, 1550, 188; AGI/P 188, r. 22, 1561, 15; P 231, no. 7, r. 14, 2; Malaga Medina, "El Virrey," p. 2; and Loredo, *Los repartos*, p. 255.

22. AGI/J 1063, no. 3, 1570, 10.

23. All quantities expressed in the various types of pesos used in the sixteenth century are converted to patacones, or pesos of 8 reales each, and are shown in parentheses for the sake of consistency and comparison. Conversions are based on Ramírez, *Provincial Patriarchs*, appendix 1 and appendix 4, p. 388, as applicable.

24. Busto, pp. 325, 384. Espinoza Soriano ("El primer informe," p. 20) states that the Cajamarquinos declared that they had given Verdugo four plates or sheets (*planchas*) of silver per day from 1535 to 1549, plus fine woolen cloth, corn, chili peppers, coca, partridge, hens, sandals, llamas, and yanaconas.

25. Gama, p. 226.

26. ART/Vega, l. 71, 13-IX-1578, 5; Falcón, p. 162; and Santillán, pp. 60, 63. Note that there are two Guayobamba (or Gallobamba) rivers shown on the map: one in Jaen that, based on the reputation of the area, is the most likely spot for panning gold, and one that as a tributary of the Chicama River is easily accessible to residents of both coast and highlands but has no reputation as a source of gold.

27. AGI/P 117, no. 1, r. 7, 2; Keith, "The Encomienda," p. 136; and Busto, p. 337.

28. Polo, "Informe," p. 157; Cieza de León, *The Travels*, p. 410; AGI/P 188, r. 22, 1561, 22v; ART/LC, 1558; and Keith, "The Encomienda," p. 139.

29. Busto, pp. 364–65; Malaga Medina, "El Virrey," p. 4; AGI/J 418, 1573, 324v; Rostworowski, *Curacas y sucesiones*, p. 17; BAH/Muñoz, A112, no. 1321, 1550, 188–188v; and Lissón y Chaves, vol. 1, pp. 190–206, especially 192.

30. Malaga Medina, "El Virrey," p. 601, and *Reducciones Toledanas*, pp. 137–38; Assadourian, "Dominio colonial," p. 10; Zevallos Quiñones, "La ropa de tributo," pp. 109–11; Lissón y Chaves, vol. 1, p. 192; AGI/P 231, no. 7, r. 14, 2; Espinoza Soriano, "El primer informe," p. 7; Levillier, *Gobernantes*, vol. 3, pp. 120–25; and Escobedo Mansilla, p. 177.

31. Malaga Medina, "El Virrey," pp. 601–2.

32. Assadourian, "La renta de la encomienda," p. 113; Escobedo Mansilla, pp. 16–17, 35–37; Lissón y Chaves, vol. 1, p. 63; and Ramírez, *Provincial Patriarchs*, chap. 3.

33. Assadourian, "La renta de la encomienda," p. 115.

34. Rostworowski, "La tasa"; Hampe Martínez, "Notas sobre población," p. 67, for the smaller part of Cajamarca in 1550; Escobedo Mansilla, p. 310–16; Zevallos Quiñones, "La ropa de tributo," p. 122; Malaga Medina, "El Virrey," pp. 8, 604; and Romero, p. 213.

35. Ramírez, "Ethnohistorical."

36. Espinoza Soriano, "El primer informe," pp. 17, 34, 35; Gama, p. 269; Loredo, "El reparto," pp. 269, 272; and ART/LC, 1558. Murra, "The Mit'a Obligations," shows that the Chupaychu Indians were even more mobile.

37. Rostworowski, "La tasa," pp. 93–94; or BAH/9-4664, 26–27.

38. ART/LC, 1558; and Robinson.

39. Spalding, *Huarochirí*, p. 160, says La Gasca ratified the existing volume of goods and labor to that which the encomenderos were already using as a means to keep the peace. Loredo ("El reparto," pp. 83–84) says that La Gasca did not try to decrease the tribute of the communities. La Gasca himself claimed, in a letter to the Council of the Indies in 1549, that the review of tribute that he ordered reduced tribute by one-third (CDIHE, vol. 50, p. 70). This claim may have been to assuage crown concerns for the welfare of its native vassals. See also Assadourian, "La renta de la encomienda," pp. 119–20; and Hampe Martínez, *Don Pedro de la Gasca*, pp. 131–38.

40. BAH/Muñoz, A112, no. 1321, 188. Hampe Martínez points out that many loyal veterans of the civil wars did not receive encomiendas, pensions, or yanaconas as rewards. Many waited, hoping to receive an award should any of the above grantees die or lose their concession (*Don Pedro de la Gasca*, pp. 127–31).

41. Escobedo Mansilla, p. 121; Jacome, p. 63; and Assadourian, "La renta de la encomienda," pp. 126–28; Hampe Martínez, *Don Pedro de la Gasca*, p. 165.

42. Malaga Medina, "El Virrey," p. 6; *Reducciones Toledanas*, p. 141; Escobedo Mansilla, p. 46; Hampe Martínez, *Don Pedro de la Gasca*, pp. 156–66; and AGI/AL 123.

43. Hampe Martínez, "Notas sobre población," p. 68.

44. Assadourian, "La Renta," p. 122; Malaga Medina, *Reducciones Toledanas*, p. 141. Table 9, however, shows that the monetary value of twelve of the fifteen communities listed increased in the inspections of the 1550s.

Note that Guambos is an ambiguous case. Could this be in part because only marketable commodities (as opposed to services) were included in the 1548 figures?

45. See Malaga Medina, "El Virrey," pp. 8, 11, for a discussion of this point. Torre Revello, vol. 8, p. 297. Note Escobedo Mansilla's caution on the problems with the tribute figures in this paragraph (p. 50) and alternative figures for 1548, presented in Hampe Martínez, *Don Pedro de la Gasca,* pp. 137–38.

46. For an example of these royal mandates, see the 1559 royal order from Gante to (1) collect information on tribute paid to the Incas and to the crown, (2) reduce all the goods and services to gold pesos (which as noted above had already been allowed in one case for the community of Huamachuco), (3) standardize the definition of tribute payer, (4) determine who was exempt from paying tribute, (5) fix the dates of payment, and (6) determine who owned land (Malaga Medina, "El Virrey," pp. 9–10). See also Assadourian, "La renta de la encomienda," pp. 122–23.

47. Escobedo Mansilla, pp. 52–54, 67; ART/LC, 1558; Ramírez, "Chérrepe en 1572"; and Assadourian, "Dominio colonial," p. 11, as the source of the quote by the Conde de Nieva near the start of the paragraph. Assadourian did not mention his primary source for the Conde de Nieva's words.

48. Apparently, placer mining of gold in the river had ended.

49. AGI/J 430, 1559, 13, 16, 29. Another document states that the total value of the Guambos in 1556 was 5,000 pesos (9,347 patacones 3 reales) (AGI/P 187, r. 20, 61).

50. Malaga Medina, "El Virrey," p. 8.

51. AGI/J 416, 1573, 210.

52. The fact that so much cloth was directly produced by the coastal communities under the direction of the curaca explains why there were no Spanish-owned and -organized *obrajes* (textile mills) on the coast in the sixteenth century (AGI/P 189, r. 11, [1566]).

53. AGI/AL 92, 1566.

54. Escobedo Mansilla, p. 49; Espinoza Soriano, "El primer informe," p. 3.

55. ART/CoO, 22-VIII-1570; AGI/J 455, 1687; J 458, 1551; P 189, r. 11, 1566; and Hampe Martínez, "Notas sobre población," p. 68.

56. ART/CoO, 22-VIII-1570; AGI/J 457, 995v and 1149v–50; J 461, 930–30v and 1121; and Remy Simatovic, "Tasas tributarias." Other estimates of Cajamarca's tribute were between 2 pesos 2 tomines (4 patacones 6 reales) and 3 pesos 2 tomines (6 patacones 7 reales) (AGI/J 461, 1020v, 1046v, 1048, 1052, 1053v).

57. BNP/A157, 1570, 140–140v; AGI/J 457, 701v. See also AGI/J 459, 3030–30v, where Lambayeque's tribute is recorded at 1,106 pesos 2 tomines 6 granos corrientes (at 324 maravedís each, 1,317 patacones 4 reales). This is the basis for the figure of Lambayeque's worth in 1566 in Table 9.

58. The 7,000–8,000 peso figures are close to the higher of the two figures for 1568, 1569, and 1570 in Table 9. In 1570, the commodities (except the fowl) were sold in Túcume for 6,555 pesos 1 tomin (pesos co-

rrientes; 8,676 patacones). Assuming fowl were chickens and sold at 1566 prices, the total value of the tribute was 7,775 pesos 1 tomin 5 granos corrientes (10,290 patacones 6 reales) (AGI/CoO, 13-VII-1570, 35v–36, 44, 119v, 301v).

59. Tribute was originally paid three times per year, *"por tercio."* This practice persisted until at least 1564 (AGI/P 97, r. 4 [1569], 16v). In Cuenca's time (1566), deliveries were made in June (San Juan) and December (Christmas, Navidad) (Escobedo Mansilla, p. 104).

60. ART/CoO, 22-VIII-1570; 15-I-1571.

61. Malaga Medina, "El Virrey," p. 11; and ART/CoHS, l. 287, 2-III-1562.

62. A fourth of a vara or a fourth of the total? AGI/J 459, 3026v–29; J 461, 1261v; and Valencia Espinoza. Also, compare these sizes with those for Pachacamac in 1549 (Escobedo Mansilla, p. 311) and for Paria (Rio, p. 408).

63. AGI/J 457, 859v, 1149v, 1252v; J 458, 1256 and 1261; J 460, 384; J 461, 930v–31, 1020v; 1121, 1453v; and P 97, r. 4 [1569], 30.

64. ART/CoO, 13-VII-1570, 166; 26-VIII-1573; AGI/J 457, 1008; J 460, 810v; J 461, 1261; J 509A, 307–7v. Assadourian reports that in other areas natives resisted commutation to cash because it was contrary to the Inca rule that commoners give only labor ("La renta de la encomienda," pp. 135–37).

65. AGI/J 457, 1253; and J 458, 1830v.

66. Larson; Ramírez, "Chérrepe en 1572"; and Spalding, *Huarochirí,* p. 160.

67. AGI/J 457, 846v–50, 1250; J 458, 1256v; J 461, 1018.

68. AGI/AL 28A, no. 45, 2v; ART/HCompa, 10-V-1698; ANP/DI, l. 4, c. 72, 1622, 110v.

69. Rostworowski, "La tasa Toledana," p. 57; AGI/AL 28A, no. 27a; AL 28B, 20 and 217; Escobedo Mansilla, pp. 69, 71.

70. Ramírez, *Provincial Patriarchs,* chap. 3, especially p. 41; and AGI/AL 28A, 28v.

71. AGI/AL 28B, 29v–30.

72. Malaga Medina, *Reducciones Toledanas,* p. 147. Escobedo Mansilla says yanaconas were first taxed under Toledo (p. 54).

73. Escobedo Mansilla, pp. 152, 154; Malaga Medina, *Reducciones Toledanas,* p. 148; and "El Virrey," pp. 19–21.

74. Escobedo Mansilla, p. 209; and BUS/R IV, no. 60, 323. See ART/CoO, 26-VIII-1573, for Túcume.

75. Escobedo Mansilla, pp. 73, 122.

76. AGI/J 457, 973; BNMadrid/Ms. 3044, 15v; Malaga Medina, "El Virrey," p. 14. Bouysse Cassagne further refines this assessment. Her research shows that communities that did not produce items the Spanish could readily turn into cash suffered more than those that did. In her study of the Urus and the Aymaras in the south, she found that the former suffered more than the latter, because they had heavier mita obligations in the mines. She argues that this was because they produced few marketable items. See, especially, p. 106.

77. Malaga Medina, "El Virrey"; ANP/R, l. 22, c. 57, 105, for Reque; and

R, l. 2, c. 5, 1582, 129–33 and 136; AGI/AL 273, 362v. José Gordillo and Mercedes del Rio come to the same conclusion for Tiquipaya (Gordillo and Rio).

78. AGI/AL 28, 1574, iv and 12.

79. ART/CoO, 26-VIII-1573; see also Huertas Vallejos.

80. AGI/AL 132, 3.

Chapter 5

1. Lockhart, *Men of Cajamarca.*

2. AGI/J 1063, no. 3, 1570, 5v; and ART/Vega, l. 71, 13-IX-1578, 5v. For an exhaustive discussion of the various definitions of *huaca*, see van de Guchte, pt. 4.

3. There is no one spelling of this name. Some of the versions found in the manuscript and other sources include Yomayuguan, Yumayugua, Yamayuguan, Yunayguan, Yomayoguan (used here throughout), and Yomayocguan. Modern spellings of topynyms are used in the text except in direct quotes. AGI/J 404, 1, 7, 10v, 108, 110v, 117v, 166, 176, and 307; and Feyjoo de Sousa, p. 25.

4. *Chaquira* (beads) were mentioned but were not entered into the calculation of the value of the treasure and in fact were given away to onlookers (an indication that the Spanish, at least, considered the beads of insignificant worth).

5. AGI/J 404, 150, 161, 425, 431, 442, 485, 512, and 571v.

6. AGI/J 404, 3, 97–97v, 101, 103v, 104v, 110, 113, 128v, 157v, and 237v.

7. AGI/J 404, 5v, 73v, 110, and 193v.

8. The fact that he hired highland Indians to help him dig at Yomayoguan may have meant he also spoke and/or understood Quechua.

9. An estado is defined by Sebastián de Covarrubias in his early seventeenth-century dictionary as a measure, the length of the height of a man (p. 561). For the purpose of this chapter, I will estimate the height of a man at five feet, six inches and use this in my calculations.

10. AGI/J 404, 111, 149v, 160, and 326. On local historical memory, see Feyjoo de Sousa, p. 24.

11. AGI/J 404, 144v and 156.

12. Ibid., 404, 1, 4, 16v, 53, 97–98, 100, 105v, 111v, 136v, 145–145v, 277, 326, and 388v.

13. Ibid., 129 and 136v.

14. Ibid., 4 and 831v.

15. Zarco said don Martín fell (ibid., 56).

16. Ibid., 129v.

17. Ibid., 138v, 141v, 162v, 201v, and 205.

18. A decree of 1537 that mentions the Moche Valley states that gold obtained from indigenous burials was to pay a fourth rather than a fifth as tax. Porras Barrenechea, *Cedulario del Perú*, vol. 2, pp. 360–61, 380. See also *ACT*, I, 334–35, where this is mentioned. This tax was in force until 1558–59, when the Viceroy Marqués de Cañete raised it to 40 percent,

which is the same percent that Matienzo says is paid on treasure. The town council sent a representative to Lima to protest the change. Subsequently, in 1561, the king ordered a tax on all items from burials and temples, including gems, of 50 percent (Matienzo, p. 131). I am indebted to Paul Ganster for this information. A petition for a license to dig in Chan Chan, dated September 11, 1816, reveals that individuals bargained with authorities over the percent the crown took. In this case the petitioner, José Garcia, offered 30 percent to Spain, besides the "fifths and rights to all that is metallic" (ART/RH, l. 146, exp. 787, 11-IX-1816).

19. AGI/J 404, 26.

20. Ibid., 59v.

21. On the numbers of workers at the site, see AGI/J 404, 24v, 25v, 56, 108v, 112, 133v, 141, 166v, 185, 195v, 256v, 328, 372–73, and 435v. These Indians were mitayos (draft labor), yanaconas (personal retainers as opposed to community Indians), and wage earners. The north coast had a specific mita distribution for huaca looting. Petitioners received 10 to 50 natives for this task. These numbers suggest a level of such activities not evident from the few extant looting licenses alone (ART/CoHS, 2-III-1562).

22. As based on Table 20 and equivalencies in Ramírez, *Provincial Patriarch*, appendix 1, p. 277, and appendix 4, p. 388. AGI/J 404, 98v, 161, 167v, and 764.

23. Lockhart, *Men of Cajamarca*, especially pp. 80–81; Cieza de León, *La crónica*, vol. 1, pp. 193–94; and Lizárraga, p. 291.

24. It is unclear whether this is huaca Tascaguan or huaca Toledo, cited by Day, p. 62, which was associated with a large treasure found during colonial times. Feyjoo de Sousa, p. 25. See also Lothrop, p. 67, on the huaca of the sun at Moche, which yielded 80,000 ducats (approximately 110,295 patacones).

25. AGI/J 404, 91, 98v, 107, 112v, 114, 117v, 128, 204v, 239v, and 554–54v.

26. Ibid., 25, 128, and 570v.

27. Ibid., 327, 462, 494v, 499, 506, 508v–10v, 559v, and 598.

28. Ibid., 422, 549v, 554–54v. The crown and high royal bureaucrats recognized the disadvantages of partnerships between excavators and local officials (AGI/AL 28B, no. 2, 216v). Rodrigo Calvillo was also in charge of getting native fishermen to supply the city of Trujillo in 1560. Additionally, he extorted money from illegal chicha-making activities. AGI/J 404, 516–17 and 580.

29. AGI/ J 404, 97v. Hojeda subsequently gave half of a (his?) share in a "guaca" (which one?) to the daughter of Alonso Ortiz, Br. Pedro Ortiz' brother (ART/LC 1559).

30. AGI/J 404, 504, and 641. It is unclear whether Pineda got another sixth of the four-twelfths ($1/6 \times 4/12 = 1/18$) that don Antonio continued to hold or a full twelfth.

31. AGI/J 404, 551v–52.

32. Ibid., 97v, 98, and 141.

33. Ibid., 379–80, 554–54v, 557v, 558v, 559v, 560, 641, and 653.

34. Ibid., 36v–37, 117v, 512, 544, and 832v.

35. Some short, terse answers suggest that the natives on the witness stand were intimidated and sought escape from an uncomfortable situation.

36. AGI/J 404, 7, 57, 254, 331v–32, 364, and 610. Compare to Lizárraga's comment on the hispanized curaca of Jayanca (p. 283).

37. Ibid., 252–52v, 420, and 516v–17. See also Silverblatt, especially p. 37.

38. I say this because encomenderos influenced the choice of succession, and there are allegations that don Antonio was not the legitimate heir. This may not have been true, since Feyjoo de Sousa said (albeit 200 years later) that he was the legitimate successor (p. 25). Viceroy Francisco de Toledo reported that indigenous religious practices continued into the 1570s (AGI/AL 28B, no. 2, 33v).

39. MacCormack, especially chap. 2.

40. AGI/J 404, 277v–78. This quote fills a void noted by Salomon, "Ancestor Cults," p. 213.

41. See Espinoza Soriano, "Un testimonio," p. 116.

42. AGI/J 404, 115v–16, 131, and 277–78.

43. Silverblatt, especially pp. 37, 40; MacCormack, especially chap. 2.

44. AGI/J 404, 495, 599, and 610–11v.

45. Ibid., 4, 41, 105v, 108v, 129, 136v, 145v, 150, 239, and 277–77v.

46. Ibid., 108 and 369v; J 458, 1468. This is consistent with Feyjoo de Sousa's version two centuries later (p. 25–26).

47. AGI/J 404, 196 and 260. The viceroy replied that it was unnecessary for natives to have a license to dig huacas (folio 252v). Was this tacit recognition of their rights to such structures?

48. AGI/J 404, 4v, 115v, 137v, 155, 159, 265, 278, 326, 361, 365, 365v, 369v, 401, and 455. A decree of the Conde de Nieva stated that no one could abandon (not work) a huaca over ten days; otherwise, other people had the right to claim and work it (dd. 26?[bre]-156? [1564]) (ART/CoO, l. 156, exp. 282, 8-1592, 17v–19).

49. AGI/J 404, 278v.

50. Feyjoo de Sousa said he was a direct descendant of ruler Chimu Chumancauchu (p. 25).

51. See Murra's discussion of this distinction ("Las etnocategorías," especially p. 438) and Chapter 3.

52. AGI/J 404, 6, 112, 145v–6, 252v, 261, and 272–73; and ANCR/1586–1611, 14v, 16v. Later manuscript documentation from Trujillo, Lambayeque, and Cuzco makes it clear that rights to excavate an indigenous structure were independent of land ownership. Thus in Cuzco, individuals received licenses to dig a site on land belonging to another individual (ANP/SG, l. 2, c. 32, and huaca licenses in section Real Hacienda of ART).

53. Feyjoo de Sousa, pp. 26; and AGI/J 404, 252v.

54. ART/CaO, l. 3, exp. 65, 15-X-1573, 3–5.

55. AGI/J 404, 106–6v, 107v, 111v, 112, 130v, and 826. All testimony in

the court case was recorded in Spanish. A check of the available dictionaries of the indigenous language of the coast (Mochica or Yunga) reveal no known words for temple or palace. The Mochica word for huaca is *töni*. Used as a suffix, the letters "an" mean "the place" or "house of." Therefore, Yomayoguan may mean the place or house of Yomayogu. The meaning of this toponym needs further investigation (Richard Schaedel, personal communication, Sept. 11, 1991).

56. Could this have been influenced by the reconquista legacy of the right to the booty of the mosques captured from the Moslem foes? If so, calling the huacas temples or shrines would have given the Spanish the right to pillage and keep the artifacts found within the structures.

57. AGI/J 404, 277.

58. Ibid., 26v. Oliva reported that Arriaga found *conopas* (statues; see my fuller discussion below) stained with blood from sacrifices made by Indians (p. 135).

59. AGI/J 404, 163v, and 253v.

60. Oliva, pp. 130, 132–34; Cobo, vol. 2, p. 149. Cobo also discusses extraordinary or unusual persons (p. 166) or items as huacas. His list of huacas refers to houses, fountains or springs, caves, hills, plains, rocks, idols, trees, places, temples, burials, lakes, cultivated fields, boundary markers, fences, resting places, and plazas (pp. 169–86). Note that Patricia Lyon has pointed out that names of huacas in Cobo's list appear to be the names of places where the huacas were located (in J. H. Rowe, "Una relación," p. 212).

61. Vargas Ugarte, *Historia de la iglesia*, vol. 1, p. 29; van de Guchte, pt. 4; Cabello de Valboa, pp. 311, 384; Betanzos, pp. 14, 67, 88, 191, 249–50, 301; Santillán, pp. 23–32; "Relación de las costumbres," pp. 157–59; and "Relación de los fundamentos."

62. Acosta, pp. 219, 221, 223, 224, 247, 270, 299; and Agustinos, pp. 11–12, 15, 17, 20–21, 23, 25, 27, 28–32, 34–37, 40–41, 44–45, 48–49, and 51.

63. "Relación de las costumbres," pp. 154, 158–60. See also Vargas Ugarte, *Historia de la iglesia*, vol. 1, pp. 34–35.

64. According to Richard Schaedel, the word *munaos* means "ancestor mummy." This is another indication that the natives were telling the truth (personal communication, Dec. 9, 1988).

65. Arriaga, xxix–xxxii, pp. 8–9, 11–12, 14, 16–17, 25, 44, 55, 59, 85, 126; Espinoza Soriano, "Un testimonio," pp. 116–17; Vargas Ugarte, *História de la iglesia*, vol. 1, pp. 34, 36; and Cobo, vol. 2, p. 336. See also Carrera, p. 68; Molina, p. 43.

66. Polo de Ondegardo, "Informaciones," pp. 6, 12, 16, 31, 34, 37, 38, 42–43, 100–101, 112–13, 194, 201; Molina, pp. 9, 10, 21–26, 29–30, 34–36, 39, 44, 46–60, 63–64, 69–73, 75–77, 80–83; Guamán Poma de Ayala, *El primer nueva corónica*, vol. 1, pp. 73 [73], 81 [81], 87 [87], 101 [101], 109 [109], 183 [185], 237 [239], 239 [241], 241 [243], 243 [245], 255 [257], 267 [269]. For the Segundo Concilio Provincial, see Mannheim, p. 295.

67. The rest of Matienzo's chapter discusses who has the right—native or

Spaniard—to excavate the tombs. He argues that the king (and by delega-tion, the Spanish colonists) have the right as the successors of the Inca. He refutes the Bishop Don Fray Bartolomé de las Casas, who thought that the natives retained the rights (pp. 128–31).

68. Matienzo, p. 128.

69. Ibid., p. 129. Trimborn, p. 17, speaks about the distinction between a "pyramid temple" and a "pyramid palace" (or tomb). Note also the use of *huaca* as meaning tomb in Ecuador in Muñoz-Bernand's study of Pindilig. Note that Classen describes Inca dead as being housed in vaults where they were accessible to descendants (p. 88).

70. Cieza de León, *La crónica*, pp. 77, 158, 175, 185, 197, 199, 205–7, 213–14, 237, 274; and *El señorío*, pp. 96, 97, 100, 262.

71. It was located at a "sand hill [çerro] that is a little over one league from the city, leaving by the road to Chicama, on the right hand side, pass-ing the large [great] hill [çerro] and in front of other smaller hills; in front of said sand hill passes an old irrigation ditch" (ART/CoO, l. 147, exp. 131, 3-IX-1563).

72. AGI/J 404, 4 and 252 (see also folios 53, 54v, 55v); ART/RH, l. 146, exp. 675, 19-II-1691; l. 146, exp. 669, 7-VII-1684; and l. 146, exp. 674, 4-XII-1690.

73. Francisco A. Loayza in Molina, pp. 9–10, especially n. 6 where he cites the Franciscan *Vocabulario políglota Incaico.*

74. Cobo, vol. 2, p. 165. See also Trimborn, p. 63, regarding Túcume and the speculation about the development of the "palace huaca" out of the "temple huaca."

75. ART/Mata, 17-II-1565; Pease, "El príncipe," especially pp. 84–87; ANP/SG, l. 2, c. 32; Duviols, "La visite," pp. 501–2, 504; Gushiken; Feyjoo de Sousa, pp. 24–25; and Dammert Bellido, p. 188.

76. Garcilaso de la Vega, vol. 1, pp. 112, 117–19.

77. Ibid., vol. 1, pp. 112, 114–15.

78. AGI/J 404, 218. In Gonzales Holguin, the Quechua term for *sepul-chro* (tomb) is *ayapucru, ayahuaci*, which incorporates the idea of burial (*aya*) and of house (*huaci*) (p. 656).

79. AGI/J 404, 252 (see also folio 362v); Cabello de Valboa, p. 328.

80. This is true for late Mochica tombs at Batan Grande (c. 600–700 A.D.). Tombs contain several generations; bodies were pushed aside to ac-commodate others. Subterranean adobe thresholds are worn, showing that people entered and left continually (Izumi Shimada, personal communica-tions, Sept. 25, 1988, Feb. 15, 1989).

81. Agustinos, p. 36; Acosta, p. 236; Cobo, vol. 2, p. 164; Santillán, p. 31, and "Relación de las costumbres," pp. 158–60. Rubiños y Andrade (p. 363) describes the palace (or casa de cacique) of Sium and truncated pyramid (also cited in Trimborn, pp. 74–75); see also Marqués de Cañete's 1557 in-structions for the visita where he asks for information on "such shrines, guacas, and houses of the dead that exist" (Espinoza Soriano, "La visita de Lima," p. 65).

82. On the use of the word *insignia* in the classical literature, see Betanzos, pp. 31, 35, 115; and Polo de Ondegardo, "Informe," p. 132. Recall also the probably biased testimony that on the surface there were bones of children and llamas, wool, and other signs of sacrifice. Were these insignias carved wooden stakes or images a la Paracas or similar signs? See also the very suggestive article by Martinez C., especially pp. 62–63.

83. AGI/J 404, 4, 24v–25, 97v, 131v, 192v, 255v–56, 337, 388–88v, 392v, 396v, 404, 635v, 826.

84. AGI/J 404, 264, and 270.

85. Ibid., 108, 252, 274; and AL 123.

86. AGI/J 404, 163, and 278v. See Betanzos' description of the treasure of the temple of the sun in Cuzco and Pachacama that had much of the same types of treasure (pp. 280, 283; see also Arriaga).

87. On human sacrifice, see Urteaga, pp. 35–40. Vargas Ugarte, *História de la iglesia*, vol. 1, pp. 43–44, summarizes the argument over whether or not the Incas practiced human sacrifice. See also Trimborn, who cites Jerez (p. 31).

88. Cieza de León, *La crónica*, vol. 1, p. 175.

89. Ibid., vol. 1, pp. 158, 213; vol. 2, pp. 91, 93, 94–95, 102; Cabello de Valboa, pp. 301, 350; Guamán Poma de Ayala, *El primer nueva corónica*, vol. 1, pp. 245 [247], 247 [249], 249 [250], 251 [253], 255 [257], 257 [259], 259 [261], 263 [265], 265 [267], 267 [269]; and Calancha, p. 1239, as cited by Rostworowski, *Estructuras Andinas*, p. 80. See also Betanzos, p. 34; Arriaga, pp. 44–45, 56–57, 60–61; Agustinos, pp. 21–22, 26–27, 34–35.

90. Cobo, vol. 2, pp. 151, 153–54, 164; Estete, p. 242; AGI/P 188, r. 22, 1561, 6v; J 404, 193, and 275; "Relación de los fundamentos," pp. 9, 43, 113; Betanzos, p. 177; Arriaga, pp. 14, 15, 35, 50, 56–57, 61; Oliva, p. 134; Cieza de León, *La crónica*, vol. 1., pp. 158, 196–97 (for Xauxa); Guamán Poma de Ayala, *El primer nueva corónica*, vol. 1, pp. 288 [290]; Acosta, pp. 221, and 227; Molina, p. 37; "Relación de las costumbres," p. 159.

91. Conrad, "The Burial Platform," pp. 99–100, 103, 105.

92. Zuidema, *Reyes y guerreros*, especially pp. 125–26 and 137–38; and *Inca Civilization in Cuzco*. Freidel shows that Mayans did not distinguish between temples and palaces. Such distinctions are those of Western archaeologists.

93. I was reminded of the symbolism of burial and mortuary practices in the Andes at a conference entitled "Tombs for the Living: Andean Mortuary Practices" held at Dumbarton Oaks, Washington, D.C., October 12–13, 1991. The papers by John H. Rowe ("Cultural Implications of Mortuary Practices in Ancient Peru") and by Frank Salomon ("The Beautiful Grandparents: Andean Ancestor Shrines and Mortuary Ritual in Ethnohistorical Perspective") were particularly helpful. The proceedings of this conference will be published.

The description of Yomayoguan suggests that it was a burial platform and walled compound as described by Conrad and by Paul Kosok (pp. 76–86). Its description as a house or houses suggests that it quite possibly was part of a larger compound (ciudadela) or shrine complex where ongoing ancestral

cults, which included ritual toasting to the dead, feasting, singing, and
dancing, were celebrated. Further north, natives continued to participate,
into the 1570s, in rituals that included dancing at the site of their "huacas"
(Ramírez, "Chérrepe en 1572"). Hermann Trimborn cites León Barandiarán, who equates guaca Sioternic to the "temple of Naymlap" and huaca
Chotuna as his palace and, by Cabello de Valboa's extension, his tomb. Indeed, this is suggested by Corregidor Feyjoo de Sousa when he relates an abbreviated and slightly adulterated version of the story of Yomayoguan, stating that huaca Yomayoguan was next to the ruined palace of the Chimu
King Chumancauchu.

Feyjoo de Sousa also states that don Antonio was a legitimate descendant
of this ruler. Testimony in the form of an allegation by Escobar in the manuscript, however, makes this statement suspect. AGI/J 404, 4, 25, 77, 97v,
131v, 252, 635v; Conrad, "The Burial Platform"; Kosok, p. 89; Trimborn,
p. 77; and Feyjoo de Sousa, p. 25.

The AGI manuscript is important because of the references to other
named structures near Yamoyoguan. Archaeological verification could determine which of the many structures in Chan Chan is Yomayoguan. Yomayoguan exists as a toponym on map 10 of the set published by Moseley
and Mackey, but the name is not associated with a structure. Different witnesses place the structure between one half and one league from the city of
Trujillo on the road to Guanchaco, the Indian fishing village on the shore of
the Pacific Ocean (AGI/J 404, 10v, 25, 166, 176, 194, 256). Other witnesses
place Yomayoguan on the "road between Trugillo to Huamachuco at an
esero [?] called mosiq[ue]" (folio 108) and "on the road to guanchaco at an
eliso [eriso?] called moro that is two leagues from Trugillo in a planted field
of this witness [don Francisco, Indian cacique of Chimu subject to don An-
tonio]" (folio 106v). The actual license to dig at Yomayoguan and the vast
majority of other descriptions place it on the "road to guanchaco," half a
league from the city. These say it is located at a spot (*sitio* or *asiento*) variously called Yomayuguan (folio 1) and Los Paredones (folios 24v, 25, 56,
255v, 337, 362v, 392v, 414v, 826) and next (*"poco mas adelante de"*) to another "huaca," which one Indian principal named as Tascaguan, which was
one league from the city (folios 23, 138v, 145, 396) and among other "huacas" (folio 204), suggesting a complex, or Chan Chan itself. If archaeologists
could find Yomayoguan and Tascaguan, the ruined palace of King Chimu
Chumancauchu might be identified. Then it would be time to return to the
archives to find more references, like the manuscript that speaks about
the "guaca" (referring specifically to a tomb) between the huaca Toledo and
the palacio del Gran Chimu in Chan Chan (ART/RH, l. 146, exp. 787, 11-
IX-1816). With perseverance and luck, many of the structures of Chan Chan
might thus be identified. Such work would open a new chapter of collabo-
rative research between archaeologists and ethnohistorians and deepen the
knowledge of the history of the area.

94. Murra, "Las etnocategorías."

Chapter 6

1. J. H. Rowe, "The Kingdom of Chimor"; and Ramírez, "The Inca Conquest."
2. Ramírez, "Social Frontiers."
3. Ramírez, "The Inca Conquest."
4. Farther north, there is evidence of women serving as paramount lords. See Díaz Rementaría, pp. 10 (for Colán), 21 (for Sechura), and 46 (for Narigualá).
5. Moseley, "Prehistoric Principles;" Ramírez, "The '*Dueño de Indios*'"; "The Inca Conquest"; and Chapter 4.
6. Chapter 2.
7. See Eling on Pacasmayo and Saña; and Ramírez, "The Inca Conquest."
8. Ramírez, "The Cajamarca Connection."
9. Zuidema, *Reyes y guerreros*, pp. 137–38, and *Inca Civilization in Cuzco*, says a lord must be remembered for four, six, and more generations. See, on the issue of reciprocity and regulation or hierarchy and control, Schaedel, especially p. 772.
10. There is a report that Diego de Almagro began granting encomiendas in 1534 to Captain Rui Barba (of Jayanca) and to Juan de Porras (of Pácora) in AGI/J 418, 1573, 114, 119. The earliest known encomienda grant in the north made by Francisco Pizarro was to Alonso Miguel de Velasco (of Reque) in 1535 (Rostworowski, *Curacas y sucesiones*, pp. 14, 73).
11. Ramírez, *Provincial Patriarchs*.
12. Hamilton, p. 50.
13. Espinoza Soriano, "La poliginia señorial."
14. Duviols, *Cultural Andina*; and Rostworowski, "Ruinas de Concón."
15. Cock, "The Lord's Control," especially pp. 1, 7, 15; and Martinez C., especially p. 64. On cosmology, see Classen; Hamilton; Patterson; Zuidema, "Inca Cosmos"; Martinez C.; Sahlins; and MacCormack.
16. Rostworowski, "Breves notas" and "El tributo indígena"; Cock, "Poder y riqueza"; Hamilton, especially pp. 18, 53; and Diez Hurtado, p. 13, emphasize the differences between highland and coastal cultures. They base their statements almost totally on the fact that colonial manuscript sources list more types of economic specialists on the coast than in the highlands. Murra, "An Aymara Kingdom," p. 124, and "El control vertical." See also Patterson, especially pp. 183–84, on Huarochirí.

Bibliography

Acosta, Padre José de. *Historia natural y moral de las Indias (1550)*. Mexico City: Fondo de Cultura Económica, 1979.

Adorno, Rolena. "Images of *Indios Ladinos* in Early Colonial Peru." In Kenneth J. Andrien and Rolena Adorno, eds., *Transatlantic Encounters: Europeans and Andeans in the Sixteenth Century*, pp. 232–70. Berkeley: University of California Press, 1991.

Agustinos. "Relación de la religión y ritos del Perú." In Joaquín F. Pacheco, Francisco de Cardenas, and Luis Torres de Mendoza, *Colección de documentos inéditos, relativos al descubrimiento, conquista y colonización de . . . América y Oceanía*, vol. 3, pp. 3–58. Madrid: Imprenta de Manuel Quirós, 1864–65.

Aibar Ozejo, Elena. "La visita de Guaraz en 1558." *Cuadernos del Seminario de Historia (Lima)* 7, no. 9 (enero 1968–diciembre 1969): 5–21.

Andrien, Kenneth J. "Spaniards, Andeans, and the Early Colonial State in Peru." In Kenneth J. Andrien and Rolena Adorno, eds., *Transatlantic Encounters: Europeans and Andeans in the Sixteenth Century*, pp. 121–48. Berkeley: University of California Press, 1991.

Angulo, Domingo. "Fundación y población de la Villa de Zaña." *Revista del Archivo Nacional [del Perú]* 1, no. 2 (mayo-agosto 1920): 280–300.

Araujo, Alejandro O. "Reseña histórica de Saña." Typescript, Eten, Peru, 29 noviembre 1957.

Arenas Pérez, Victor J., and Héctor E. Carmona. *Anuario de Lambayeque*. Chiclayo: Editorial "Minerva," 1947.

Arriaga, Padre Pablo José de. *La extirpación de la idolatría en el Perú* [1621]. Colección de libros y documentos referentes a la historia del Perú. Second Series. Vol. 1. Lima: Sanmartí, 1920.

Arroyo, Luis. *Los Franciscanos y la fundación de Chiclayo*. Lima, 1956.

Assadourian, Carlos Sempat. "Dominio colonial y señores étnicos en el espacio Andino." *HISLA: Revista Latinoamericana de Historia Económica y Social* 1 (1983): 7–20.

{tab}. "La renta de la encomienda en la decada de 1550: Piedad cristiana y desconstrucción." *Revista de Indias* 48, nos. 182–83 (1988): 109–46.

Bandera, Damián de la. "Relación del origen é gobierno que los Ingas tuvieron y del que habia antes . . . (1557)." In *Biblioteca Peruana: El Perú a través de los siglos*, vol. 3, pp. 491–510. First series, 3 vols. Lima: Editores Técnicos Asociados, S.A., 1968.

Barriga, Padre Victor M. *Los mercedarios en el Perú.* Arequipa: Editorial La Colmena, 1939–42.

Bastien, Joseph W. "Land Litigations in an Andean Ayllu from 1592 to 1972." *Ethnography* 26, no. 2 (1979): 101–31.

Baudin, Louis. *Daily Life in Peru Under the Last Incas.* London: Allen & Unwin, 1961.

Betanzos, Juan Diez de. *Suma y narración de los Incas (1551).* Madrid: Atlas, 1987.

Borah, Woodrow. *Early Colonial Trade and Navigation Between Mexico and Peru.* Ibero-americana, vol. 38. Berkeley: University of California Press, 1954.

Bouysse Cassagne, Thérése. "Tributo y etnias en Charcas en la época del Virrey Toledo." *Historia y cultura: Revista de la Sociedad Boliviana de Historia* 2 (1976): 97–113.

Brüning, Enrique. *Estudios monográficos del Departamento de Lambayeque.* Chiclayo: D. Mendoza, 1922–23.

Burga, Manuel. *De la encomienda a la hacienda capitalista.* Lima: Instituto de Estudios Peruanos, 1976.

Busto, José Antonio del. "El Capitán Melchor Verdugo, Encomendero de Cajamarca." *Revista histórica* 24 (1959): 318–87.

Cabello de Valboa, Miguel. *Miscelánea antártica [1586].* Lima: Instituto de Etnología, Universidad Nacional Mayor de San Marcos, 1951.

Cabero, Marco A. "El corregimiento de Saña y el problema histórico de la fundación de Trujillo." *Revista histórica* 1, nos. 2–4 (1906): 151–91, 336–73, 485–514.

Carrera, Padre Fernando de la. *Arte de la lengua Yunga de los Valles del Obispado de Truxillo . . . [1644].* Tucumán: Instituto de Antropologia, 1939.

Castro, Fray Cristóbal de, and Diego de Ortega Morejón. "Relación de Chincha (1558)." In *Biblioteca Peruana: El Perú a través de los siglos*, vol. 3, pp. 465–89. First series, 3 vols. Lima: Editores Técnicos Asociados, 1968.

Centro de Estudios de Historia Eclesiástica del Perú. *Monografía de la Diócesis de Trujillo.* 3 vols. Trujillo: Imprenta Diocesana, 1930–31.

Cieza de León, Pedro de. *La crónica del Perú, Primera Parte (1553).* Lima: Pontificia Universidad Católica del Perú, 1984.

———. *El señorio de los Incas, Segunda parte de la Crónica del Perú (1550).* Lima: Instituto de Estudios Peruanos, 1967.

————. *The Travels of Pedro de Cieza de León.* London: Hakluyt Society, 1864; and New York: Burt Franklin, 1964.

Classen, Constance. *Inca Cosmology and the Human Body.* Salt Lake City: University of Utah Press, 1993.

Cline, S. L. *Colonial Culhuacan, 1580–1600: A Social History of an Aztec Town.* Albuquerque: University of New Mexico Press, 1986.

Cobo, Bernabé. *Historia del Nuevo Mundo (1653).* 2 vols. Biblioteca de autores españoles. Madrid: Gráficas ORBE y Estades, Artes Gráficos, 1956.

Cock, Guillermo A. "The Lord's Control of Artisans, Craftsmen and Labor Specialization in the Jequetepeque Valley, North Coast of Peru." Paper presented at an unidentified conference, n.d. (typed copy courtesy of the author).

————. "Poder y riqueza de un Hatun Curaca del Valle del Jequetepeque en el Siglo XVI." *Historia y cultura [Lima]* 17 (1984): 193–55.

————. "Power and Wealth in the Jequetepeque Valley during the Sixteenth Century." In C. B. Donnan and G. A. Cock, eds., *The Pacatnamu Papers,* vol. 1, pp. 171–80. Los Angeles: Museum of Cultural Anthropology, University of California at Los Angeles, 1986.

Comisión del estatuto y redemarcación territorial, Ley 10553. *La demarcación territorial y política del Departamento Lambayeque, Informe de la Asesoria Técnica.* Lima: Imprenta D. Miranda, 1947.

Conrad, Geoffrey W. "The Burial Platform of Chan Chan: Some Social and Political Implications." In Michael E. Moseley and Kent Day, eds., *Chan Chan, Andean Desert City,* pp. 87–118. Albuquerque: University of New Mexico Press, 1982.

————. "The Inca Imperial Expansion." In G. W. Conrad and Arthur A. Demarest, eds., *Religion and Empire,* pp. 81–151. Cambridge, England: Cambridge University Press, 1984.

Conrad, Geoffrey W., and Arthur A. Demarest, eds. *Religion and Empire.* Cambridge, England: Cambridge University Press, 1984.

Cook, Noble David. "The Indian Population of Peru, 1570–1620." Ph.D. diss., University of Texas, Austin, 1973.

————. "La visita de los Conchucos por Cristóbal Ponce de Leon, 1543." *Historia y cultura [Lima]* 10 (1976–77): 23–45.

Covarrubias, Sebastián de. *Tesoro de la lengua Castellana o Española (1611).* Barcelona: S. A. Horta, 1943.

Craig, Alan K. "Origins and Development of Andean Mining." In Izumi Shimada, ed., *Sican Metallurgy: Cultural and Technological Dimensions of Ancient Andean Metallurgy.* New York: Cambridge University Press, in press.

Cuneo-Vidal, Rómulo. "El cacicazgo de Tacna." *Revista histórica* 6, no. 4 (1919): 309–24.

Cunow, Heinrich. *La organización social del Imperio de los Incas.* Lima: Librería y Editorial Peruana de D. Miranda, 1933.

Dammert Bellido, José. "Procesos por supersticiones en la Provincia de Cajamarca en la segunda mitad del siglo XVIII." *Allpanchis* 20, no. 23 (1984): 177–200.

Davies, Keith. *Landowners in Colonial Peru*. Austin: University of Texas Press, 1984.

———. "The Rural Domain of the City of Arequipa, 1540–1665." Ph.D. diss., University of Connecticut, Storrs, 1974.

Day, Kent C. "Ciudadelas: Their Form and Function." In Michael Moseley and Kent Day, eds., *Chan Chan: Andean Desert City*, pp. 55–66. Albuquerque: University of New Mexico Press, 1982.

Diaz del Castillo, Bernal. *The True History of the Conquest of Mexico*. La Jolla: Renaissance Press, 1979.

Díaz Rementería, Carlos J. *El cacique en el virreinato del Perú: Estudio historica-jurídico*. Sevilla: Departamento de Antropología y Etnología de América, Universidad de Sevilla, 1977.

Diez Hurtado, Alejandro. *Pueblos y caciques de Piura: Siglos XVI y XVII*. Piura: Centro de Investigación y Promoción del Campesino, 1988.

Duviols, Pierre. *Cultura Andina y represión*. Cuzco: Centro de Estudios Rurales Andinos, 1986.

———. "La visite des idolatries de Concepción de Chupas (Pèrou, 1614)." *Journal de la Sociètè des Amèricanistes* 55, no. 2 (1966): 497–510.

Eling, Jr., Herbert H. "Interpretaciones preliminares del sistema de riego antiguo de Talambo en el Valle de Jequetepeque, Perú." In Ramiro Matos M., ed., *III Congreso Peruano "El hombre y la cultura Andina": Actas y Trabajos*, vol. 2, pp. 401–19. Lima: Secretaria general del III Congreso Peruano del hombre y la cultura Andina, 1977.

Escobedo Mansilla, Ronald. *El tributo indígena en le Perú, Siglos XVI–XVII*. Pamplona: Ediciones Universidad de Navarra, 1979.

Espinoza Soriano, Waldemar. *La destrucción del imperio de los Incas*. Lima: Amaru Editores, 1981.

———. "Los huancas, aliados de la conquista. Tres informaciones inéditas sobre la participación indígena en la conquista del Perú, 1558–1560–1561." *Anales científicos de la Universidad Nacional del Centro del Perú (Huancayo)* no. 1 (1972): 1–407.

———. *Los Incas, economia, sociedad y estado en la era del Tahuantinsuyo*. La Victoria, Peru: Amaru Editores, 1987.

———. "Los mitmas yungas de Collique en Cajamarca[,] Siglos XV, XVI[,] y XVII." *Revista del Museo Nacional [del Perú]* 36 (1969–70): 9–57.

———. "La poliginia señorial en el reino de Caxamarca, siglos XV y XVI." *Revista del Museo Nacional [del Perú]* 43 (1977): 399–466.

———. "El primer informe etnológico sobre Cajamarca, Año de 1540." *Revista Peruana de Cultura* 11–12 (1967): 1–37.

———. "Los señorios étnicos de Chachapoyas y la alianza hispano-chacha. Visitas, informaciones y memoriales de 1572–1574." *Revista histórica* 30 (1967): 224–332.

———. "Un testimonio sobre los idolos, huacas, y dioses de Lampa y Cajatambo, Siglos XV–XVII." *Scientia et Praxis (Revista de la Universidad de Lima)* (1980): 115–30.

———. "El Valle de Jayanca y el reino de los Mochica: Siglos XV–XVI." *Bulletin de l'Institut Français d'Etudes Andines* 4, nos. 3–4 (1975): 243–74.

———. "La visita de Lima en 1557." *Cuadernos del Seminario de Historia* 12 (1980): 53–68.

Estete, Miguel de. "Noticia del Perú (1535)." In *Los cronistas de la conquista,* vol. 2, pp. 195–251. Biblioteca de Cultura Peruana. First series, no. 2. Paris: Desclee, de Brouwer, 1938.

Falcón, Licenciado Francisco. "Representación hecha por el Licenciado Falcón al Concilio Provincial sobre los daños y molestias que se hacen a los indios [1567]." In Horacio H. Urteaga, ed., *Informaciones acerca de la religion y gobierno de los Incas,* vol. 11, pp. 133–76. Colección de libros y documentos referentes a la historia del Perú. Lima: Sanmartí, 1918; and in Luis Torres de Mendoza, ed., *Colección de documentos inéditos relativos al descubrimiento, conquista y organización . . . ,* vol. 7, pp. 451–95. Madrid: Imprenta de Frias y Compania, 1867.

Farrington, Ian S. "Irrigación prehispánica y establecimientos en la costa norte del Perú." In Rogger Ravines, comp., *Tecnología andina,* pp. 117–28. Lima: Instituto de Estudios Peruanos, 1978.

Farriss, Nancy M. *Maya Society Under Colonial Rule: The Collective Enterprise of Survival.* Princeton: Princeton University Press, 1984.

Fernandez-Santamaria, José A. "Juan Gines de Sepulveda on the Nature of the American Indians." *The Americas* 31, no. 4 (Apr. 1975): 434–51.

Feyjoo de Sousa, Miguel. *Relación descriptiva de la Ciudad y Provincia de Truxillo del Perú.* Madrid: Imprenta del Real y Supremo Consejo de las Indias, 1763.

Freidel, David A. "The Trees of Life: Ahau as Idea and Artifact in Classic Lowland Maya Civilization." In Arthur A. Demarest and Geoffrey W. Conrad, eds., *Ideology and Pre-Columbian Civilizations,* pp. 115–33. Santa Fe: University of New Mexico Press, 1992.

Friede, Juan. *El indio en lucha por la tierra, historia de los resguardos del macizo central colombiano.* Bogotá: Ediciones Espiral Colombia, 1944.

Gama, Sebastián de la or da. "Visita hecha en el Valle de Jayanca [Trujillo] [1540]." *Historia y cultura* 8 (1974): 215–28; and "Visita de Jayanca [1540]." In Waldemar Espinoza Soriano, trans., "El Valle de Jayanca y el reino de los Mochica, Siglos XV y XVI." *Bulletin de l'Institut Français d'Estudes Andines* 4, nos.3–4 (1975): 243–74.

Garcilaso de la Vega. *Los comentarios reales de los Incas (1586).* 5 vols. Lima: Libreria y Imprenta Gil, S.A., 1941–46.

Gibson, Charles. *The Aztecs Under Spanish Rule: A History of the Indians of the Valley of Mexico, 1519–1810.* Stanford: Stanford University Press, 1964.

González de San Segundo, Miguel Angel. "El Doctor Gregorio González de Cuenca, Oidor de la Audiencia de Lima, y sus ordenanzas sobre caciques e indios principales (1566)." *Revista de Indias* 42, nos. 169–70 (julio–diciembre 1982): 643–67.

———. "Pervivencia de la organización señorial aborígen (contribución al estudio del cacicazgo y su ordenacíon por el derecho indiano)." *Anuario de estudios Americanos [Sevilla]* 29 (1982): 47–92.

Gonzalez Holguin, Padre Diego. *Vocabulario de la lengua general de todo el Peru llamada lengua Qquichua o del Inca (1608).* Lima: Imprenta Santa María, 1952.

Gordillo, José M., and Mercedes del Rio. *La visita de Tiquipaya (1573).* Cochabamba, Bolivia: Universidad Mayor de San Simon, 1993.

Guamán Poma de Ayala, Felípe. *Nueva corónica y buen gobierno [c. 1613].* Paris: Institut d'ethnologíe, 1936.

———. *El primer nueva corónica y buen gobierno.* J. V. Murra and Rolena Adorno, eds. 3 vols. Mexico, D.F.: Siglo XXI Editores, S.A., 1980.

Guillén Guillén, Edmundo. *Versión inca de la conquista.* Lima: Editorial Milla Batres, 1974.

Guilmartin, Jr., John F. "The Cutting Edge: An Analysis of the Spanish Invasion and Overthrow of the Inca Empire, 1532–1534." In Kenneth J. Andrien and Rolena Adorna, eds., *Transatlantic Encounters: Europeans and Andeans in the Sixteenth Century,* pp. 40–69. Berkeley: University of California Press, 1991.

Gushiken, José. "La extirpación de idolatrias en Santiago de Carampoma." *Boletín del Instituto Riva-Aguero* 9 (1972–74): 151–65.

Hamilton, Joe. "Plebe and Potentate: History and Society of Prehispanic North Central Coast Peru." Typescript, Jan. 1978.

Hampe Martínez, Teodoro. *Don Pedro de la Gasca, Su obra política en España y América.* Lima: Pontificia Universidad Católica del Péru, 1989.

———. "Notas sobre población y tributo indígena en Cajamarca." *Boletín del Instituto Riva-Aguero* no. 14 (1986–87): 65–81.

Harrington, John P. "Yunka, Language of the Peruvian Coastal Culture." *International Journal of American Linguistics* 11, no. 1 (1945): 24–30.

Harris, Olivia. "*Phaxsima y qullqi.* Los poderes y significados del dinero en el Norte de Potosí." In Olivia Harris, Brooke Larson, and Enrique Tandeter, comps., *La participación indígena en los mercados surandinos, siglos 16–20,* pp. 235–80. La Paz: Centro de Estudios de la Realidad Económica y Social, 1987.

Hartmann, Roswith. "Mercados y ferias prehispánicos en el área andina." *Boletín de la Academia Nacional de Historia* 54, no. 118 (1971): 214–35.

Hartmann, Roswith, and Udo Oberem, eds. *Estudios Americanistas: Libro jubilar en homenaje a Hermann Trimborn.* 2 vols. St. Augustin, Germany: Haus Volker und Kulturen, Anthropos-Institut, 1978.

Haskett, Robert. *Indigenous Rulers: An Ethnohistory of Town Government in Colonial Cuernavaca.* Albuquerque: University of New Mexico Press, 1991.

Herr, Richard. *Rural Change and Royal Finances in Spain at the End of the Old Regime.* Berkeley: University of California Press, 1989.

Horn, Rebecca. "Postconquest Coyoacan: Aspects of Indigenous Sociopolitical and Economic Organization in Central Mexico, 1550–1650." Ph.D. diss., University of California, Los Angeles, 1989.

Huertas Vallejos, Lorenzo. *Ecología e historia: Probanzas de indios y españoles referentes a las catastróficas lluvias de 1578, en los corregimientos de Trujillo y Saña.* Chiclayo: CES Solidaridad, 1987.

Jacome, Nicanor. "La tributación indígena en el Ecuador." *Bulletin de l'Institut Français d'Etudes Andines* 3, no. 1 (1974): 49–80.

Jiménez de la Espada, Marcos, ed. *Relaciones geográficas de Indias.* 4 vols. Biblioteca de Autores Españóles. Madrid: Tip. de M. G. Hernandez, 1881–97.

Julien, Catherine J. "Inca Decimal Administration in the Lake Titicaca Region." In George A. Collier, Renato I. Rosaldo, and John D. Wirth, eds., *The Inca and Aztec States, 1400–1800,* pp. 119–51. New York: Academic Press, 1982.

Keatinge, Richard W. "The Pacatnamú Textiles." *Archaeology* 31, no. 2 (1978): 30–41.

Keith, Robert Gordon. *Conquest and Agrarian Change.* Cambridge, Mass.: Harvard University Press, 1976.

———. "The Encomienda and the Genesis of a Colonial Economy in Spanish America." *Research in Economic Anthropology* 3 (1980): 135–60.

———. "Origins of the Hacienda System on the Central Peruvian Coast." Ph.D. diss., Harvard University, 1969.

Kosok, Paul. *Life, Land and Water in Ancient Peru.* New York: Long Island University Press, 1965.

Larson, Brooke. *Colonialism and Agrarian Transformation in Bolivia: Cochabamba, 1550–1900.* Princeton: Princeton University Press, 1988.

Latcham, Ricardo E. *La existencia de la propiedad en el antiguo imperio de los Incas.* Anales de la Universidad de Chile. Santiago: Imprenta i Litografia Universo, 1923.

Lechtman, Heather. "A Metallurgical Site Survey in the Peruvian Andes." *Journal of Field Archaeology* 3 (1976): 1–42.

Lecuanda, José Ignacio de. "Descripción del partido de Saña o Lambayeque." In Manuel A. Fuentes, ed., *Biblioteca Peruana de historia, ciencias y literatura [Lima],* vol. 2, pp. 238–68. Lima: Bailly, 1861.

León Barandiarán, Augusto D. *Mitos, leyendas y tradiciones lambayecanas.* n.p. [Lima?], n.d. [1938?].

———. *Tradiciones Lambayecanas.* Chiclayo, 1959.

León-Portilla, Miguel, ed. *Broken Spears: The Aztec Account of the Conquest of Mexico.* Boston: Beacon Press, 1962.

Levillier, Roberto. *Don Francisco de Toledo: Supremo Organizador del Perú, su vida, su obra (1515–1582).* Madrid: Espasa-Calpe S.A., 1935.

———. *Gobernantes del Perú: Cartas y Papeles del Siglo XVI.* 14 vols. Madrid: Sucesores de Rivadeneira, 1921–26.

Lévi-Strauss, Claude. *The Raw and the Cooked.* Chicago: University of Chicago Press, 1983.

Lissón y Chaves, Emilio. *La iglesia de España en el Perú.* 4 vols., Sevilla, 1943–46.

Lizárraga, Fray Reginaldo de. "La descripción y población de las Indias (1604)." *Revista histórica* 2, nos. 3–4 (1907): 260–383, 459–543.

Lockhart, James. *Men of Cajamarca.* Austin: University of Texas Press, 1972.

———. *The Nahuas After the Conquest: A Social and Cultural History of the Indians of Central Mexico, Sixteenth Through Eighteenth Centuries.* Stanford: Stanford University Press, 1992.

———. *Nahuas and Spaniards: Postconquest Central Mexican History and Philology.* Stanford: Stanford University Press and UCLA Latin American Center Publications, 1991.

———. *Spanish Peru.* Madison: University of Wisconsin Press, 1968.

Loredo, Rafael. "El reparto de Guaynarima." *Revista histórica* 13 (1940): 78–124.

———. *Los repartos: Bocetos para la nueva historia del Perú.* Lima, 1958.

Lothrop, Samuel K. *Inca Treasure as Depicted by Spanish Historians.* Los Angeles: Southwest Museum, 1938.

McBride, George McCutchen. *Chile: Land and Society.* American Geographical Society Research Series, vol. 19. Port Washington, N.Y.: American Geographical Society, 1936.

MacCormack, Sabine. *Religion in the Andes: Vision and Imagination in Early Colonial Peru.* Princeton: Princeton University Press, 1991.

MacLachlan, Colin M. *Spain's Empire in the New World: The Role of Ideas in Institutional and Social Change.* Berkeley: University of California Press, 1988.

Malaga Medina, Alejandro. *Reducciones Toledanas en Arequipa: Pueblos tradicionales.* Biblioteca de Autores Arequipeños. Arequipa: Publiunsa, 1989.

———. "El Virrey don Francisco de Toledo y la reglamentación del tributo en el virreinato del Perú." *Anuario de estudios Americanos [Sevilla]* 29 (1972): 597–623.

Mannheim, Bruce. *The Language of the Inka Since the European Invasion.* Austin: University of Texas Press, 1991.

Martínez C., José Luis. "Kurakas, rituales e insignias: Una proposición." *Histórica* 12, no. 1 (July 1988): 61–74.

Matienzo, Juan de. *Gobierno del Perú (1567).* Paris/Lima: Institut Français d'Etudes Andines, 1967.

Mayer, Enrique. "Censos insensatos: Evaluación de los censos campesinos en la historia de Tangor." In Iñigo Ortiz de Zúñiga, *Visita de la Provincia de Leon de Huánuco en 1562,* vol. 2, pp. 341–65. Huánuco: Facultad de Letras y Educación, Universidad Nacional Hermilio Valdizán, 1972.

Mellafe, Rolando. "The Importance of Migration in the Viceroyalty of Perú." In Paul Deprez, ed., *Population and Economics,* pp. 303–13. Winnipeg, Canada: University of Manitoba Press, 1970.

———. "La significación histórica de los puentes en el virreinato peruano del siglo XVI." *Historia y cultura [Lima]* 1, no. 1 (1965): 65–113.

Melo, Garcia de, et al. "Informacion . . . acerca de las costumbres que tenian los Incas del Perú, antes de la conquista española . . . [1582]." In Roberto Levillier, ed., *Gobernantes del Perú*, vol. 9, pp. 268–96. Madrid: Sucesores de Rivadeneyra, S.A., 1925.

Millon, René F. "Trade, Tree Cultivation and the Development of Private Property in Land." *American Anthropologist* 57 (1955): 698–712.

Mogrovejo, don Toribio Alfonso de. "Diario de la segunda visita pastoral . . . 1593." *Revista del Archivo Nacional [del Perú]* 1, nos. 1–2 (1920): 49–81, 227–79; vol. 2, no. 1 (1921): 37–77.

Molina, Cristóbal de. "Relacíon de las fabulas y ritos de los Incas [1574]." In *Las crónicas de los Molinas*. Lima: Librería y imprenta D. Miranda, 1943.

Moore, Sally Falk. *Power and Property in Inca Peru*. Morningside Heights, N.Y.: Columbia Universty Press, 1958.

Morales, Adolfo de. "Repartimiento de tierras por el Inca Huayna Capac." Cochabamba, Bolivia: Departamento de Arqueología, Universidad Mayor de San Simon, 1977.

Moseley, Michael E. "Introduction: Human Exploitation and Organization on the North Andean Coast." In Michael E. Moseley and Kent Day, eds., *Chan Chan: Andean Desert City*, pp. 1–24. Albuquerque: University of New Mexico Press, 1982.

———. "Prehistoric Principles of Labor Organization in the Moche Valley, Peru." *American Antiquity* 40 (1975): 191–96.

Moseley, Michael E., and Kent C. Day. *Chan Chan, Andean Desert City*. Albuquerque: University of New Mexico Press, 1982.

Moseley, Michael E., and Carol J. Mackey. *Twenty-Four Architectural Plans of Chan Chan, Peru*. Cambridge: Peabody Museum Press, 1974.

Muñoz-Bernand, Carmen. "Autoctonia y descendencia: Contribución al estudio de las huacas." In Roswith Hartmann and Udo Oberem, eds., *Estudios Americanistas: Libro jubilar en homenaje a Hermann Trimborn*, vol. 2, pp. 81–91. St. Augustin, Germany: Haus Volker und Kulturen, Anthropos-Inst., 1979.

Murra, John V. "Andean Societies Before 1532." In Leslie Bethell, ed., *The Cambridge History of Latin America*, vol. 1, pp. 59–90. New York: Cambridge University Press, 1984.

———. "An Aymara Kingdom in 1567." *Ethnohistory* 15, no. 2 (1968): 115–51.

———. "Cloth and Its Functions in the Inca State." *American Anthropologist* 64, no. 4 (1962): 710–28.

———. "El control vertical de un máximo de pisos ecológicos en la economia de las sociedades andinas." In Iñigo Ortiz de Zúñiga, *La visita de la Provincia de Leon de Huánuco en 1562*, vol. 2, pp. 427–76. Huánuco: Facultad de Letras y Educación, Universidad Nacional Hermilio Valdizán, 1972. Also in Murra, *Formaciones económicas y políticas del mundo andino*, pp. 59–116.

———. "Derechos a las tierras en el Tawantinsuyu." *Actas del XXXVI Congreso Internacional de Americanistas (1964)*, vol. 2, 31–34. Seville: 1966.

Also in *Revista de la Universidad Complutense de Madrid* 28, no. 117 (1980): 237–87.

―――. *The Economic Organization of the Inka State.* Greenwich, Conn.: JAI Press, 1980.

―――. "Las etnocategorías de un khipu estatal." In Heather Lechtman and Ana Maria Soldi, *La tecnología en el mundo andino,* vol. 1, pp. 433–42. Mexico: Universidad Nacional Autonoma de Mexico, 1981.

―――. *Formaciones económicas y políticas del mundo andino.* Lima: Instituto de Estudios Peruanos, 1975.

―――. "The Mit'a Obligations of Ethnic Groups to the Inca State." In George Collier, et al., eds., *The Inca and Aztec States,* pp. 237–62. New York: Academic Press, 1982.

―――. "Nueva información sobre las poblaciones yana (1964)." In Murra, *Formaciones económicas y políticas del mundo andino,* pp. 225–42.

―――. "El tráfico de *mullu* en la costa del Pacífico [1971]." In Murra, *Formaciones económicas y políticas del mundo andino,* pp. 255–68.

Murúa, Fray Martín de. *Historia del orígen y genealogía real de los Reyes Incas del Perú [1590].* Madrid: Instituto Santo Toribio de Mogrovejo, Consejo Superior de Investigaciones Científicas, 1946.

Neale, Walter C. "Land Is to Rule." In Robert Eric Frykenberg, ed., *Land Control and Social Structure in Indian History,* pp. 3–15. Madison: University of Wisconsin Press, 1969.

Netherly, Patricia J. "Local Level Lords on the North Coast of Peru." Ph.D. diss., Cornell University, 1977.

―――. "The Management of Late Andean Irrigation Systems on the North Coast of Peru." *American Antiquity* 49, no. 2 (Apr. 1984): 227–54.

―――. "Los señores tardíos en la costa y sierra norte." Paper presented at the Segundo Congreso Peruano del Hombre y la Cultura Andina, Trujillo, Oct. 27–Nov. 2, 1974.

Nietschmann, Bernard. "When the Turtle Collapses, the World Ends." In Johnnetta B. Cole, ed., *Anthropology for the Eighties,* pp. 281–90. New York: Free Press, 1982.

Noejovich, Hector Omar. "El régimen de bienes en la América precolombina y el hecho colonial." Paper presented at the VII Simpósio Internacional de Historia Económica, Lima, Junio de 1986.

Nuñez Anavitarte, Carlos. *El cacicazgo como supervivencia "esclavista-patriarchal" en el seno de la sociedad colonial.* Cuzco: Invierno, 1955.

Oliva, Reverendo Padre Anello. *Historia del reino y provincias del Perú, de sus Incas reyes . . . [1598].* Lima: Imprenta y librería de San Pedro, 1895.

Orrego H., Augusto. "Palabras del mochica." *Revista del Museo Nacional [del Perú]* 27 (1958): 80–95.

Ossio, Juan M. "La propiedad en las comunidades Andinas." *Allpanchis* 19, Año 17, no. 22 (1983): 35–59.

Pagden, Anthony. *The Fall of Natural Man: The American Indian and the Origins of Comparative Ethnology.* Cambridge, Mass.: Cambridge University Press, 1982.

Parkerson, Philip T. "The Inca Coca Monopoly: Fact or Legal Fiction?" *Proceedings of the American Philosophical Society* 127, no. 1 (1983): 107–23.

Patterson, Thomas C. "Andean Cosmologies and the Inca State." In Christine Ward Gailey, ed., *Civilization in Crisis: Anthropological Perspectives*, vol. 1, pp. 181–93. Washington, D.C.: American Anthropological Association, 1992.

Pease, Franklin. "Los Incas en la colonia." In *El mundo Andino en la época del descubrimiento*, pp. 191–206. Lima: Comisión Nacional Peruana de V Centenario del Descubrimiento-Encuentro de Dos Mundos, 1990.

———. "La noción de propiedad entre los Incas: Una aproximación." In Shozo Masuda, ed., *Etnografía e historia del mundo andino continuidad y cambio*, pp. 3–34. Tokio: University of Tokio, 1986.

———. "El príncipe de Esquilache y una relación sobre la extirpación de idolatría." *Cuadernos del Seminario de Historia [Lima]* 7, no. 9 (enero 1968–diciembre 1969): 81–118.

Platt, Tristan. *Estado Boliviano y ayllu Andino: Tierra y tributos en el norte de Potosí*. Lima: Instituto de Estudios Peruanos, 1982.

Polo de Ondegardo, Licenciado Juan. "Del linage de los ingas y como conquistaron (1571)." In Horacio H. Urteaga, *Colección de libros y documentos referentes a la historia del Perú*, vol. 4, pp. 45–94. Lima: Imprenta y Librería de Sanmartí y Ca., 1917.

———. "Informaciones acerca de la religión y gobierno de los Incas [1571]." In Horacio H. Urteaga, *Colección de libros y documentos referentes a la historia del Perú*, vol. 4, pp. 161–204. Lima: Imprenta y Librería de Sanmartí y Cia., 1916–17.

———. "Informe del Licenciado Juan Polo de Ondegardo al Licenciado Briviesca de Muñatones sobre la perpetuidad de las encomiendas en el Perú (1561)." *Revista histórica [Lima]* 13 (1940): 125–96.

Poole, Stafford. "The Declining Image of the Indian Among Churchmen in Sixteenth-Century New Spain." In Susan E. Ramírez, ed., *Indian-Religious Relations in Colonial Spanish America*, pp. 11–20. Syracuse: Maxwell School of Citizenship and Public Affairs, Syracuse University, 1989.

Porras Barrenechea, Raúl. *Cedulario del Perú*, 2 vols. Lima: Departamento de Relaciones Culturales del Ministerio de Relaciones Exteriores del Perú, 1944.

———. *Los cronistas del Perú (1528–1650)*. Lima: Banco de Crédito del Perú, 1986.

———. *Fuentes historicas Peruanas: Apuntes de un curso universitario*. Lima: Instituto Raul Porras Barrenechea, 1963.

Powers, Karen. "Resilient Lords and Indian Vagabonds: Wealth, Migration, and the Reproductive Transformation of Quito's Chiefdoms, 1500–1700." *Ethnohistory* 38, no. 3 (Summer 1991): 225–49.

———. "Seeing Beyond the Numbers: Indian Demography, Colonialism and Ethnogenesis in the Northern Andes, 1500–1700." Typescript, 1992.

Ramírez, Susan E. "The Cajamarca Connection: A Geo-Historical Guide to Northern Peru." Paper presented at a symposium entitled "An Interdisciplinary Perspective on Andean Ecological Complementarity," Cedar Key, Fla., May 18–25, 1983.

———. "Chérrepe en 1572: Un análisis de la Visita General del Virrey Francisco de Toledo." *Historia y cultura* 11 (1978): 79–121.

———. "The '*Dueño de Indios*': Thoughts on the Consequences of the Shifting Bases of Power of the '*Curaca de los Viejos Antiguos*' under the Spanish in Sixteenth-Century Peru." *Hispanic American Historical Review* 67, no. 4 (1987): 575–610.

———. "Ethnohistorical Dimensions of Mining and Metallurgy in Sixteenth-Century Northern Peru." In Alan K. Craig and Robert C. West, eds., *In Quest of Mineral Wealth: Aboriginal and Colonial Mining and Metallurgy in Spanish America*, pp. 93–108. Geoscience and Man, vol. 33. Baton Rouge: Louisiana State University, 1994.

———. "The Inca Conquest of the North Coast: A Historian's View." In Michael E. Mosely and Alana Cordy-Collins, eds., *The Northern Dynasties: Kingships and Statecraft in Chimor*, pp. 507–37. Washington, D.C.: Dumbarton Oaks Research Library and Collection, 1990.

———. "Indian and Spanish Conceptions of Land Tenure." Paper delivered at the annual meeting of the American Historical Association, Cincinnati, Ohio, Dec. 1988.

———. "Land Tenure and the Economics of Power in Colonial Peru." Ph.D. diss., University of Wisconsin, Madison, 1977.

———. "'Myth' or 'Legend' as Fiction or Fact: A Historian's Assessment of the Traditions of North Coastal Peru." Paper presented at the Fourth International Symposium on Latin American Indian Literatures, Mérida, Mexico, Jan. 9, 1986.

———. "La organización económica de la costa norte: Un análisis preliminar del periódo prehispánico tardío." In Amalia Castelli et al., eds., *Etnohistoria y antropología Andina*, pp. 281–97. Lima: Centro de Proyección Cristiana, 1981.

———. "De pescadores y agricultores: Una historia local de la gente del Valle de Chicama Antes de 1565." *Bulletin de l'Institut Français d'Etudes Andines [Lima]* 24 (1995).

———. *Provincial Patriarchs: Land Tenure and the Economics of Power in Colonial Peru.* Albuquerque: University of New Mexico Press, 1986.

———. "Retainers of the Lords or Merchants: A Case of Mistaken Identity?" In Luis Millones and Hiroyasu Tomoeda, eds., *El hombre y su ambiente en los Andes Centrales*, pp. 123–36. Senri Ethnological Studies X. Osaka, Japan: National Museum of Ethnology, 1982.

———. "Social Frontiers and the Territorial Base of Curacazgos." In Shozo Masuda, Izumi Shimada, and Craig Morris, eds., *Andean Ecology and Civilization: An Interdisciplinary Perspective on Andean Ecological Complementarity*, pp. 423–42. Tokyo: University of Tokyo Press, 1985.

Ravines, Rogger, ed. *Tecnología andina.* Lima: Instituto de Estudios Peruanos, 1978.

Ravines, Tristán. *Noticia y memoria de Cajamarca, 1532–1950.* Cajamarca: Instituto Nacional de Cultura, 1986.

"Relación anónima sobre el modo de gobernar de los Incas (1583)." In Roberto Levillier, ed., *Gobernantes del Perú*, vol. 9, pp. 289–96. Madrid: Sucesores de Rivadeneyra, 1925.

"Relación de las costumbres antiguas de los naturales del Pirú." In Francisco Esteve Barba, ed., *Biblioteca de autores españoles*, vol. 209, pp. 151–89. Madrid: Gráfica Norte, 1968.

"Relación de los fundamentos acerca del notable daño que resulta de no guardar a los indios sus fueros (Junio 26, 1571)." In Luis Torres de Mendoza, ed., *Colección de documentos inéditos relativos al descubrimiento, conquista y organización . . . de América y Oceanía*, vol. 17, pp. 5–177. Madrid, Imprenta de Manuel B. de Quiroz, 1872.

"Relación de Piura [1571?]." In Marcos Jiménez de la Espada, ed., *Relaciones geográficas de Indias*, vol. 2, pp. 225–42. Madrid: Tip. de M. G. Hernandez, 1885.

Remy Simatovic, Pilar. "Organización y cambios en el Reino de Cuismancu, 1540–70." In Fernando Silva Santisteban, Waldemar Espinoza Soriano, Rogger Ravines, comps., *Historia de Cajamarca*, vol. 2, pp. 35–68. Cajamarca: Instituto Nacional de Cultura, 1986.

———. "Tasas tributarias pretoledanas de la provincia de Cajamarca." *Historia y cultura* 16 (1983): 69–82.

Reyeros, Rafael. "El 'tupu' y sus modalidades." *América Indígena* 32, no. 3 (julio–septiembre 1972): 830–36.

Ricard, Robert. *The Spiritual Conquest of Mexico*, trans. Lesley Byrd Simpson. Berkeley and Los Angeles: University of California Press, 1966.

Rio, Mercedes del. "La tributación indígena en el repartimiento de Paria (Siglo XVI)." *Revista de Indias* 1, no. 189 (1990): 397–429.

Rivero-Ayllon, Teodoro. *Lambayeque, sol, flores y leyendas.* Chiclayo: Gráfica Jacobs, 1976.

Robinson, David, ed. *Migration in Colonial Spanish America.* Cambridge, England: Cambridge University Press, 1990.

Romero, Emilio. *Historia económica del Perú.* Buenos Aires: Editorial Sudamericana, 1949.

Rossel Castro, Alberto. "Los cacicazgos de Ica." In *Anales del III Congreso Nacional de historia del Perú*, pp. 242–47. Lima: Centro de Estudios Historico-militares del Perú, 1963.

Rostworowski de Diez Canseco, María. "Breves notas sobre la estructura socio-económica en la costa peruana precolombiana." In Roswith Hartmann and Udo Oberem, eds., *Estudios americanistas: Libro jubilar en homenaje a Hermann Trimborn*, vol. 2, pp. 207–11. St. Augustin, Germany: Haus Volker und Kulturen, Anthropos-Inst., 1979.

———. *Curacas y sucesiones, Costa norte.* Lima: Imprenta "Minerva" Miraflores, 1961.

———. "Dos manuscritos inéditos con datos sobre Manco II: Tierras personales de los incas y mitimaes." *Nueva coronica [Lima]* 1 (1963): 223–39.

————. *Estructuras Andinas del poder.* Lima: Instituto de Estudios Peruanos, 1983.

————. *Etnía y sociedad: Costa peruana prehispánica.* Lima: Instituto de Estudios Peruanos, 1977.

————. "Las etnías del Valle de Chillón." In *Etnía y sociedad: Costa peruana prehispánica,* pp. 21–95. Lima: Instituto de Estudios Peruanos, 1977.

————. *Historia del Tahuantinsuyu.* Lima: Instituto de Estudios Peruanos, 1988.

————. "Mercaderes del Valle de Chincha en la época prehispánica: Un documento y unos comentarios." In *Etnía y sociedad: Costa peruana prehispánica,* pp. 97–140. Lima: Instituto de Estudios Peruanos, 1977; and *Revista Española de Antropología Americana [Madrid]* 5 (1970): 135–77.

————. "Nuevos aportes para el estudio de la medición de tierras en el virreynato e incario (1711–1714)." *Revista del Archivo Nacional [del Perú]* 28, nos. 1–2 (enero–diciembre 1964): 31–58.

————. "Patronyms with the Consonant F in the Guarangas of Cajamarca." In Shozo Masuda, Izumi Shimada, and Craig Morris, eds., *Andean Ecology and Civilization,* pp. 401–21. Tokyo: University of Tokyo Press, 1985.

————. "Pescadores, artesanos y mercaderes costeños en el Perú prehispánico." In *Etnía y sociedad: Costa peruana prehispánica,* pp. 211–63. Lima: Instituto de Estudios Peruanos, 1977; and *Revista del Museo Nacional [del Perú]* 41 (1975): 311–49.

————. "Plantaciones prehispánicas de coca en la vertiente del Pacífico." In *Etnía y sociedad: Costa peruana prehispánica,* pp. 155–95. Lima: Instituto de Estudios Peruanos, 1977.

————. "Ruinas de Concón: Derrotero etnohistorico." In *Etnía y sociedad: Costa peruana prehispánica,* pp. 141–54. Lima: Instituto de Estudios Peruanos, 1977; *Revista del Museo Nacional [del Perú]* 38 (1972): 315–26; and *Costa Peruana prehispánica,* pp. 167–74. Lima: Instituto de Estudios Peruanos, 1989.

————. "El señorio de Changuco." *Bulletin de l'Institut Français d'Etudes Andines [Lima]* 5, nos. 1–2 (1976): 97–147.

————. "La tasa ordenada por el Licenciado Pedro de la Gasca (1549)." *Revista histórica* 34 (1983–84): 53–102.

————. "La tasa Toledana de Capachica de 1575." *Revista histórica* 35 (1985–86): 43–79.

————. "Testamento de don Luis de Colan: Curaca en 1622." *Revista del Museo Nacional del Perú* 46 (1982): 507–43.

————. "Las tierras reales y su mano de obra en el Tahuantinsuyu." *Actas y memorias del XXXVI Congreso Internacional de Americanistas [1964],* vol. 2, 31–34. Seville: 1966.

————. "El tributo indígena en la primera mitad del siglo XVI en el Perú." In *Jornadas Americanistas: Estudios sobre política indigenista española en América,* vol. 2, pp. 393–99. Valladolid: Seminario de Historia de América, Universidad de Valladolid, 1976.

————. "Visitas de indios en el siglo XVI." *Cahiers du monde Hispanique et Luso-Brésilien* 7 (1966): 85–92.

Rowe, Ann Pollard. *Costumes and Featherwork of the Lords of Chimor: Textiles from Peru's North Coast.* Washington, D.C.: Textile Museum, 1984.

Rowe, John Howland. "Cultural Implications of Mortuary Practices in Ancient Peru." Paper presented at a Dumbarton Oaks Conference entitled "Tombs for the Living: Andean Mortuary Practices," Washington, D.C., Oct. 12–13, 1991.

———. "Inca Culture at the Time of the Spanish Conquest." In Julian H. Steward, ed., *Handbook of South American Indians*, vol. 2, pp. 183–330. Bureau of South American Ethnology, Bulletin 143. Washington, D.C.: U.S. Government Printing Office, 1947.

———. "The Kingdom of Chimor." *Acta Americana [Mexico]* 6, nos.1–2 (enero–junio, 1948): 26–59.

———. "Una relación de los adoratorios del antiguo Cuzco." *Histórica [Lima]* 5, no. 2 (diciembre 1981): 209–61.

Rubiños y Andrade, Licenciado Justo Modesto. "Un manuscrito interesante: Succesión cronologica . . . de los curas de Pacora y Morrope en la Provincia de Lambayeque . . . 1782." *Revista histórica* 10, no. 3 (1936): 289–363.

Sahlins, Marshall. *Islands of History.* Chicago: University of Chicago Press, 1985.

Salinas y Cordova, Fray Buenaventura de. *Memorial de las historias del Nuevo Mundo Piru.* Lima: Universidad Nacional Mayor de San Marcos, 1957.

Salomon, Frank. "Ancestor Cults and Resistance to the State in Arequipa, ca. 1748–1754." In Steve J. Stern, ed., *Resistance, Rebellion, and Consciousness in the Andean Peasant World, Eighteenth to Twentieth Centuries*, pp. 148–65. Madison: University of Wisconsin Press, 1987.

———. "Ancestors, Grave Robbers, and the Possible Antecedents of Cañari 'Inca-ism.'" In H. O. Skar and F. Salomon, eds., *Natives and Neighbors in South America. Anthropological Essays*, pp. 207–32. Gothenburg, Sweden: Goteborgs Etnografiska Museum, 1987.

———. "The Beautiful Grandparents: Andean Ancestor Shrines and Mortuary Ritual in Ethnohistorical Perspective." Paper presented at a Dumbarton Oaks Conference entitled "Tombs for the Living: Andean Mortuary Practices," Washington, D.C., Oct. 12–13, 1991.

———. *Ethnic Lords of Quito in the Age of the Incas: The Political Economy of North Andean Chiefdoms.* Dissertation Series. Ithaca, N.Y.: Latin American Studies Program, Cornell University, 1978.

———. *Native Lords of Quito in the Age of the Incas.* Cambridge, Eng.: Cambridge University Press, 1986.

———. "Vertical Politics on the Inka Frontier." In John V. Murra, Nathan Wachtel, and Jacques Revel, eds., *Anthropological History of Andean Polities*, pp. 89–117. Cambridge, England: Cambridge University Press, 1986.

Salomon, Frank, and Sue Grosboll. "Names and Peoples in Incaic Quito: Retrieving Undocumented Historic Process Through Anthroponymy and Statistics." *American Anthropologist* 88, no. 2 (1986): 387–99.

Santillán, Licenciado Hernando de. "Relación del orígen, descendencia, política y gobierno de los Incas (c. 1563–1572)." In Francisco Estete Barba, ed., *Crónicas peruanas de interés indígena*, pp. 97–150. Madrid: Ediciones Atlas, 1968; or in Horacio Urteaga, ed., *Colección de libros y documentos referentes a la historia del Perú*, vol. 9, pp. 1–124. Second series, 12 vols. Lima: Imprenta y Librería Sanmarti y Ca., 1927.

Sanz Tapia, Angel. "El cacique don Felipe Ramírez y su obtención de tierras baldías." In *Jornadas americanistas: Estudios sobre política indigenista española en América (1974)*, vol. 3, pp. 275–89. Valladolid: Seminario de Historia de América, Universidad de Valladolid, 1975.

Schaedel, Richard P. "Andean World View: Hierarchy or Reciprocity, Regulation or Control." *Current Anthropology* 29, no. 5 (1988): 768–75.

Schroeder, Susan. *Chimalpahin and the Kingdoms of Chalco*. Tucson: University of Arizona Press, 1991.

Sevilla Exebio, Julio César. "Ferreñafe 1795: Un movimiento anti-tributario." Mimeograph. Ferreñafe, 1983.

Shimada, Melody, and Izumi Shimada. "Prehistoric Llama Breeding and Herding on the North Coast of Peru." *American Antiquity* 50, no. 1 (1985): 3–26.

Silverblatt, Irene. "Dioses y diablos: Idolatrías y evangelización." *Allpanchis* 16, no. 19 (1982): 31–47.

Spalding, Karen. "Los escaladores sociales: Patrones cambiantes de movilidad en la sociedad andina bajo el régimen colonial." In *De indio a campesino: Cambios en la estructura social del Perú colonial*, pp. 61–87. Lima: Instituto de Estudios Peruanos, 1974.

———. *Huarochirí, An Andean Society Under Inca and Spanish Rule*. Stanford: Stanford University Press, 1984.

———. "La red desintegrante." In *De indio a campesino: Cambios en la estructura social del Perú colonial*, pp. 89–123. Lima: Instituto de Estudios Peruanos, 1974.

———. "Resistencia y adaptación: El gobierno colonial y las élites nativas." *Allpanchis* 15, nos. 17–18 (1981): 5–21.

Stern, Steve J. *Peru's Indian Peoples and the Challenge of Spanish Conquest*. Madison: University of Wisconsin Press, 1982.

———. "The Rise and Fall of Indian-White Alliances: A Regional View of 'Conquest' History." *Hispanic American Historical Review* 61, no. 3 (1981): 461–91.

Taylor, William B. "Cacicazgos coloniales en el valle de Oaxaca." *Historia Mexicana* 20, no. 1 (julio–septiembre 1970): 1–41.

———. *Landlord and Peasant in Colonial Oaxaca*. Stanford: Stanford University Press, 1972.

TePaske, John J., and Herbert S. Klein. *The Royal Treasuries of the Spanish Empire in America*. 3 vols. Durham, N.C.: Duke University Press, 1982.

Topic, Jr., John R. "Lower-class Social and Economic Organization at Chan Chan." In Michael E. Moseley and Kent Day, eds., *Chan Chan: Andean*

Desert City, pp. 145–75. Albuquerque: University of New Mexico Press, 1982.

Torre Revello, José. "Un resumen aproximado de los habitantes del Virreinato del Peru en la segunda mitad del siglo XVI." *Anuario del Instituto de Investigaciones Historicas* 18 (1960), pp. 297–300.

Torres, José Amilcar. "Propietarios de tierras de la Provincia del Valle de Jequetepeque hace 300 años." *La Unión [Pacasmayo, Perú]* 46, no. 14 (May 1959) 20-v-1959, pp. 3, 6, 8; 11-v-1959, pp. 1, 3; 14-v-1959, p. 1; 16-v-1959, p. 1; 12-v-1959, p. 3.

Trelles Aréstegui, Efrain. *Lucas Martínez Vegazo: Funcionamiento de una encomienda Peruana inicial.* B.A. thesis, Pontifícia Universidad Católica del Perú, 1980.

Trimborn, Hermann. *El reino de Lambayeque en el antiguo Perú.* Collectanea Instituti Anthropos XIX. St. Augustin, Germany: Hans Volker und Kulturen, Anthropos-Institut, 1979.

Trujillo, Peru, Consejo Provincial. *Actas del Cabildo de Trujillo, 1549–1604.* 3 vols. Lima: Talleres Gráficos P. L. Villanueva S.A., 1969–70.

Ulloa Sotomayor, Alberto. *La organización social y legal del trabajo en el Perú.* Lima: Imprenta La Opinión Nacional, 1916.

Urteaga, Horacio H. *Colección de libros y documentos referentes a la historia del Perú,* vol. 3, pp. 3–204. Lima: Imprenta y Librería de Sanmartí y Ca., 1916–17.

———. *El Perú: Bocetos historicos.* Second series. Lima: E. Rosay, 1919.

Vaca de Castro, Licenciado Christóbal. "Ordenanzas de tambos distancias de unos a otros, modo de cargar los indios y obligaciones . . . 1543." *Revista histórica* 3 (1908): 427–92.

Valdez de la Torre, Carlos. *Evolución de las comunidades indígenas.* Lima: Ed. Euforion, 1921.

Valencia Espinoza, Abraham. *Pesos y medidas Inkas.* Cuzco: Centro de Estudios Andinos, 1982.

Valera, Blas. *Las costumbres antiguas del Perú y la historia de los Incas (siglo XVI).* In Francisco A. Loayza, ed., *Los pequeños grandes libros de historia americana,* vol. 8, first series. Lima: Editorial de Domingo Miranda, 1945.

van de Guchte, Maarten. "'Carving the World': Inca Monumental Sculpture and Landscape." Ph.D. diss., University of Illinois, Urbana, 1990.

Vargas Ugarte, Rubén. "Fragmento de una historia de Trujillo." *Revista histórica* 8, nos. 1–2 (1925): 86–118.

———. *Historia de la iglesia en el Perú (1511–1568).* 5 vols. Lima: Imprenta Sta. María, 1953.

———. "Los mochicas y el cacicazgo de Lambayeque." In *Actas y trabajos científicos del 27 Congreso Internacional de Americanistas [1939],* vol. 2, pp. 475–82. Lima: Librería y Imprenta Gil, 1942.

Varón Gabai, Rafael, and Auke Pieter Jacobs. "Peruvian Wealth and Spanish Investments: The Pizarro Family During the Sixteenth Century." *Hispanic American Historical Review* 67, no. 4 (1987): 657–95.

Vassberg, David E. "Concerning Pigs, the Pizarros, and the Agro-Pastoral Background of the Conquerors of Peru." *Latin American Research Review* 13, no. 3 (1978): 47–61.

———. *La venta de tierras baldias: El comunitarismo agrário y la corona de Castilla durante el siglo XVI.* Madrid: Servicio de Publicaciones Agrárias, 1983.

Vega, Garcilaso de la. *Los comentarios reales de los Incas [1586].* 6 vols. Lima: Librería y Imprenta Gil, 1941–46.

Villamarin, Juan A., and Judith E. Villamarin. "Kinship and Inheritance Among the Sabana de Bogota Chibcha at the Time of the Spanish Conquest." *Ethnology* 14 (Apr. 1975): 173–79.

Vollmer, Gunter. *Bevolkerungspolitik und Bevolkerungsruktur im Vizekonigreich Peru su Ende Kolonialzeit (1741–1821).* Zurich/Berlin: Gehler, 1967.

Wachtel, Nathan. *Vision of the Vanquished: The Spanish Conquest of Peru Through Indian Eyes, 1530–70.* New York: Barnes & Noble, 1977.

Weeks, David. "European Antecedents of Land Tenure and Agrarian Origins in Hispanic America." *Journal of Land and Public Economics* 22, no. 1 (Feb. 1947): 60–75.

Wightman, Ann M. *Indigenous Migration and Social Change: The Forasteros of Cuzco, 1570–1720.* Durham, N.C.: Duke University Press, 1990.

Wood, Stephanie. "Corporate Adjustments in Colonial Mexican Indian Towns: Toluca Region, 1550–1810." Ph.D. diss., University of California, Los Angeles, 1984.

Zevallos Quiñones, Jorge. *Los cacicazgos de Lambayeque.* Trujillo: Consejo Nacional de Ciencia y Tecnologia, 1989.

———. *Un diccionario Castellano-Yunga.* Estudios Yungas II. Lima: Imprenta del Ministerio de Educación Pública, 1947.

———. *Los gramáticos de la lengua Yunga.* Estudios Yungas III. Lima: Cia. de Impresiones y Publicidad, 1948.

———. "La ropa de tributo de las encomiendas Trujillanas en el siglo XVI." *Historia y cultura [Lima]* 7 (1974): 107–22.

———. *Toponímia preincaica en el Norte del Perú.* Estudios Yungas I. Lima: Libreria e Imprenta Gil, 1944.

———. "Una nota sobre el primitivo idioma de la Costa Norte." *Revista histórica* 14, Entrega 3 (1941): 376–79.

———. "La visita del pueblo de Ferreñafe [Lambayeque] en 1568." *Historia y cultura [Lima]* 9, (1968): 155–78.

Zuidema, R. Tom. *The Ceque System of Cuzco.* Leiden: E. J. Brill, 1964.

———. "Hierarchy and Space in Incaic Social Organization." *Ethnohistory* 30, no. 2 (1983): 49–75.

———. *Inca Civilization in Cuzco.* Austin: University of Texas Press, 1990.

———. "Inca Cosmos in Andean Context." In Robert V. H. Dover, Katherine E. Seibold, and John H. McDowell, eds., *Andean Cosmologies Through Time*, pp. 17–45. Bloomington: Indiana University Press, 1992.

———. "Kinship and Ancestor Cult in Three Peruvian Communities: Her-nández Príncipe's Account of 1622." *Bulletin de l'Institut Français d'Etudes Andines* 2, no. 1 (1973): 16–33.

———. "The Lion in the City: Royal Symbols of Transition in Cuzco." *Journal of Latin American Lore* 9, no. 1 (1983): 39–100.

———. *Reyes y guerreros: Ensayos de cultura Andina.* Lima: FOMCIEN-CIAS, 1989.

Zurkalowski, Erich. "El establecimiento de las encomiendas en el Perú y sus antecedentes." *Revista histórica* 6, Entrega 3 (1919): 254–69.

Index

In this index "f" after a number indicates a separate reference on the next page, and "ff" indicates separate references on the next two pages. A continuous discussion over two or more pages is indicated by a span of numbers, e.g., "57–59." *Passim* is used for a cluster of references in close but not consecutive sequence.

Library of Congress Cataloging-in-Publication Data

Ramírez, Susan.
  The world upside down : cross-cultural contact and conflict in sixteenth-century
Peru / Susan Elizabeth Ramírez.
    p. cm.
  Includes bibliographical references (p.   ) and index.
  ISBN 0-8047-2416-4 (cl.) : ISBN 0-8047-3520-4 (pbk.)
    1. Indians of South America—Peru—History—16th century—Sources.
2. Indians of South America—Peru—Land tenure. 3. Indians of South
America—Peru—Taxation. 4. Encomiendas (Latin America)—
History—16th century. 5. Spain—Colonies—America—
Administration. 6. Peru—History—Conquest, 1522–1548.   I. Title.
F3429.R35   1996   95-39791
985'.02—dc20   CIP

Original printing 1996
Last figure below indicates year of this printing:
05   04   03   02   01   00   99   98